DEFYING THE MARKET

Profiting in the Turbulent
Post-Technology Boom

Stephen Leeb and Donna Leeb

McGraw-Hill

New York   San Francisco   Washington, D.C.   Auckland   Bogotá
Caracas   Lisbon   London   Madrid   Mexico City   Milan
Montreal   New Delhi   San Juan   Singapore
Sydney   Tokyo   Toronto

Library of Congress Cataloging-in-Publication Data
Leeb, Stephen.   Leeb, Donna.
    Defying the market : profiting in the turbulent
      post-technology boom / by Stephen Leeb and Donna Leeb.
    Includes bibliographical references
      p.   cm.
    ISBN 0-07-134110-2 (alk. paper)
    1. Stocks—United States. 2. Investment analysis—United States.
HG4910.L449 1999
332.63/22–dc21   99-024141
                                        CIP

McGraw-Hill

*A Division of The **McGraw·Hill** Companies*

1 2 3 4 5 6 7 8 9 0 DOC / DOC 9 0 4 3 2 1 0 9

ISBN 0-07-134110-2

Printed and bound by R.R. Donnelley & Sons Company.

This book is printed on recycled, acid-free paper
containing a minimum of 50% recycled de-inked fiber.

McGraw-Hill books are available at special quantity discounts to
use as premiums and sales promotions, or for use in corporate
training programs. For more information, please write to the
Director of Special Sales, McGraw-Hill, 11 West 19th Street, New
York, NY 10011. Or contact your local bookstore.

We dedicate this book with love to our two sons, Tim and Will. Thanks for your interest, patience, and tolerance.

CONTENTS

PART II
CASHING IN

PART III
HEDGING YOUR BETS

PART IV
INVESTMENT WRAP-UP

PREFACE

Much of this book—an investment guide to the late 1990s and the first part of the twenty-first century—has to do with technology, a topic of endless fascination and debate. Everyone has an opinion on technology. You love it, you hate it; you must have the latest version of Windows, you still use a manual typewriter; you're plugged into the Internet, you still use a rotary telephone. It takes all kinds.

As one of the authors of this book, I happen to like technology. In fact, I've always liked to have the latest and the best, at least in those areas I care about. Take computers, for example. Since I bought my first personal computer in the early 1980s, I've probably upgraded at least 20 times, moving from an Apple II through a 386 and most recently to a Pentium II 400 megahertz with 384 megs of memory and two monitors. I'm also an avid biker and was one of the first to buy a titanium bike when it came out a few years ago. I bought a Mercedes 500E not because I had any interest in whatever prestige might be associated with the name Mercedes—if that were my motivation there were bigger and flashier models around—but because it was so technologically sophisticated. And I'm passionate about music and have sought out the most advanced sound system technology could provide.

As part of my interest in technology and science, I read everything I can get my hands on. For instance, I subscribe to or buy such magazines as *Science, Nature, New Science,* and *Science News,* to name a few, and read them cover to cover. I also am a sucker for any book, obscure or well received, that has a technologic or scientific theme. Just mention to me a book with a title such as *Technology, Pessimism, and Postmodernism,* and I'm in the bookstore like a flash.

My interest in technology is part hobby but is also highly complementary to my work as an investment adviser. Technology is part and parcel of today's world, and no one can understand the economy and the financial markets or make intelligent stock recommendations without an extensive awareness of technological developments.

There's a reason that I'm proclaiming my good technological credentials right up front. For in the last few years, somewhat to my bemusement and amid the hoopla of books and articles proclaiming the imminent onset of digital nirvana, I have become aware of the latest and most significant trend in technology. It's not a new generation of electronic devices or a higher level of automation in factories. Rather it is an across the board slowdown in technological progress. And I have become convinced that this slowdown will turn out to be one of the key investment realities of the late twentieth and early twenty-first centuries and maybe beyond.

Investors who recognize the slowdown in tech and understand how it relates to financial markets around the world will have a big head start when it comes to winning the investment sweepstakes. Investors who fail to take the slowdown into account, risk picking the wrong stocks or the wrong industries and missing out on the biggest opportunities.

In the chapters that follow, we explain what this slowdown in technological progress—in conjunction with other key trends— means for you as investors. But first, a few more words on exactly what we mean by the limits of technology, because we don't want you to get the wrong idea. You could write a book about the downside to technological progress—the glitches, the risks, the impact of technology on social relationships and education, and so on. Nearly every day, in fact, I come across an article or televised discussion dealing with one or more of these areas.

The glitches? We've all experienced them—the computer that abruptly crashes, erasing hours' worth of work, the VCR that tapes the wrong show (we'd concede that the latter might be a case of operator error). The Y2K problem could be a glitch on a super-large scale.

As for the potential risks, the Internet alone raises fears ranging from child molesters scouting for victims to hackers finding their way into your bank accounts. Too much time at the computer keyboard can cause carpal tunnel syndrome, while there is considerable evidence that overuse of cellular phones can cause cancer.

These and others like them are all legitimate concerns. But while the particulars are different, this type of concern is really nothing new, in the sense that technological progress has always been a question of trade-offs. We love our cars but bemoan pollution, reckless drivers, and maddening traffic jams. We couldn't do without electricity but every so often, when experiencing a blackout, discover there is something inexplicably appealing in being forced to do nothing but gather around a candle-lit table once night comes on. In the end it comes down to which technologies you're used to. One generation's innovations are the next generation's necessities, for better or worse.

As for the social and psychological impact of new technologies, as in the past you could debate this forever. E-mail has been extolled for bringing families closer together in ways that apparently were never possible by mail or phone. On the other hand, educators and parents worry about how well children will become socialized when, from an early age, they are more accustomed to playing computer games than to playing with other kids in someone's back yard.

Some people rhapsodize about the Internet's potential to make the whole world a village. (The comedian Jackie Mason, on the other hand, muses that people praise the Internet because they say it can bring someone from Siberia right into your home. But, he asks, suppose an actual Siberian came knocking on your door. Would you let him in?) On a more serious note, a recent study by researchers at Carnegie Mellon University found that spending even a few hours a week online apparently causes increased feelings of depression and loneliness.

As I said, someone could write a book on all these topics and, in fact, many people have. But this book is not one of them. Basically, this book is neutral when it comes to the highly charged and personal questions of whether technology is good or bad or in what ways it is either. Those are essentially moral and philosophical issues, and while they're fascinating, this is an investment book.

Rather, in this book we stand back and look at the rarely perceived fact that however you feel about technology, it happens to be reaching certain limits. I have no preconceived bias against technology and no axe to grind. I'm simply interested in reporting the development I've noted—which is that technology to a significant extent is losing its edge—and tracing what this will mean for investors.

We're not Luddites, and it's not a question of going back to a simpler past or divesting ourselves of the technology we already have. We'll continue to live with all the technological advances of the past, which will continue to surround us and define our world. Moreover, technology will keep evolving in ways that on a superficial level might seem new and different, and many of the forms it takes will make life more convenient or more fun or possibly more complicated.

The point, though, is that for now—the popular impression notwithstanding—the true technological breakthroughs are behind us. And this, together with other key trends that we will describe, will have a pervasive impact on all your investments.

STEPHEN LEEB

ACKNOWLEDGMENTS

We're grateful to Darryl Bohning and Michael Pukchanski for their informative discourses on physics and chess, respectively. We'd also like to thank Steve Fishman, Wade Black, and Gregg Early for their insightful and encouraging comments on our initial manuscript; Trae Underwood for her cheerful help with the charts and tables; Iris Aronson for her competent handling of innumberable details; and Roger Conrad and all Steve's other co-workers at KCI. We benefited from and enjoyed our many provocative conversations with Noah Shaw, Steve Rittenberg, and Herb Wyman. We appreciate our agent Al Zuckerman's invaluable guidance through all stages of this project. Finally, our thanks go to our editor Jeffrey Krames for so astutely keeping us on track.

DEFYING THE MARKET

INTRODUCTION

Being an investor is a tough job. Just when you think you know what you're doing, the world suddenly changes. And if you fail to anticipate these changes, or don't understand them when they occur, you can see your profits evaporate in a flash.

Say you've been making money hand over fist by buying and holding the big blue chips—as in the 1990s, when from late 1990 to mid-1998, the Dow Jones Industrial Average rose from about 2000 to over 9000, with few interruptions. Great—a piece of cake. But wait—here comes the tumultuous summer of 1998. Your stocks tumble. Is it temporary? Is it permanent? How do you know, and what can you do about it?

These kinds of questions are particularly relevant, in fact, urgent, in the late 1990s. For most of this decade, investors have enjoyed the longest bull market in history. Moreover, it was a market that favored the biggest and safest stocks—so you could make big money without taking big risks. It was an investor's dream. What made it possible was an unusually benign economic environment, characterized by steady and relatively strong noninflationary growth, that by a happy coincidence of factors managed to persist year after year.

For a variety of reasons it was clear when we first began planning and writing this book in late 1997, months before the market began to experience its first serious shaking up in many years, that this extraordinary era was drawing to a close. The events of the summer of 1998, when Japan and Russia were on the skids and stocks slid, merely brought home how close we were to the end. And they showed how important it was to understand what exactly was changing, in order to have the best chance of getting on the right side of the new investment order.

There is no escaping it. The key to successful investing, always, is to understand the underlying trends in the real world—to be able to look at the world around you and discern what is significant and what is irrelevant. Sure, there are self-referential investment "systems" that are propounded with tremendous confidence and enjoy great vogue—buying value, buying when one stock market average contradicts another stock average, buying when the moon is full. But ultimately, a successful system of investing has to be in synch with the underlying macroeconomic realities. A system that works well when inflation is low isn't likely to work as well if inflation starts to soar. An approach that makes you money when, say, General Motors is the bellwether stock will be less effective when Microsoft becomes the biggest-cap stock.

THREE KEY TRENDS

Over the past several years, we have become increasingly aware of certain underlying trends that have been quietly gathering force. Moreover, we have become convinced that these trends are likely to be the key to investment success over the next decade or so. The trends are as follows: (1) a pervasive slowdown in technological progress; (2) a mandate for economic growth, in the developing and the developed world alike; (3) the result of the coming together of these two trends—a rise in inflationary pressures.

At first blush, you might doubt these trends. You also might think them somewhat removed from the nitty gritty world of investments, and you might wonder if they're really something you need to know about. The answer is yes. For these trends, in a big way, will help shape the investment scene for many years to come. They will be essential in determining which investments will soar and which will tank.

In fact, we would argue that making the effort to understand these three trends—all of which are highly controversial—is the most important thing you can do for yourself as a serious investor. This book is a guide to what these trends are and how you should use them to your benefit.

The book is divided into four main parts. Part I, "The Big Picture," concentrates mainly on the essential investment background— the trends themselves. What do we mean when we claim that technology is slowing down—are we nuts? Why is worldwide economic growth almost certainly wired in? And how can we make a case for inflation when it has been so widely accepted that inflation has been tamed? This part of the book gives you the theoretical background for understanding our specific investment advice. It will give you the basis for accepting our recommendations—or, if you think we fail to make our case, for rejecting them. It will also give you the necessary tools for evaluating stocks that you might find on your own, or that your neighbor or brother-in-law might urge you to buy.

Part II, "Cashing In," focuses on the specific investments that will let you take advantage of the changing market environment that these trends will bring about. If technology is slowing down, what does it mean, for instance, for computer stocks? Why is a major drug company like Pfizer a great investment while the biotech group stinks? Will oil stocks ever make a comeback? Why will rising inflation mean that small growth companies will become market leaders, while the big blue chips will mostly fade? Which blue chips will buck the trend? In this section, we tell you exactly what stocks and groups of stocks you should buy and which you should avoid.

Any investment adviser quickly learns humility. Whenever you recommend a particular stock, a particular industry, or a particular investment philosophy, you always have to ask yourself what if anything could change or go wrong and how you protect yourself from getting burned if it does. In Part III, "Hedging Your Bets," we tell you how to round out your investments to protect yourself in case the picture changes—particularly, to guard against the possibility that deflation instead of inflation might become the predominant reality. We discuss such choices as straight bonds versus zero coupon bonds and tell you what unique very big and very safe investment lets you have it both ways—an inflation beneficiary and deflation hedge all in one. This section also contains a chapter on stocks that provide protection of a different sort, against an environmental disaster—the odds of which, as we'll explain, are increasing as economic growth collides with technological limits.

Finally, in Part IV, "Investment Wrap-Up," we sum up all our investment advice in one simple package of six sample portfolios, designed to meet the needs of investors with varying goals and with different amounts of money to invest.

Keep in mind, at all times, the overriding point we made earlier: Change is coming. The era of noninflationary growth that we've enjoyed so long is over, gone, kaput. The only question is what will replace it. As we'll describe in more detail throughout the book, the only plausible alternatives are inflationary growth, on the one hand, or a devastating period of deflation, on the other. In this book we tell you why we think the former is the more likely and how to position yourself to take advantage of it—while protecting yourself against the possibility of the latter.

THE SLOWDOWN IN TECH

If there's one thing in this book that is likely to prove more controversial, more hotly resisted, more laughed at than anything else, it will be our view that the world is now experiencing a widespread slowdown in technological progress. We're convinced that technological progress is stagnating across the board, in areas ranging from computers to drug research to energy and just about everything in between. Everything we know and read tells us the slowdown is for real and will not be reversed anytime soon. Technology on all fronts is bumping into limits. Technological gains will be fewer and farther between, and when they do occur, they will be less significant and more marginal.

We are aware that this may be hard to swallow—for it goes against the grain of the prevailing faith that technology is indomitable. You may relish technology or find some of its manifestations baffling or annoying, but like most people in today's industrialized, electronicized world, you probably assume that continued technological progress is inevitable. If so, that's hardly surprising. For hundreds of years technology has transformed our world time and time again. Whenever a breakthrough was needed, it seemed to occur—from the steam engine to the cotton gin to the airplane to the atomic bomb to the computer.

In our era alone, millions of people have personally experienced both the dawn of the television age and the onset of the Internet. An astounding 43 percent of homes in the United States have personal computers, most or all of them with more computing power than any mainframe in the 1960s. No wonder that many people today, even if they've never thought about it consciously, believe that technology will continue to progress by leaps and bounds.

In fact, it may seem to you that the pace of technology has accelerated in recent years, and now more than ever we take for granted a continual stream of amazing advances. Just a few years ago, if you had sat down next to someone on a bus and realized he was talking aloud to something in his hand, you'd have been alarmed and probably would have thought it prudent to shift to another seat. Today you'd barely notice—it would be just one more salesperson or yuppie using a cellular phone. We've created talking cars and are exploring Mars, and every day the newspapers seem to announce that we've decoded one more gene, cloned one more mammal, or found a seemingly promising treatment for one more disease. How then can we assert, just when science and technology seem poised to take even greater strides forward, that we are suddenly hitting a stone wall?

Moreover, it might seem that technology has firmly insinuated itself into the stock market, and that to win big in the investment arena you need to jump on the technological bandwagon. Stocks such as Microsoft and Intel have been dominant investments, and hot new Internet issues have shot up to the moon. If anything, it would seem that the age of technology is just coming into its own.

That's the popular perception. But it's wrong. We'll show in Chapters 1 and 2 that in a variety of areas technology is basically spinning its wheels. For instance, since their inception, computers have made amazingly rapid progress. However, in the last few years, improvements have slowed dramatically as computer technology has approached certain physical limits. This has major implications for investing in computer-related stocks.

But that's just the start. Appearances to the contrary, there have been no true breakthroughs in recent years in medical research, in drug development, in weather forecasting, or in other key areas. One telling statistic, for instance, is that increases in life expectancies have slowed dramatically in the United States for key demographic groups. The original discovery of antibiotics in the 1920s was a genuine breakthrough, but since then nothing new and better has come along—and now there is growing evidence that many virulent forms of bacteria are starting to win the battle against the antibiotics we've been counting on.

Ironically, as we'll explain in Chapter 2, one reason for the general slowdown in technological progress is the computer itself. The computer has such allure that it has become the research tool of choice for nearly all scientists—and it has been a fatal choice. In any effort that pits the abilities of the computer, even the fastest super-computer that ever can be developed, against the complexities of nature, nature will win out.

That's a major theme of this book, and while at first it might seem to have little to do with investment decisions, there's a critical tie-in. The natural world is incredibly complex. Technology seeks to manipulate the natural world for the benefit of humankind—to increase food yields, for instance, or to create drugs that work in tandem with the human genome. But for any meaningful success in these and other areas, we need to understand the natural processes with which we are interfering. And we don't—they are too complex. Even processes that you might think we have learned all about, like photosynthesis or evolution, continue to elude our understanding at any deep level. We have theories about what goes on, but they are really only the barest sketch of an explanation, a rough first draft. We can't duplicate these natural processes in the lab, and we can't improve upon them. As we'll show, our repeated efforts to do so through the use of computers are almost laughable—the natural world simply can't be cracked through the hit-and-miss tactics of supercomputing.

What's the investment tie-in? The first is that if technological breakthroughs are not in the offing—and our overreliance on computer-directed research means they are not and will not be—then any company that rises or falls on the success of a new technology is likely to prove disappointing. Yes, there will be exceptions. But they will be few and far between, and it's simply not worth betting that any one company will be the exception to the rule. The message: Stay away from pure tech plays—the chance that any one company will develop a genuinely new and usable product or process is far too small. However, this doesn't mean that you should avoid tech stocks altogether. Certain large and well-established companies that are commonly thought of as tech companies are a different matter entirely. In this section we'll explain the difference and tell you which tech companies might still be worth your investment dollar.

It's possible that some of this section may seem somewhat heavy going, because to discuss the slowdown in tech we include a fair amount of what might seem like pure science. If so, we apologize in advance. But we hope you'll stick with it, because it provides the underpinning for a lot of the investment advice that follows.

WHY INFLATION?

The slowdown in technological progress is just part of the big picture. What makes it particularly significant is the way it will interact with a second trend—a worldwide push for economic growth, on the part of developing and developed nations alike.

In Chapter 3, we describe this trend and explain why policymakers will almost certainly find themselves opting for highly stimulative measures that will keep growth going at any cost. The way we put it is that growth has shifted from being a luxury to being a necessity. A reversal in growth anywhere threatens growth everywhere and poses the risk of an economic meltdown. As a result, the powers that be will be under tremendous pressure to prop up growth whenever it threatens to falter. We saw this in 1998, when policymakers responded to an economic slowdown in Asia with a host of monetary and other initiatives designed to get growth back on track.

How does the necessity for growth relate to the slowdown in technological progress? For one thing, economic growth entails rising demand for basic commodities. If through improvements in technology we were able to increase the supply of these commodities, it would be no big deal. World economies would hum along, and the period of noninflationary growth we've enjoyed so long could continue.

But with technology making only marginal gains, the continued push for economic growth will lead to rising and eventually fairly high levels of inflation. In other words, if we're right about technology, it has far broader investment implications than just a go-slow attitude toward a group of tech stocks. It means there will be nothing to help keep the lid on inflation. And once inflation starts to rise, it will have an impact on every investment you can think of, some for better, some for worse.

In Chapter 4 we look at the final part of the big picture—a slow-down in productivity gains in the United States and other developed nations. Once again, technological progress or the lack of it is the crucial piece of the puzzle. A lot of people, including those in high governmental and policy-making positions, believe, or hope, that an ongoing stream of improvements in technology and specifically the computer will lead to increases in productivity. But this is wishful thinking. With technology faltering, productivity gains simply won't materialize—and, as we'll explain, efficiency gains, which are not the same thing, are now running their course. If productivity gains aren't there, the upshot will be further inflationary pressures on top of those that will sharply boost commodity prices.

How high will inflation go and when will it start? It probably hit bottom in 1998. The eventual top is hard to predict, but it is likely that price increases will at some point reach at least the double-digit levels of the 1970s.

CASHING IN

Technological limits plus a push for growth equal rising inflation: That's the basic equation. In Part II, we get to the payoff—how to apply this equation to making the right investment choices. Under-standing the underlying trends is just the essential first step to know-ing what to buy and what to avoid. In this section we look at a wide range of investment opportunities and pitfalls.

Chapters 5 and 6 zero in on two commodities whose prices should soar as worldwide growth, and especially growth in develop-ing economies, accelerates. They are energy and food. Oil stocks, which have been among the market's worst laggards, are nearly sure bets to come into their own with a bang. The connection is obvious:

Economic development requires energy, and without technological breakthroughs that might, for example, result in viable alternatives, the chief available energy source for now and for the foreseeable future remains oil. Ergo, oil prices will rise, and oil stocks should be part of every investor's portfolio. We discuss exactly which oil stocks to buy and look at the advantages and the risks of particular segments within the industry.

Food stocks—quick, can you name any?—are a whole other group of commodity plays that will benefit from the twin reality of technological limits and economic growth. You might think the pressures on food prices will come largely from population growth, but actually that's not the main worry. The real impetus will be economic development in Third World countries, which tends to slow down population growth—but also leads to increased demand for better, more protein-intensive sources of food. Once again, technology will be unable to bail us out in the form of significantly increased food supplies. The built-in limits are simply too formidable and have to do both with our inability to understand at any deep level the food production process and with physical limits such as how much water is available for growing food. Again, these broad trends have concrete investment repercussions. Food stocks aren't a particularly cohesive or well-known group at the moment—but selected examples will do surprisingly well in the new investment age now dawning.

Commodity plays are direct beneficiaries of the push for worldwide growth. But that's just the start of how technological limits combined with the push for growth will help and hurt a wide array of stocks and other investments. Remember, the main economic outcome will be a rise in inflation across the board. How will this affect stocks and other investments overall? In every way that you can imagine. One clue is to look at what investments were winners and losers during the inflationary years from the mid-1960s to the early 1980s. If you came of investment age in the late 1980s or later, it might stun you to realize that in the 1970s the big blue chips—the stocks that have been such exuberant performers in recent years—

were disasters, ending up below water. Instead, it was small growth stocks that led the way to explosive gains. Chapter 7 is your guide to which investments flourish during inflationary times—not just small growth companies but also gold and certain real estate plays—and how to pick the best of them.

But before you unload your big-cap stocks entirely, read Chapter 8. A select handful of the best and most secure big caps will buck the trend—they have such a hold on their markets that even in inflationary times they can post the strong revenue and profit growth that will lead to stock market gains. Every investor should have some of these safe giants.

HEDGING YOUR BETS

We're very confident that we're right about the slowdown in technology. We're equally confident that we're right about the necessity for growth—without ongoing strong growth around the world, economies will unravel quickly, weakness in one country triggering weakness in another. But there is one caveat to all that we've said so far about how these factors will lead to a new era of inflation, and it's not something to ignore. All our analysis is based upon the assumption that policymakers will act rationally and with foresight to avert economic disaster. In other words, we're assuming that they will see matters the way we do and act accordingly.

There always is the possibility, however, that they won't—that there will be a slip-up. Policymakers may underestimate the consequences of a slowdown in growth, or they may act too little or too late when growth is threatened. In that case, we lose our bet. We won't get inflation—we would get something far worse and more difficult to handle or reverse: virulent deflation and economic contraction. Stocks would weaken, banks would collapse, and consumers would have no money to spend, in an ever-worsening down cycle.

We don't expect policymakers will be that short-sighted, which is why we are stressing inflationary beneficiaries as the investments of choice. However, there are two points. First, you always should have insurance against something going wrong—never bet the house on any one outcome no matter how probable. And second, in the coming era of inflationary growth, there may be periods of deflationary scares, when it *looks* as if deflation may be in the offing. During those times, your inflation-oriented stocks may suffer, while investments that benefit most in times of deflation will begin to outperform. To keep your portfolio afloat during those times and to let yourself sleep at night, you should balance your inflation beneficiaries with some deflation hedges. We describe these in detail in Chapter 9.

In Chapter 10 we look at another kind of investment that offers protection against the possibility of something going wrong—only in this case it is environmental, not economic, insurance that we recommend. In recent years we've experienced a spate of environmental jolts, many of them weather related, from a heat wave in the southwestern United States to devastating floods in China. As economic growth accelerates, one unfortunate consequence will be to put further stress upon our planet—increasing the likelihood of a major environmental disaster. With technology hitting limits, we won't be able either to avert such disasters or to come up with quick fixes if they occur. One result will be that certain environment-friendly companies—such as forest products companies—will gain new respect. In Chapter 10 we discuss our favorites among the breed.

MODEL PORTFOLIOS

Putting together an actual portfolio is trickier than it might seem. By the time you've reached Chapter 11, we hope you'll be convinced that you need to own, at a minimum, some energy and/or food stocks, some small growth companies, maybe some gold, a few tried-and-true big-cap giants, an environmental issue or two, and at least some bonds. (We also hope you'll say a firm no to anyone who tries to sell you a fledgling high-concept technology company.) But how do you know how much of each you should own, in relative and absolute terms? To what extent should you diversify within each category? And should every investor buy the exact same mix?

In this final chapter we give answers that are as explicit and detailed as possible. We offer six sample portfolios, geared toward investors with between $50,000 and $2 million and designed to take into account different life situations and different tolerances for risk. Of course, these portfolios aren't the final word. There's plenty of room within them for substitutions and some creative tinkering—if you wish. But they'll also serve you just fine if you take them just as they are (with the caveat, of course, that investments always need to be monitored for ongoing developments).

There you have it—a quick preview of what lies ahead in the rest of the book. But before moving on, we want to offer two additional thoughts on technological limits. We know that many people resist the idea that technology is slowing down. It's worth examining why. We think that one reason is that people commonly confuse gains in our ability to accumulate data with genuine technological break-throughs. It's indisputable that, thanks to computers, researchers are generating reams of data never before possible. We have lots more information about a lot of things, and it's easy to assume that this represents impressive technological progress. But the ultimate value of all this data remains questionable. Without the ability to make sense of it, a glut of information can be not only meaningless, but harmful.

On May 5, 1998, the *Wall Street Journal* carried an illustrative little article about supposed technological advances in our ability to predict tornadoes. In the late 1980s, the newspaper recounted, the National Weather Service prevailed upon Congress to upgrade its radar system, at a cost of $4.5 billion. One major argument for the new Doppler radar technology was that it would greatly increase forecasters' ability to track tornadoes, by giving them information not previously obtainable about the movement of raindrops within a storm.

Unfortunately, it turned out that forecasters had no reliable way to interpret what the various raindrop patterns meant—some of the time a particular pattern would result in a tornado and some of the time it would not. To be safe, whenever forecasters observed a particular configuration of raindrop movements, they would issue a tornado warning—and as a result, the number of false warnings zoomed. The result of *that* was that many people in those areas began turning a deaf ear to all tornado warnings. Meanwhile, because the National Weather Service had invested so much in the new technology, it had reduced the number of volunteers it trained to gather information about storms in the field. "We've got this wonderful piece of technology giving us lots of information, but we don't have the ability to interpret it at all," the *Journal* quoted Brian Peters, a meteorologist in the Birmingham office of the National Weather Service. "You hope and pray your interpretation is correct. It's not quite reading tea leaves, but it is a close kin."

There's a second and even more basic reason why the notion of technological limits is resisted. When it comes to technology, many people simply go on faith, and faith is hard to eradicate. There is an ingrained belief that when push comes to shove, technology will come to the rescue. Jane Brody, in a personal health column in *The New York Times* on June 2, 1998, talked about smokers in the 1960s who shrugged off the warnings of the Surgeon General that smoking causes lung cancer. Their reasoning was that by the time they got old enough to develop cancer, science would have come up with a cure. If that isn't blind faith in technology, I don't know what is. And guess what—30 years later people are still dying of lung cancer.

Today, all of us who drive large gas-guzzling cars are implicitly guilty of the same attitude. We know that oil is finite but deep in our gut can't believe we'll ever have to worry about running out. Surely, by the time we get close to that point, we'll have found an alternative. Ditto for water and ditto for polluted air. When things get down to the wire, technology will bail us out—or so we'd like to believe.

The main goal of this book is to point you toward investment success in the coming era of inflationary growth. But if the book also helps spread the realization that technological progress is facing limits, that, too, will be a good thing. Only when the limits are recognized will there be any hope of reorienting research so that some of them may be overcome. We'll then have a better shot at solving some of the problems facing the world—and for investors, it also may bring back the fun of investing in small tech!

But enough of philosophical musings. Now on to the good stuff—the underlying trends and the investments that will allow you to benefit from them.

THE BIG PICTURE

1

THE COMPUTER REVOLUTION SLOWS DOWN

The slowdown in technology at large begins with a slowdown in computers, which are at the heart of modern technology. Computers have been a phenomenal success story. In just a few decades they have swept through the world, while computer companies have become major presences in the stock market. But now the computer revolution is finally winding down as miniaturization—the driving force behind it—reaches limits. For investors, one message is that only the most entrenched and best capitalized computer companies are worthy of their investment dollars. Marketing is in. Innovation is out.

George Bush once irritated countless voters by emerging from a supermarket and commenting in tones of awe on the wonders of the price scanning equipment at the checkout counter. Many Americans understandably took this to mean that he was woefully out of touch with ordinary lives, given that scanners had been common in stores for many years.

Yet there was something touching about his reaction, because while most of us already took scanners for granted, if you think about it they *are* miraculous little machines, and Bush's wonder had an innocently childlike quality to it. If any one of us had been transported directly from, say, the 1960s to the present era, we'd probably all be marveling, too, not just at scanners but at all the ways that computers are routinely used in today's world.

In fact, it's not even open to question. When you think of technology in the second half of the twentieth century, the first thing you think of is the computer. In less than four decades the computer has gone from a gigantic, unwieldy, exotic machine available only to a few large institutions to a ubiquitous part of everyday life.

At the same time, computers have made their mark in a big way on the investment scene. Today two companies in the computer field—Intel and Microsoft—together are bigger in terms of their capitalization than any single other company in the world. Moreover, the computer revolution, in a very direct way, has contributed to the amazing bull market of the 1990s. The reason is that as computers have become ever smaller, more powerful, and more affordable, they have been used by more and more companies to achieve efficiencies that they otherwise could not have effected. Thus computers have led directly to increased corporate profits, which have been behind the rise in stocks.

Now, though, the computer revolution is winding down. The reverberations will be felt in the stock market and in the economy at large. The slowdown in computer technology is the first, critical piece in an amalgam of trends and developments that ultimately will transform the entire investment arena.

THE INCREDIBLE SHRINKING CHIP

To understand the significance of the slowdown, you first have to appreciate the incredible rate at which computers have progressed up to now. Since their inception, computers have improved at an exponential rate. The fastest computers today, the supercomputers, operate nearly a *billion* times faster than the early computers—performing close to five trillion operations a second compared with about five thousand operations a second for machines in the early 1940s and 1950s.

If cars had progressed at the same pace, we'd be able to drive around the world in under an hour. Or if the number of miles per gallon had improved at a like rate, we'd be able to drive to the moon and back on less than one gallon of gas. But they haven't—only the computer has made such giant strides, at a remarkably consistent and headlong rate.

Moreover, early versions of the computer by virtue of their large size and multimillion-dollar price tags were available to only a handful of government agencies, universities, and big corporations. Today computers are so compact and affordable that they are in hundreds of millions of homes and businesses around the world. Even small children are frequently given their own personal computers, which in some circles are considered as much a right and necessity as a backpack.

The key to the computer revolution has been relentless miniaturization. Early versions were gigantic—one known as the ENIAC, for instance, came in at about 70 feet long and seven feet high. These early models were built around vacuum tubes and by today's standards would be considered agonizingly slow.

One breakthrough came in 1947 with the discovery by Bell Lab scientists of the transistor, which within a few years began to replace vacuum tubes in computers. Like vacuum tubes, transistors transmit electrical impulses, but they are smaller, use less energy, and give off less heat, which means they can be safely packed into smaller containers.

In the 1960s computer technology was transformed yet again by the invention of the integrated circuit, in which all the different electronic components are manufactured as a single unit. In 1971, Intel, founded three years earlier, introduced the world's first microprocessor, or computer on a chip—an integrated circuit containing everything necessary to serve as a central processing unit, or CPU. All these developments helped shrink the computer to a convenient desktop size, making possible the advent of the personal computer and bringing the computer into the home while challenging the dominance of the mainframe.

But this was just the start. Over the past three decades there has been a dazzling progression of ever faster and more powerful chips. In 1965, Gordon Moore, a founding partner of Intel, the dominant producer of microchips, predicted that every 18 months computer chips would double in speed and power. And for a long time Moore's law held sway. By continually finding ways to shrink the size of transistors, Intel and other chipmakers were able on a regular basis to keep introducing new, improved chips that contained about twice the number of transistors as the preceding version and that could run computers about twice as fast. Moreover, these gains in speed and power came at no extra cost to the consumer, because it costs no more to manufacture a chip with more transistors than with fewer. The cost per transistor actually was being halved with each new version.

For instance, in 1982 Intel introduced the 286, the chip used in the first mass market machine. It contained 200,000 transistors and performed 1 million operations a second.

The next generation chip was the 386: It contained about a half million transistors, and some versions could perform 8 million operations a second. (The same basic chip in terms of its architecture generally goes through several versions, with later ones offering more power.)

In 1989, the 486 came on the scene with about 1 million transistors. Some versions could process 50 million operations a second.

In 1993, Intel unveiled the 586, also called the Pentium. With 3.2 million transistors per chip, it was twice as fast as the 486. Moreover, starting with the 486 and the Pentium, Intel users, for the first time, had access to a mouse. Until then, the only operating system used in Intel-based machines was the far more cumbersome DOS (disk operating system), in which users had to remember a complicated series of commands rather than simply pointing to a cute little icon. In 1990, however, Microsoft, which supplies the operating software for Intel machines, introduced Windows 3.0, which was soon followed by Windows 3.1. In conjunction with the faster microchips, this new software finally gave Intel users the ability to keep more than one program open at a time and to switch back and forth easily among them. (Of course, users of Apple computers had enjoyed this advantage right from the start, and many Apple devotees would still swear the original Apple system remains far superior to Windows.)

REPEALING MOORE'S LAW

The Pentium, however, marked a fundamental turning point. Since then, Moore's law has become inoperative, as computer technology approaches an array of fixed physical limits. It is getting more technically difficult and hence more expensive to keep fitting more transistors onto a chip. Moreover, doubling the number of transistors per chip no longer translates into a chip that runs twice as fast, because of other physical limits that act as a constraint on overall speed.

As a result, after the Pentium, progress in Intel's chips has been relatively insignificant, as the chart titled "Processor Performance" shows. In recent years, the newest computers haven't been that much better than older models. The gains in speed and power have been incremental, not exponential. And the measurable benefits to users have been far fewer.

The next chip was the 686, called the Pentium Pro. The name itself could be seen as a tip-off to the fact that the new chip was merely a refined version of the previous offering, not a brand new animal. On the surface the Pentium Pro seemed to be a major leap forward, in that it contained about 6 million transistors compared with 3.2 million for the Pentium. But this was misleading, because in terms of performance it was only marginally better. For instance, a Pentium Pro/200 is less than 20 percent faster than the Pentium/200. By contrast, the Pentium/200 was two to three times as fast as the

SPOTLIGHT ON MICROSOFT

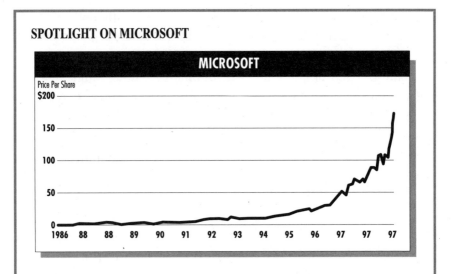

- Microsoft is the leading software company in the world.
- A version of its Windows software serves as the operating system in more than 90 percent of the world's personal computers.
- Microsoft is the leader in applications software such as spreadsheets and word processing and in consumer software such as Encarta.
- Microsoft is likely to extend its leadership to the Internet, where its Explorer browser should lead the pack.
- In the 1990s both profits and revenues grew by more than 40 percent yearly.
- Microsoft has a pristine balance sheet.
- Microsoft stock appreciated more than 50-fold during the 1990s.
- Growth will slow in the years ahead but should still remain above 25 percent a year well into the first decade of the new century.
- The stock's price to earnings ratio (P/E) should be at least twice that of the Standard & Poor (S&P) 500.

comparable 486 chip. And on some tasks—especially on games and software developed for the Pentium—the Pentium was actually faster than its successor.

The Pentium Pro was followed by the Pentium II, and again the name suggests the relative insignificance of the change. Overall the differences among the various Pentiums have proved small. On many but not all tasks, the later Pentiums are faster. But the differences have always been relatively small and never the quantum leaps that were the norm in the past.

Even confirmed technophiles have seen the writing on the wall. John Dvorak, columnist for *PC Magazine*, wrote in its May 27, 1997 issue, "I've always advocated that people keep up with technology by buying the newest and fastest system they can afford. But it's hard to make this recommendation when there's no logical reason to do so. . . Right now, I see no reason to recommend anything faster than a midrange Pentium PC."

In 1997 Intel previewed its next chip, the Merced. Originally expected to be on the market in 1999, the chip's introduction has been delayed because of manufacturing-related problems. Though the Merced is designed to be compatible with existing software, the plan is not to market it as a substitute or replacement for the Pentium II, no doubt because as with the Pentium Pro it will not run existing software faster. Rather, Intel has targeted it to the very high-end cor-

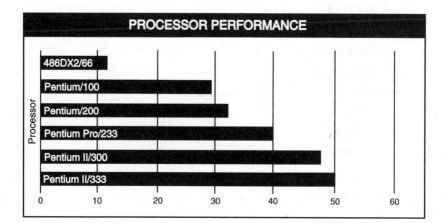

porate market, and it is being cast as a rival to existing Reduced
Instruction Set Computing (RISC) chips, produced by competing
chipmakers. These chips are used in high-end workstations—computers that perform highly sophisticated graphical and numerical
analysis—and in servers or computers that serve as a link to a corporate network of smaller computers.

The Merced is likely to be the end of the line. Early versions will
probably contain as many as 20 million transistors, more than twice
as many as on today's Pentium II chips. Later versions, according to
Byte magazine, may contain more than 100 million transistors. But
because of various physical limits, it is almost certain that the fivefold jump in transistors per chip, if it happens, will not translate into
a fivefold jump in processing power. Moreover, even if it did, it
would still be true that the jump between the early Merced and later
incarnations would be far less than the jump between the 486 and the
Pentium II. And viewed even more broadly, the jump to 100 million
from 20 million is peanuts compared with the 20-million-fold
increase we've seen up to now in the speed of personal computers.
Clearly, no matter how you look at it, we're closer to the end than to
the beginning.

THE PHYSICAL LIMITS

We keep referring to physical limits that computers are encountering.
What exactly are these mysterious limits? One has to do with lithog-
raphy—printing through light. Light waves, emitted from various
materials, are used to etch silicon, the raw material from which chips
are made. The more finely it can be etched—in computer jargon, the
smaller the chip's "features"—the more transistors can be fitted in.

The laws of physics dictate, however, that whatever light is used
must have a wavelength no bigger than the smallest feature of a chip.
Thus, to etch silicon ever more finely, you need to keep switching to
lights that emit shorter wavelengths. But such lights are both more
expensive and more difficult to manage.

Moreover, as the feature size shrinks beyond a certain point, other technical problems loom large. For instance, the transistors will begin leaking current, even when computers are turned off.

As a result, using current lithographic methods, a feature size of about 0.1 micron is considered the limit. (A micron is one-millionth of a meter.) Early versions of Intel's Merced chip have a feature size of about 0.18 micron. That is extremely close to the 0.1 micron limit, which is why past rates of progress in transistor packing simply aren't sustainable.

Physical laws also explain why in recent years doubling the number of transistors per chip no longer means doubling the computer's speed and power. The reason is that to take advantage of the faster chips, the whole system has to be made faster. For instance, you must increase something known as bus speeds—the speeds at which the microprocessor communicates with other parts of the computer, such as computer memory. If bus speeds can't be increased, gains in the microprocessor itself will have little impact. But bus speeds are limited by the necessity of dealing with the electromagnetic fields created when electrical signals are sent from the microprocessor to other parts of the computer. Because of electromagnetic interference, bus speeds have less potential for improvement than processor speeds and act as a constraint on the entire system.

Physical limits are inextricably intertwined with financial limits, because as physical limits are neared, it becomes ever more expensive to wring out extra units of speed. Each new generation of chip requires construction of a new fabrication plant. Intel recently spent $1.3 billion on a plant in Arizona. Gordon Moore has estimated that it may cost up to $10 billion to build a plant to produce the next generation of chip, which will use current lithographic methods. To construct a plant that would use a revolutionary lithographic method, such as printing through X-rays, would cost a lot more, assuming such a process even proved physically feasible. Moreover, it becomes less and less likely that potential buyers will feel the need to upgrade, because the relatively small increases in power won't bring any tangible benefits.

LIMITS TO SOFTWARE

Limits in computer hardware are only part of the story. Hardware is useless without the software to go with it, and software, too, is hitting limits.

In fact, one of the most striking things about recent computer history is how much effort and money have been poured into making so little real progress in developing improved operating systems. It took Microsoft years to produce its original Windows software, which, while a boon for the users of Intel-based computers, did nothing more than give them the capabilities that Apple users had had all along. Then it took many more years for Microsoft to come up with a successor to Windows 3.1. Microsoft introduced Windows 95 in 1995 with great fanfare (and two years later than planned). But one of the most noteworthy things about it was that, while somewhat more convenient to use than Windows 3.1, it ran existing applications slower than its predecessor. All in all, the product took about five years and countless hours to produce—just to come up with a package that at best was just a bit easier to use than the one already available.

Why is progress in software so slow? One answer is that software is developed by human beings. Asking why we can't keep developing better and better software is, to some extent, like asking why musicians can't keep composing better and better symphonies, or playwrights write better and better plays. A large part of software development is creative. It can be automated only to the extent that we understand the creative process.

In addition, software has become increasingly cumbersome. This is partly out of a frantic need to keep adding new features to distinguish the latest software from earlier versions and partly to ensure that the new software will work seamlessly with the increasingly complex chips it is designed to run. Thomas Landauer, in his book *The Trouble with Computers* (MIT Press, 1995), notes that software productivity, as measured by the number of lines of code a programmer can write in a set time, has been increasing by about 5 percent a year. However, the length of software packages has been increasing by many times that. One result is that we need a growing number of programmers just to keep up. Another is that computer operating sys tems have become so complex that, inevitably, on at least some applications they act as a drag on how fast the latest microprocessors can run. Windows 3.1 required 20 megabytes of space, roughly equal to a 2700-page book. Windows 95 requires about 60 megs—three times more code for very little improvement. Windows NT, which is the corporate version of Windows 95 and the version of Windows designed to make the fullest use of the latest generation of processor, requires over 215 megs, the equivalent of about 30,000 pages of text.

Much of the productivity gains in writing software programs have resulted from languages that allow programmers to identify chunks of an existing program and insert them into a new program. Java and C++ are the main examples. But these object-oriented programs, as they are known, are losing their effectiveness. They are very useful in writing software that can be used by many different types of computers. When attempts have been made to combine them with complex applications such as relational databases, however, the problems have been intractable, as the sad saga of Sybase illustrates. Sybase, based in Emeryville, California, was once a major rival to database leader Oracle. But in the mid-1990s it made the mistake of trying to merge object-oriented programming with relational databases. The stock price plunged, with the company losing nearly 90 percent of its value, and almost overnight the company went from a stellar growth vehicle to a deficit-ridden organization struggling to survive.

In 1998, Microsoft introduced Windows 98 as well as plans for Windows NT 5.0 for corporate users. Again, though years in the making, these latest versions are only marginally different from their predecessors. In other words, the best that Microsoft could come up with, after huge investments of time and money, were mind-bogglingly complex operating systems that are only slightly better than what it offered before—and that may be inferior to competitors' products.

You may have noticed that there is a relationship between new chips and new software that also serves as a drag on faster progress in computers. New chips are designed to run not just "legacy" software (i.e., existing software), but also new software. But as we pointed out, new software is designed to be compatible with operating systems that are many times more complex than previous operating systems. In other words, the far greater complexity of the chip is necessary in part just to make the system compatible with the more complex software. Why not stick with the simpler operating system? Because a simpler operating system will not take full advantage of the more complex chip. It's a Catch 22 situation, in that the more complex the chip, the greater the need for a complex operating system. But the more complex the operating system, the less likely the chip will perform at maximum speed for a wide range of tasks.

SUPERCOMPUTER STRUGGLES

At any given time the fastest and most powerful calculating machines around are known as supercomputers. In talking about the slowdown in computer technology, we've focused so far on personal computers. But as microchips have become ever smaller and more densely packed, they not only have made possible the conveniently sized personal computer, they also have led to explosive gains in the speed and power of supercomputers, where size is not an issue. Supercomputers are an ever-shifting target. The supercomputers of the 1960s, for instance, had far less calculating power than the personal computer sitting on our desk today. But the fastest supercomputers of today are more than 10,000 times faster than that same personal computer.

Today the fastest supercomputers consist of hundreds of microprocessors operating in tandem and thus are called massively parallel processing machines. They can operate at enormous speeds. But they also are unwieldy and difficult to program. Because of this they typically are dedicated to very specific, well-defined tasks. Currently, for example, one of their major uses is simulated atomic weapons tests for the military. There is only a relative handful of supercomputers around, and in the United States their use is allocated between major civilian research centers and various military and governmental agencies.

How fast are supercomputers and how much faster will they get? Intel first announced it had developed a usable computer capable of doing a trillion operations a second at the end of 1996. A trillion operations a second is, of course, almost unimaginably fast. At one operation a second it would take more than 400 human lifetimes to perform a trillion operations. And as of early 1999, the very top-of-the-line machines were performing at five times that speed. Still, it appears that with these leaps forward, computer hardware is reaching the outer limits of its potential speed—and that it is much closer to the end than to the beginning. Current thinking is that a quadrillion (a thousand trillion, known as a petaflop) calculations a second will eventually be possible, but that it will take at least 10 years for that to happen. It's noteworthy that 10 years—which may be an optimistic projection—is longer than it took to go from a billion to a trillion operations a second.

Even after petaflop supercomputers are developed, our predictive powers are not likely to increase all that much. Using chess as an example, a petaflop machine would be able to analyze just one additional move ahead compared to today's machines.

One telling fact about supercomputers is that there are no supercomputer companies left, which is probably the market's way of telling us that supercomputers are running into a variety of limits. The supercomputer companies of the past have either gone bankrupt or merged into other companies. The last stand-alone supercomputer company was Cray Research, which became part of Silicon Graphics. Cray Research was one of the technology stars of the 1970s and early 1980s. Founded by the brilliant Seymour Cray, the stock rose to fame and fortune on the heels of its franchise in supercomputing. But it ran into hard times at the end of the Cold War, when the Defense

Department's needs for creating nuclear attack scenarios lessened and other research projects were given less funding. Commercial demands were not enough to sustain the company. Seymour Cray then launched a new supercomputer company, Cray Computer, which at the time of Cray's accidental death in 1996 was on the verge of closing its doors.

There have been other attempts to start supercomputer companies. One of the best known was Thinking Machines, founded in the early 1990s by Danny Hillis. Hillis made headlines in 1989 when he predicted that massively parallel processing supercomputers would soon replace conventional computers. Thinking Machines staked its future on just such a machine, called the Connection Machine. It did not take long, however, before the company went out of business. Today supercomputers are produced almost as a sideline by a few companies whose primary business is personal computers.

The essential point is that inherent limits in technology mean that it now requires tremendous amounts of money and effort to produce computers that, compared to the advances of the past, are just somewhat faster than earlier versions. Even more important is that the fastest machines don't provide that much more in the way of tangible benefits to the user. As a result, the commercial market for such machines is not enough to sustain the companies that make them.

THE INTERNET AND TECHNOLOGICAL LIMITS

If the computer itself is the invention that most epitomizes technology in the last three decades of the twentieth century, then the Internet probably most encapsulates technology in the latter part of the 1990s. In the last few years the Internet has insinuated itself into everyone's consciousness to an amazing degree—there even is a charming hit movie based upon the romantic possibilities of e-mail. It seems as if everyone is rushing to get online, and clearly Internet use is expanding rapidly. Initially used by scientists as a convenient way to exchange information about research results, today the Internet is becoming both a consumer and a commercial medium. As of early 1999 in the United States alone more than 60 million people were hooked up to the Net, and the number of Web sites had climbed from about 15,000 in 1993 to around 1.5 million. Businesses establish addresses on the World Wide Web as a matter of course, and the Net has become another medium for personal and business communications, shopping, browsing, and more.

Yes, the Internet is hot. And reflecting this, Internet stocks have been *the* big story in the stock market in 1998 and beyond. Internet stocks have come on like gangbusters, with stocks leaping 30 or 40 points or more in a day. Some of this activity has come from hyperactive day traders getting in and out of Internet stocks more than once within a single day, while some has come from investors convinced that the Internet will have a major impact on the business world—that they are in the forefront of a new frontier.

What does it all really mean? We'll have more to say about investing in the Internet later this chapter. But from the point of view of technological advances, all this mad activity probably means less than you might think. For from a technological perspective, one of the most relevant facts about the Internet is that the technology establishing it—enabling computers to communicate with one another via phone lines—has been pretty much fixed since the early 1980s. So while its use is expanding rapidly, both in terms of how many people are using it and for what purposes, Internet technology has more or less matured. And as you'll see, this has implications for which Internet stocks should be long-term winners and which you should approach with particular caution.

What of the Internet's impact on the world in which we live? It is clearly having an effect on how we do business, though there is no evidence that it is actually increasing business productivity. Shopping on the Internet isn't fundamentally different from shopping through interactive TV, which has been around a while. Nor is it likely that electronic commerce ever will completely replace standard forms of commerce. For instance, one of the areas where the

Internet has been most useful is travel. It can show consumers all available flights to a particular area as well as available rates. But even here there are limits. Lists of flights and prices are fine, but a good travel agent's individual knowledge of the world and of his or her customers counts, too.

Beyond its impact on commerce, though, some people have high hopes for the Internet's role in leading to a better future. They see it as an information highway that, by encouraging a rapid exchange of ideas from all around the world, will stimulate creative thinking and lead to major scientific breakthroughs—in effect, a technological key that could get technology moving again.

Maybe so. It seems more probable, though, that just the opposite may be true—the very glut of information available through the Internet may stifle creativity. David Shenk, in his book *Data Smog: Surviving the Information Glut,* makes a similar point and does so by quoting seventeenth-century philosopher Spinoza. Spinoza argued that in tackling knowledge, the first step is to comprehend what we are told. The next step is to accept what we comprehend. Only then can we begin to evaluate critically what we have accepted. In other words, Shenk concludes, the overwhelming amount of information the Internet generates makes creative analysis more difficult, because we're likely to remain forever caught in the early stages of comprehending and accepting. Ironically the Internet, which is working toward becoming a comprehensive catalog of human knowledge, may forestall the creation of new knowledge.

Many people have taken happily to the Internet, while others think it is a time-consuming distraction. From our point of view, however, the key fact is that the technology you see is what you'll be getting for the foreseeable future. As with computers themselves, improvements will be evolutionary, not revolutionary. The Internet will get much faster, and search engines may get a bit more efficient. But it will not be radically different from what it is today. And this bears directly on which Internet stocks to buy and which to avoid, as you'll see later.

THE INVESTMENT MESSAGE

COMPUTER LESSONS: TECH LOSERS VS. A MARKETING WINNER

Nothing more clearly illustrates our point that marketing, not technology, has become the key to success in the computer area than a comparison of the fate of some leading-edge computer companies in the 1990s with that of Dell Computer, a spectacular success story of the same period. In 1987, computer stocks being followed by Value Line included such names as Altos Computer, Apollo Computer, Amdahl, Prime Computer, and Ramtek, all of them technological leaders. But don't bother looking them up today—either they've gone bankrupt or they've merged with other companies. They couldn't make it on their own.

Probably the best known was Digital Equipment, which was taken over by Compaq in 1998. In the mid-1990s, DEC—one of the stars of the 1970s and still a research powerhouse in the 1990s—introduced a chip dubbed Alpha. It was widely considered to be better than any other chip around, including all those produced by Intel. It didn't matter—DEC couldn't compete when it came to marketing and service, and the company couldn't survive intact.

On the software side, one of the most technologically advanced companies was MacNeal-Schwendler, a clear leader in computer-aided engineering. With millions of lines of proprietary computer code, this seemed to be a can't-miss company. In mid-1984 it was trading at about eight dollars a share. As of early 1999, it remained the clear leader in its field—and its stock price was under six dollars a share. In other words, for over 12 years the company has held a technological edge in what would seem to be a big arena, and yet the stock has been a disaster. In terms of investment results, superior technology couldn't hold a candle to superior marketing.

Now look at Dell Computer. This computer manufacturer, based in Round Rock, Texas, is one of the roaring success stories of the 1990s. Its share price rose from about $.10 a share in 1990 to over $60 in 1998—a 600-fold gain that made millionaires out of many investors. During those years the company was a sales powerhouse, with both revenues and profits rising over 30-fold.

But was Dell really the technological leader you might imagine? Not at all. To simplify only a little, Dell buys hardware from the likes of Intel and software from the likes of Microsoft and metal boxes from anyone who sells them cheaply. It puts these pieces together and presto, a personal computer is born and shipped. Some technological skill might be required to assemble and test these parts, but it's a level that many a computer-savvy kid could achieve. What that kid could not do is control inventories as skillfully as Dell or, even more important, market its wares as shrewdly. In other words, Dell is a marketing and business marvel but in no way a true tech company. It spends less on research and development as a percentage of revenues than do companies that produce business forms. In 1977 the company spent roughly seven times more on share repurchases than on research and development. The most rewarding tech company of the 1990s is no more a tech company than is Coke or a dozen other successful consumer product marketing companies.

In the preceding pages we've detailed how computer technology, after decades of propulsive improvements, at last is reaching limits. What does this mean for investing in general and for computer stocks in particular? Your first guess might be that it is a negative. Then again, looking at Bill Gates, founder and head honcho of Microsoft and computer slowdown or not still the richest man in America, you might conclude that it's not. Which answer is right? Actually, both are. The slowdown will hurt some computer-related companies but in many ways will actually be a positive for others. Keep the following points in mind and you'll be in a position to evaluate computer-related investments with a steely eye and clear head.

Big is beautiful. The slowdown in computer technology is a negative for a broad range of small computer companies. By the same token, though, it favors a few big established companies—such as Intel on the hardware side, Microsoft on the software side, and Cisco on the communications side—because it makes it all the more certain that they will be able to retain their ascendancy.

Here's why. With computer technology now advancing at a slowing pace, there is little risk of a new and improved technology coming along to topple today's leaders. It's like musical chairs—if you're in possession of a chair when the music stops, you win. The computer giants like Microsoft and Intel have all the chairs, and the music has stopped. They are natural beneficiaries of the slowdown in tech because they can keep pushing the familiar products they have already established. Young upstarts will be able to compete with them only to the extent that they can come up with strikingly better products, and with technology slowing down, such products simply aren't in the offing.

Marketing is in, innovation is out. This obviously is closely related to the first point, because bigger and more established companies have the wherewithal to come up with the best marketing programs. It explains why it's all but irrelevant that Microsoft's latest versions of Windows are not significantly better than earlier incarnations. It doesn't matter—Microsoft's marketing muscle ensures that those versions will gain wide acceptance. Windows 98, for instance, has been aggressively promoted as an essential upgrade. And while in many ways—for example, adaptability for use with different types of computers—Windows NT 5.0 is inferior to competing operating systems such as UNIX, it, too, is almost certain to become the dominant corporate operating system, thanks to its familiar look and, again, Microsoft's marketing might.

In other words, the new systems will be widely accepted for reasons that have nothing to do with better technology. It's worth noting that both Microsoft and Intel have been spending less money on research and development than on marketing and stock repurchases. For the fiscal year ended June 30, 1997, for instance, Microsoft spent more than twice as much on share repurchases as on research and development, while marketing outlays exceeded research and development expenditures by about 20 percent. The figures were similar for Intel. For both companies, developing new technology is becoming less important than capitalizing on what's already out there. And this makes perfect sense, because the returns the companies can expect from technology per se are becoming increasingly limited as technology itself reaches limits. When innovation is out of the picture, marketing becomes king. And established companies that are marketing juggernauts are in a position to continue to dominate. If you do come across a smaller company that seems promising, don't get too carried away by its research department—just make sure it has a surefire marketing program.

Ditto for Internet companies. As we noted previously, since late 1998 explosive moves in Internet stocks have been one of the big stories in the stock market. At times it has seemed as if virtually any company with a "dot com" after its name has cast a magical spell on investors, and the numbers have been phenomenal. Between September 1998 and January 1999, for instance, the total valuation of the 12 stocks making up the Chicago Board of Options Exchange (CBOE) Internet Index climbed from a bit over $100 billion to more than $500 billion. And this despite the fact that most of these stocks have no earnings. Through big moves up and big dips down, these stocks clearly have to be reckoned with.

Obviously, the key question is, What next? Is it a question of Internet mania, or are these investments for the long term? The answer comes back to the point we made earlier, that the technology establishing the Internet is pretty much fixed. As with computer companies in general, this means that the companies that already have a leading position in controlling the technology will remain the leaders. These include those Internet companies that control the Internet's routers, switches, and cables. In other words, even when it comes to such a hot technological area as the Internet, where if anywhere you might think that small technologically innovative companies can flourish, not so—here, too, established is in, because existing leaders won't be outmoded by technological innovation.

One established company that fits the bill is Cisco. This telecommunications giant has a firm grip on Net infrastructure, supplying some 85 percent of the routers, the ultra-high-powered modems that link computers up with one another. A second leader in Net infrastructure is MCI WorldCom, a business telecommunications provider whose assets include fiber cable that crisscrosses the oceans. Both these companies are positioned to maintain their hold on their markets and to grow rapidly.

Another way to play the Net is through the content providers. But the same approach holds—bigger is better. The two companies best positioned to leverage their assets into Net profits are giants Disney and TimeWarner. With sites ranging from ESPN to ABC, Disney already is a major and rapidly growing Net presence. TimeWarner, which in addition to its growing Net sites also is a cable provider, is potentially a vertically integrated complete telecommunications provider.

But what about the supercharged Net plays that rocketed to stock market success in the past year—America Online, Amazon.com, and Yahoo? Are they the exceptions to the rule, and should investors get or stay aboard? We'd urge caution. Obviously, their valuations have been pushed to breathtakingly high levels, and we think they assume a level of future growth that appears unrealistically optimistic. One key point is that a significant chunk of the growth in the Net in the United States already has occurred, and these three companies have little in the way of profits to show for it. While more and more households will continue to hook up to the Net, much of the cream of the revenue-produc-

SPOTLIGHT ON CISCO

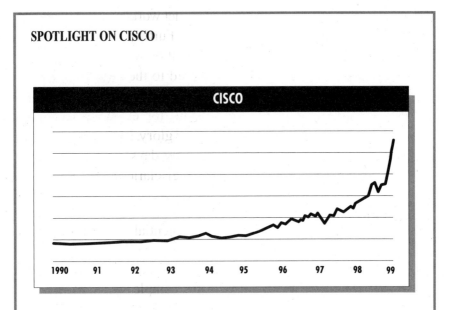

- Cisco is the leading maker of networking products—the hardware used for the Internet and for corporate intranets.
- Cisco supplies 85 percent of all routers in use, high-powered modems used to connect computers to one another.
- Since its public debut in 1990, earnings and revenues have grown at better than 100 percent per year.
- Cisco has no long-term debt despite the fact that some of its growth has come from acquisitions.
- Its stock price has climbed more than 200-fold in the 1990s.
- Growing use of the Internet and telecommunications services in general assures future growth that could be as high as 30 percent annually through 2005.
- With a growth rate more than three times that of the market, the company would not be overvalued with a P/E multiple twice or even three times that of the market.

ing crop in this country—that is, the high net worth and relatively free-spending households—already is online. Further growth will come, but the going will get tougher, and competition will increase.

The Internet has often been compared to the interstate highway system, and this is not a bad comparison. The initial retail successes—Montgomery Ward and Kresge, for example—are either gone or are mere shadows of their former glory, superseded by companies that were not around in those early days, such as Wal-Mart and the Gap. Today's initial Internet beneficiaries on the retail side may suffer similar fates.

What could go wrong. There are a few potential pitfalls for the large and established computer companies. In the case of Microsoft, and also Intel, one obvious concern is the government, whose antitrust suits against the two companies could have unpleasant consequences. It's worth noting, however, that the very fact that tech companies now can threaten to become monopolies or near monopolies shows that factors other than dynamic innovation are defining the market. Remember the old phrase, build a better mousetrap and the world will beat a path to your door? When better mousetraps still can be built, their creators can outsell even the most entrenched maker of existing mousetraps. Only when the differences between the best mousetrap and the next best are minimal can the entrenched stay that way.

A second thing to be alert for is any sign that a dominant company is losing its touch, making critical mistakes in judgment, as IBM did in the early 1980s when, fearful of cannibalizing its mainframe market, it chose to downplay personal computers. It was this miscalculation that caused IBM to lose its leadership position in the computer industry. It's always possible that today's leaders will make a comparable error. The point, though, is that apart from problems with the government, they control their own destinies. They could make a mistake, but they won't be brought down by better technologies that overtake them. The message, again, is that investors should focus on the skills of management, not the prospects for technologically exciting products.

In the case of Microsoft, there is one other potential threat, which ironically is the exact opposite of new and better technology emerging—rather, it is the possibility that older technology might come to seem like a respectable alternative. We've noted that each new generation of Microsoft software is strikingly more complex than earlier versions. One result is to virtually ensure that new programs are somewhat unstable—that they are "buggy" and prone to crashing now and again.

This opens the door to simpler programs that are based on much earlier software versions. One such newcomer is an operating system called Linux, which is based on UNIX and was developed by hundreds of independent programmers working collaboratively. The source code for Linux is in the public domain, and the operating system is virtually free to any company, meaning that its cost is whatever is required to implement the product on a companywide basis. As a stand-alone product, Linux lacks a graphical user interface (GUI), which is at the heart of Windows. But GUIs also are being developed separately in the same open and free fashion as Linux. Will these alternatives to Windows—more stable and possibly cheaper—turn out to be a real threat to Microsoft's dominance? Probably not, given Microsoft's marketing clout. But it's interesting that if Linux does prove a surprise contender, it will be a case not of new technology overwhelming the old but of older technology proving its worth all over again.

Even the biggest and best computer stocks shouldn't top your investment list. Okay. If you're going to invest in computer stocks, big is better and marketing is king. But, you might be wondering, should you bother investing in these stocks at all? With technological progress slowing down, how do they compare with the best stocks not in the computer area?

It's a very good question. We'd answer it the following way. If you can buy only five stocks, we wouldn't include any in the computer area—there are too many others we like more. If you can buy only 10 stocks, the same thing—you could do better. But if your portfolio is large enough to accommodate around 15 stocks or more, you could include a few tech leaders like Microsoft or Cisco. They should be good solid performers, because strong worldwide growth will mean growing markets for computers, and Internet growth, which is clearly wired in, will benefit them as well.

Why wouldn't we rate them as our top picks? Because the slow-down in computer technology means that computer buyers will not feel the same need to replace their computers, or computer software, with newer versions at the same rapid pace as in the past. In other words, computers are becoming more like durable goods and less like disposable items. By contrast, the big consumer companies—which we discuss in Chapter 8—deal in products that need continual replenishment. If you drink a Coke on Tuesday, you're likely to want to drink another one on Wednesday.

2

THE PERILS OF SMALL TECH

It's not just small computer companies that should be avoided—the same goes for small tech companies across the board. A few might make it, but they're low-percentage plays, and the great majority will be disappointing. The reason: To succeed over the long haul, tech companies are dependent upon technological breakthroughs that can lead to genuinely innovative products—and such breakthroughs simply aren't in the offing. Why the general slowdown in tech? Ironically, a major reason is the computer's increasing dominance in research labs—which, for reasons we'll explain, is actually short-circuiting the chances of meaningful discoveries.

Recently we picked up a copy of Value Line from 1987 to see which technology companies the service was following at the time.

Among those featured were eight companies providing advanced
telecommunications products, designed to transmit voice and data
more quickly and easily over phone lines. These were by no means
fly-by-night start-ups—they were solid enough that Value Line
deemed them worthy of ongoing coverage.

FATE OF TELECOMMUNICATIONS			
Companies Being Followed by Value Line in 1987			
	1983 Price	1998 Price	% Change
ADC Telecommunications	$0.7	$24	3,329%
Andrew Cp.	5	16	220
DSC Comm.	12	24	100
Gandalf Technologies	12	0	-100
Graphic Scanning*	10	5	-50
M/A Com.**	26	12	-54
Mitel	15	8	-47
Northern Telecom	9	40	344
Total Return S&P 500			900

*GSCC acq at 5 in 91; **M/A acq by AMP in 95.

How have they fared since then? The chart titled "Fate of Telecommunications" tells the story, and clearly you wouldn't want to have had
most of these companies in your portfolio. Only one of them outperformed the S&P 500; we'll get to that one in a minute. Of the three
companies that spent the highest portions of their revenues on research
and development, one, Gandalf Technologies, went belly up in the
early 1990s. The other two, M/A Com and Graphic Scanning, were
acquired at prices well below those that prevailed in 1983. And that's
despite the fact that all three of them were widely regarded at the time
as having products that were a step ahead of competitors' offerings.

The second most successful of the group was Northern Telecom,
Canada's largest and North America's second-largest telecommuni-

cations equipment company. The one true success story was a relatively small company called ADC Telecommunications, which in subsequent years outperformed the S&P 500 by a wide margin. At first glance it appeared as if this might challenge the view that small tech is the road to nowhere. But a closer look showed that nothing could be further from the truth. As Value Line put it, ADC was not really a tech company at all, in that it was not built around technological products. Rather, it provided a variety of marketing and consulting services to other technology companies.

In other words, of the two companies that were not major disappointments, one was large and well-established enough to have a major edge in marketing its products, and the other was actually in the business of marketing. The pure tech plays, on the other hand, just couldn't cut it.

And here's why. When technological progress is incremental rather than explosive, it is unlikely that any gain will be meaningful enough to overcome the advantages of size and marketing. The companies that fared so disappointingly had state-of-the-art products, but it didn't matter—the products weren't so dramatically much better that they could propel the companies to success. It's just as we saw in Chapter 1 with computer companies. The relevant question isn't whether Microsoft's software is technologically the best available. It's whether any other software company can compete with Microsoft in terms of marketing. The same goes with tech companies in general. And the clear conclusion is that investors should view any small tech company with the utmost caution.

SURVEYING THE SLOWDOWN IN TECH

Clearly, the first big trend we've identified—a broad-based slowdown in technology—has major investment repercussions. But we don't expect you to take this trend on faith. In this chapter we first lay out how technology is slowing down and why. Then we'll return to some of the further ramifications for investors.

PREDICTING EL NINO

One of the most publicized weather/climate events of the 1990s was the El Nino of 1997–1998. El Nino, which means Christ Child, is identified by unusually warm water off the coast of Peru. El Ninos probably have been occurring for centuries but got little notice until the early 1970s, when a severe drought allegedly caused by an El Nino resulted in major worldwide food shortages.

How much have we really learned about predicting El Ninos since then? Not much, despite sophisticated computer models. It's true that the El Nino of 1997–1998 was forecast earlier than similar occurrences in the past. But that wasn't because of superior climate models. Rather, scientists realized that if they put in more ocean temperature monitors, they could tell sooner when the ocean was getting warmer. It's like predicting the temperature of a bath by measuring the temperature of the water as it is coming out of the faucet—it involves common sense more than science.

Nor were scientists particularly prescient at predicting how this particular El Nino would affect weather around the globe. This became clear one night in October 1997 while we were watching a Ted Koppel *Nightline* show devoted to El Nino and featuring a panel of respected scientists. Their discussion resembled nothing so much as the ones we used to have with college friends during football season, when we'd all heatedly debate the significance of the scores of past games to predict the outcome of the upcoming weekend's games. The Koppel discussion was similarly enlightening (i.e., not very). The most telling remark came from Richard Andrews, head of California's effort to prepare for El Nino: "In my mind every probability [of a natural disaster] is 50-50. Either it will happen or it won't happen." This is quite a comment on technology's ability to make helpful predictions.

In the broadest terms, we look to technology to help us in three basic ways. First, it should help us predict the future better—for example, to give us longer-term and more accurate weather forecasts. Second, it should increase our control over nature—through creating drugs to combat disease, for instance, or fertilizers to increase food production. And third, we want technology to increase productivity—to increase the output of individual workers.

It turns out that after big leaps forward earlier in this century, technology is not making notable progress in any of these areas. In this chapter we'll focus on the first two ways technology should help us and save our discussion of productivity for Chapter 4.

Weather forecasting.   You might think that we've made great strides in our ability to predict certain aspects of the future—and the weather would seem a prime example. After all, we're a long way from the days of consulting the *Farmer's Almanac*. Today we have supercomputers that can process data at the rate of several trillion operations a second, and one of the major applications of supercomputers has been in the field of weather forecasting. If we could make accurate forecasts sufficiently in advance, there would be major benefits to farmers, airlines, city officials, and so on. And these could translate into significant profit gains for companies that depend in one way or another on the weather, as well as for those that produce weather-predicting instruments and programs.

Computers have made progress in this area, but their forecasting ability is now increasing at a slowing rate, and further improvements will be harder to come by yet. In the early 1980s, according to an article in the September 20, 1996 issue of *Science*, when supercomputers were roughly 10,000 times slower than today, weather forecasts were fairly accurate to within five or six days. Today, with our much faster machines, we've added just one extra day or so. An extra day can certainly be significant in preparing for a weather disaster. But the time and increased calculating ability required to peer just one extra day in the future suggest limits more than open-ended progress.

The same goes for efforts to predict longer-term changes in climate. For example, supercomputers have been used to try to predict both future levels of greenhouse warming and the effect on overall climate. The results haven't been spectacular. According to Klaus Hasselman, writing in the November 20, 1997 issue of *Nature,* "model predictions of future greenhouse warming are still uncertain to within around 50 percent."

HIV and other viruses. When it comes to controlling and not just predicting nature, technology also has been making less headway than is generally assumed. Take viruses, for example, which are the simplest of all living organisms. How much progress have we really made in understanding and dealing with them? Not much. Forty years ago a single researcher, Jonas Salk, working without a computer, was able to conquer the curse of polio with a simple vaccine of dead cells. Like the live Sabin vaccine that eventually replaced it, it provided nearly complete, lifelong protection against polio, in effect eradicating the disease. Moreover, the vaccine was inexpensive and easy to administer, had no side effects, and was soon available worldwide.

Compare this to the situation today with AIDS, which is reaching pandemic proportions in parts of the world. AIDS also is caused by a virus, the HIV virus. If you have paid superficial attention to the science section of your daily newspaper, you might think that recently we've made great strides in treating AIDS and that it's only a matter of time before a complete cure is found. Strikingly, at year-end 1996, *Time,* the leading popular news magazine, and *Science,* the erudite publication of the American Institute for the Advancement of Science, concurred on the year's greatest accomplishment. For both, it was progress in the war on AIDS.

And it's true that there had been progress. For the first time since the disease had been diagnosed in the early 1980s, it could be treated with some success. Researchers had come up with a cocktail of assorted drugs that in combination could ease the symptoms and prolong lives. What's striking, though, is how limited the solution has been. The drugs neither prevent the disease nor provide a complete cure. They have debilitating side effects and, moreover, are prohibitively expensive, leaving most of the Third World out in the cold.

Most fundamental of all, we have no greater insight into the AIDS virus today than before and thus no reason to think a more complete treatment will soon be found. AIDS is devastating increasingly large areas of the Third World. Moreover, evidence is mounting that new strains of the AIDS virus are successfully resisting the drugs that up to now have worked best.

Bacterial infections. Similarly, we've also made little progress in conquering bacterial infections since Fleming's serendipitous discovery of penicillin in 1928. Remarkably, penicillin, which was first marketed in the early 1940s, is still regarded as the safest and best of the antibiotics. One disease that didn't respond to penicillin was tuberculosis. The most effective antibiotic against that disease is streptomycin, which was introduced just shortly after penicillin. "New" antibiotics are basically just refined versions of older ones. In other words, when it comes to dealing with bacterial infections, the big magic occurred decades ago.

Cancer. One of the most striking signs of the limits of technology in the medical area has been lack of progress in the war on cancer. Some 30 years ago President Nixon declared an all out war on cancer. Today, billions of dollars later, we have made little progress in either understanding or combating the disease, as is brilliantly discussed by Stephen Hall in his book *Commotion in the Blood*. The two chief protagonists of his book are William B. Coley and Steven Rosenberg, both surgeons who sought to battle cancer by marshaling the body's immune system. Both achieved only limited success. One difference is that Coley practiced in the nineteenth century while Rosenberg was schooled in the most advanced techniques of the twentieth century. Hall's point is that in over a hundred years our knowledge of cancer has advanced very little.

His conclusion is echoed by many others, including Sir David Weatherall, chaired Oxford professor. Weatherall states, "We seem to have reached an impasse in our understanding of the major killers of Western society, particularly . . . cancer . . . . Although we have learned more and more about the minutiae of how these diseases make patients sick, we have made little headway in determining why they arise in the first place." And while we have made progress in treating some forms of cancer, such as childhood leukemia, these positive developments are offset by increases in other kinds of cancer, such as melanomas.

Moreover, even to the degree that cancer death rates have been falling, it's not because of technological strides. Writing in the March 20, 1998 issue of *Science,* Eliot Marshall notes, "Basic research *may* have resulted in an explosion of new knowledge about the molecular processes that lead to cancer, but these findings have had little impact on overall cancer figures." Instead, the marginal improvement stems from "smoking trends and early detection."

Life expectancies. The limits of modern medicine perhaps can be best summarized in one depressing statistic. Life expectancies for the longest lived group of human beings, adult women, have stopped increasing, according to the most recent period for which data are available, 1990 to 1995. This is the longest stretch of time in at least a century in which life expectancies for this group have not risen. Moreover, throughout the world the rate of gain in life expectancies has been decelerating, and for the United States as a whole, life expectancies have been advancing barely at all. Furthermore, whatever small gains in longevity have been achieved stem not from technological advances in medicine but—as detailed in *Science* in its May 8, 1998 issue, in an article by James Vaupel and other researchers—from demographic factors such as trends in child-bearing age.

Superconductivity. Medicine is far from the only area where technology's ability to control nature is stalling. Do any readers recall the names Johannes Bednorz and Karl Muller? They are two scientists who in 1986 apparently cracked the problem of superconductivity, which refers to a quality of matter that allows electrons to travel virtually unimpeded through materials. Before then, superconductivity could be demonstrated only at temperatures near absolute zero, which greatly limited its potential uses. At higher temperatures, though, superconductivity promised such technological miracles as super-fast magnetic trains and nearly free electricity.

HURT BY HYPE

SUPERCONDUCTOR FLOPS				
		Five Year Price Change		**% Change**
American Superconductor	AMSC	22	10	-54.55
Superconductor Technologies	SCON	6	4	-33.33
Conductus	CDTS	10	1.5	-85.00
Illinois Superconductor	ISCO	15	1	-93.33
Intermagnetics General	IMG	11	5.5	-50.00
				-63.24

*11/93 through 11/98

In the wake of the discovery that it was possible to achieve superconductivity at temperatures considerably above absolute zero, several companies were formed to exploit the "untold" commercial benefits. Most of the investors that bought into the hype were devastated. As the chart titled "Superconductor Flops" shows, the five companies involved in these efforts have an average five-year loss of more than 60 percent in the stock market. The best of the bunch posted a loss of "only" 33 percent. It's true that several of the stocks experienced periods of speculative frenzy when share prices rose severalfold in relatively short periods of time. For example, the worst performer of the group, Illinois Superconductor, jumped about fivefold in a 12-month period in 1995 and 1996 on news that it had completed development of its first product. If you had gotten in and out at the right time you'd have done very well, but that kind of finesse is hard to count on. And in the end the market is ruthless. If the technology is not up to snuff, technology stocks will end up in the gutter.

Bednorz and Muller discovered that materials containing copper oxide could conduct current without any resistance at temperatures far higher than previously recorded. This seemed like such a breakthrough that it was assumed that further progress was inevitable. On Wall Street, companies expected to benefit from gains in superconductivity went wild.

What's happened since then? Not a whole lot. Recently researchers have been able to come up with a few limited applications of the original discovery, but, using supercomputers, they have not made further progress in discovering new materials that are superconductive at higher temperatures. Meanwhile, superconductor stocks have tanked.

EXPLAINING THE SLOWDOWN

What accounts for the pervasive slowdown in technological progress? For investors, this is not an academic question. If the reasons involve random or temporary factors, there might be hope of a change at any time. The pace of progress might once again pick up, and, among other repercussions, small tech companies might be worth buying after all. If something more basic is inhibiting technological progress, though, the outlook for small tech stocks will remain thumbs down, and there will be other investment implications as well.

And something more basic is at work. A major reason for the slowdown in technological progress is the whole approach to research today—specifically, the fact that most research is computer driven. That's a negative, because there is a fatal mismatch between the capabilities of the computer—even the very fastest supercomputer available or ever likely to be available—and the complexity of the problems we expect it to solve.

Computers are geared toward making stupendously rapid comparisons among huge numbers of variables in the hopes of finding matches. They can solve problems brilliantly as long as the problems are finite in nature. For instance, computers were used to help solve the famous four-color problem. Mathematicians had long speculated that any two-dimensional map could be colored using just four colors (i.e., it seemed intuitively clear that four colors would be enough to ensure that no two adjacent areas ever had the same color). But for a long time no one could actually prove this hypothesis. Then, in 1976, two University of Illinois professors used a computer to enumerate all types of possible maps, thereby solving the problem. For a relatively closed-ended problem such as this one, computers were the ideal tool.

Most real-world problems, though, from the weather to disease to food production, involve variables that for all practical purposes are infinite. And when it comes to infinity, even 5 trillion operations a second is pretty slow. But we haven't come to grips with this fact. Instead, the lure of computers, with their ability to build up and deal with huge amounts of data, is so strong that scientific research has been pushed almost exclusively in their direction. This has resulted in a tremendous amount of labeling and information but has not deepened our understanding of basic processes or resulted in true scientific breakthroughs.

An excellent example of how research is being skewed is the vast human genome project, to which so many hopes have been pinned. Funded by Congress in 1990 as a 15-year multibillion-dollar effort to map the human genome completely, this project is likely to give us huge amounts of data—without really deepening our understanding. The project's goal is to segment the approximately 3 billion bases of the DNA molecule into the 100,000 or so genes that define the human genome. This might seem like a potentially stunning achievement. But it is akin to isolating the letters of an alphabet with no clue as to how they work together to form words, sentences, and paragraphs.

The main problem is that genes rarely work in isolation—by and large they interact with one another. And the number of potential interactions among 100,000 genes is astronomically higher than the number of particles in the universe. It would be written as 1 followed by 30,000 zeroes, an unfathomably big number. It is so big that if we assume that the universe continues for a trillion more years—about 80 times its estimated life span so far—a supercomputer capable of doing a quintillion calculations a second could get to only an infinitesimal fraction of 1 percent of these possibilities. Moreover, this doesn't take into account the possibility of partial interactions among genes or of mutations. Finally, it also doesn't take into account the fact that the portion of the human genome that comprises the 100,000 genes is probably less than 10 percent of our total DNA. The other 90 plus percent has been termed "junk" DNA. No one knows for sure how junk DNA interacts with the "good" DNA.

The point is that the potential number of possibilities involving genes is basically infinite, and no computer will be able to sort them out. The human genome project may result in fragmentary insights, but not the explosion of knowledge that is expected. Listing and labeling genes is not the same as understanding them. Still, researchers are racing to decode. But as for making real break-throughs in understanding and treating disease—we wouldn't bet on it. And we also wouldn't bet on any companies that are built around the hope of such breakthroughs.

Drug companies, too, have embraced the computer with enthusiasm. They are focusing their research on genetic manipulation and on the mass testing of various combinations of chemicals, hoping to stumble upon a combination with positive effects on particular diseases. In this new world of combinatorial chemistry, researchers use computers to screen large databases for any chemicals known to react in particular ways with cells, proteins, or the genomes of bacteria or viruses. If by chance a desired activity is found, the chemical is studied and modified. It's a scatter-gun approach—creating hundreds of thousands of different compounds at a time in hopes of finding one that works.

What's wrong with that? It's that the range of potential chemicals in the world is not for practical purposes all that much different from infinity. It's true that through computer-based research, drug companies can test many more compounds than in the past. But they are still just a small fraction of the possibilities. And typically the combinations are random rather than based upon theories about how diseases operate and what might work against them. What are the chances that randomly creating even many hundreds of thousands of chemical combinations will result in the discovery of wonderful medicines? Not good, given that the body is able to generate about a trillion antibodies to defend itself against invaders. If these haven't worked already, the chances of randomly coming up with something that will work are low indeed. Not to mention that even if we were to find something that worked against a particular disease, there would be a good chance that it also would generate some unwanted side effects.

A BETTER APPROACH

If the computer isn't the answer, what is? One answer comes from looking at where the greatest progress has been made in recent years—which is not the computer lab but through efforts to probe the natural world. In May 1998 the American Society of Clinical Oncology met in Los Angeles. The most exciting and definitive results centered on Taxol and Camptosar, two drugs based on substances found in nature. What's essential to realize about these drugs is that they could *not* have been created by computer-driven laboratory techniques, because their structures are simply too complex. As Colin Macilwain, writing in the April 9, 1998 issue of *Nature,* explains, all the synthetic molecules created by modern, computer-generated combinatorial methods are polymers—relatively simple structures. "The understanding of structural biology doesn't allow for the creation of anything with such a novel structure as, say, Taxol, which consists of four intricately entwined carbon rings," he concludes. It's true that even these drugs at best extend the lives of cancer sufferers and are not cures. But the point is that they are better than anything the computer has been able to generate.

A related answer is to devote more time and effort to theorizing about what is found in nature and then investigating those theories. Returning for a moment to AIDS, the British physician Frank Ryan, author of *Virus X,* has speculated that there is often a special relationship between a virus and its host. One big question that science is making little effort to answer—probably because it is beyond the scope of current technology—is how far a virus's symbiotic relationship with its host extends. It is possible, and indeed, in the case of AIDS, probable, that a virus can exist peacefully in one host but attack the cells of another host. The AIDS virus apparently is harmless in a monkey's cells but becomes vicious in human cells. Ryan makes the interesting if speculative argument that the AIDS virus is protecting monkeys from harm from human predators. Attempting to explore such a possibility by listing possible viruses or virus types, which is where most current research is focused, is like trying to understand why a pool of water reflects an image by counting the number of water molecules in the pool.

AN ALIEN GIFT?

We're not the first to point out the overwhelming complexity of genetic material and, by extension, of the proteins that both create and are created by such material. In 1981 Francis Crick—who along with James Watson helped get the whole genetic revolution going in the first place, sharing the Nobel Prize for deciphering the shape of the DNA molecule—wrote a book called *Life Itself: Its Origins and Nature.* His take on the complexity of nature was to observe that particular proteins are so complex that they could not have emerged by chance even in the billions of years over which life has evolved on this planet. The conclusion of this gifted scientist was that DNA must have come to us via an alien civilization. We don't necessarily go that far—but the point is that the basic building blocks of life and matter on this planet are so complex that the computer's hit or miss approach to understanding and improving upon them is almost certain to prove inadequate.

ANATOMY OF COMPLEXITY: THE HIV VIRUS

How complex is the HIV virus? It consists of approximately 9700 separate nucleotides, the basic components of genes. Each nucleotide can consist of one of four possible elements. The problem is that the nucleotides are not stationary—they mutate. This means that as the virus divides, one or more elements in any of the 9700 positions may spontaneously change to another element. The number of potential life forms that can be created with 9700 spots, each of which can consist of any one of four nucleotides, is *astronomically higher than the number of elementary particles in the entire universe—by which we mean every component of every atom in every galaxy.*

However, not all these possible mutations are a problem, since some will actually destroy the virus, rendering it harmless. In some viruses, including the polio virus, the vast majority of the potential mutations do destroy the basic virus. The remaining mutations are of a manageable level, making it possible to develop a vaccine.

This isn't true of the HIV virus. The number of potential mutations that won't destroy the underlying virus is far too great for any computer to cope with, which is why efforts to develop a vaccine have been unsuccessful so far. Using computers, researchers are frantically trying to catalog various combinations of genes, hoping they will stumble upon a pervasive weakness in the virus through this hit or miss strategy. But the chances are almost overwhelming that they won't. A vaccine is theoretically possible—but it is more likely to result from our finding some indirect way of attacking all possible variants of the HIV virus. This, however, would require us first to develop a better understanding of how viruses function and mutate. Such an understanding is unlikely given our fixation with computer labeling rather than with efforts to get at the workings and interactions of genes or to understand how viruses interact with their hosts.

Moreover, using hit or miss strategies to try to develop medicines or vaccines for a constantly mutating virus runs the huge risk that we may unknowingly provoke the development of mutated forms that are far more virulent than the original virus. The nightmare scenario for AIDS would be a strain that is airborne, like flu and cold viruses. While it may be unlikely that we will inadvertently cause such a strain to be produced, the point is that our current knowledge of viruses does not allow us to rule out the possibility.

CLONING AND HYPE

Wait a minute, you might be saying at this point. Maybe it's true that we're making less progress than generally believed in such areas as treating disease, and maybe the computer is not the white knight of research that many people think it is. But not all the headlines can be wrong. What about cloning, for instance? Isn't that a genuine breakthrough that has the potential to lead to wondrous things?

Once again, there's more hype than substance, and, in fact, the whole issue of cloning illustrates how simplistic much of the thinking on technology and progress is. For one thing, cloning is not as absolutely new as you might think. We've cloned animals from fetal cells in the past and made near clones of mice simply through inbreeding. Studies have shown that even identical twins are not perfect copies, simply because their position in the womb and their experience in coming out of the womb are never identical, and the same would be even more true for clones—they actually would be less identical to the parent than are identical twins to each other, because they would share a completely different birth environment.

Some people have written about cloning as if it will lead directly to genetic engineering that will enable us to create animals and ultimately human beings with any characteristics we want—the ability to do math, say, or to compose a symphony—but this is naïve. The complexity of the human genome is such that if we attempt to manipulate one characteristic, we'd likely wind up affecting other characteristics as well, given that genes are interrelated in such complex ways. Moreover, many of the expectations for cloning ignore the whole subject of interactions between genes and the environment.

In other words, most of the discussion of cloning simply illustrates how simplistic much of the thinking about technology is. It doesn't advance our understanding but rather makes our lack of understanding more obvious.

THE INVESTMENT MESSAGE

Once again, bigger is better and marketing carries the day. As with the computer stocks discussed in Chapter 1, when it comes to technology-related stocks in general, the slowdown in tech means don't take a flier. Avoid small tech companies that depend upon the success of pure research. Instead, stick with the big established companies that have the financial resources and marketing capabilities to sell the products they have.

To see why this is good advice, look at the chart titled "Pfizer vs. the Biotechs," which compares the performance of the biotech stocks with that of giant drug manufacturer Pfizer from the years 1992 through mid-1998. As you can see, the performance of the biotechs—a group that epitomizes small tech, research-dependent stocks—was dismal. The group as a whole ended lower than where it began. And this was in a period when the market as a whole was soaring, with the S&P 500 tripling in price.

Pfizer's performance presents a much prettier picture. While the biotechs were tanking, Pfizer rose nearly sixfold. What explains the difference? Like the biotechs, Pfizer and the other major drug companies carry out research, and they, too, are increasingly wedded to the techniques of computer-driven research. In the case of the drug companies, though, the actual results of their research are far less significant. Even though they are unlikely to come up with genuinely new products, they have the marketing clout to sell whatever they do

come up with as new and improved. In Chapter 8 we discuss this phenomenon in more detail and recommend the best of the big tech
stocks along with other big-cap winners. For now, though, just keep
the following in mind. Small tech stocks like the biotechs, which
depend on genuine breakthroughs and progress, are for masochists
only. They may soar briefly on a story but are unlikely to be there for
the long haul. Stick with the tried and true.

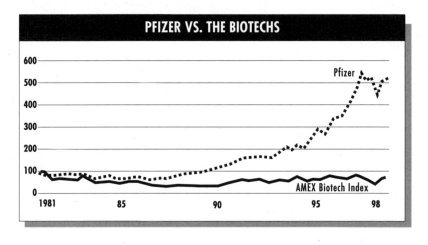

Inflationary pressures will build. The slowdown in technological progress is the first big underlying trend that eventually will lead
to rising inflation. What's the connection? The key point is that technology is not the omnipotent force that many people think. It can't
come up with solutions on demand to whatever problems we face.
Meanwhile, as we'll discuss in Chapter 3, over the next decade and
beyond there is likely to be a tremendous worldwide push for economic growth. One effect will be rising demand for all kinds of
resources, and if technological innovation can't keep pace in helping
to meet that demand, prices will rise. The slowdown in technology is
setting the stage for a new era of inflation—and a long-term reshuf-
fling of the investment deck.

PSYCHED BY DEEP BLUE

One event that both played into and furthered belief in the open-ended power of technology and the computer was the 1997 six-match chess showdown between IBM's Deep Blue and world chess champion Gary Kasparov. For the first time a computer apparently had triumphed over a top-ranked human player, and it seemed as if technology had taken a giant leap forward. The reality, however, was quite different. Big Blue didn't outthink Kasparov—it merely spooked him.

Kasparov won the first game. In the second, though he played with unusual caution, he still managed a draw. But then in a bizarre development Kasparov resigned, giving Deep Blue an unearned win. Why? Because he assumed the computer would not have played into a position in which it traded an obvious advantage for a forced draw. In fact, though, the computer had not seen what Kasparov had assumed any decent player would see and there was indeed a forced draw.

The fifth game shook Kasparov because it led him to suspect IBM programmers might be altering Deep Blue's program in between games, which turned out to be the case. In the sixth and final game, Kasparov—either demoralized or in protest against what he considered cheating by the other side—simply played a dumb game. He didn't so much lose the game as concede it before it began.

All in all, it is clear that if Kasparov had merely treated the computer like any other opponent, the score would have been at worst one win for Kasparov and five draws. Moreover, this assumes that the four games in which Kasparov had advantages would not have turned into wins. The result is very similar to previous computer–human contests and suggests that when it comes to chess, the computer hasn't made notable progress. IBM must have recognized the same thing. After the

Kasparov match the company retired Deep Blue, even though Kasparov offered to play it again and to take money only if he beat it.

There's a footnote. In 1998, to no fanfare whatsoever, the Germans put the most powerful chess program, Fritz 5, onto a computer that made use of five Pentium II processors. The result was likely comparable to Deep Blue in that Fritz 5 with just one processor had given Deep Blue a run for its money. This super-silicon gamester was trounced by Indian grandmaster Anand, who several years earlier had lost a world championship match to Kasparov. Deep Blue may have garnered media adulation, but it turns out that even in a game like chess, in which a theoretical road to mastery is through greater calculating power, computers have stopped making any real progress. And the possible number of chess moves is a joke compared to the possible number of combinations the computer is expected to cope with in the research lab.

3

THE NEW
IMPERATIVE
FOR GROWTH

Along with a slowdown in technological progress, the second big trend that will shape the investment arena as we approach the millennium is surging economic growth, in the developing and developed world alike. Growth has become a necessity, because if growth fails, the whole economic house of cards will come tumbling down everywhere. The investment implications are broad— ranging from burgeoning profits for companies positioned to take advantage of worldwide growth to gains for companies that benefit from inflation, which is a corollary of strong growth.

The economy today is like an airplane that has plenty of gas in the tank but no landing gear. As long as economic growth remains strong, the economy can continue to fly, and all of us—the passengers—will be fine. But if we ever run out of fuel—if growth ever were to slow—then God help us. It would take a miracle for us to land safely. We need growth as much as that plane needs fuel, because there's no alternative economic path that would let us survive in any acceptable fashion.

To put it more directly, in today's world—which is more economically interdependent than ever before and more dependent upon financial assets—growth has become *the* economic necessity. Growth, for the world as a whole and for the United States itself, has become not just desirable but essential, for the consequences of any failure to keep growth going would be dire.

MARKET REACTIONS: 1997 AND 1998

This new necessity for growth was demonstrated clearly by the behavior of the stock market in 1997 and 1998—and by the actions of policymakers in those periods.

Between the spring of 1991 and the fall of 1997, the United States stock market was on a nearly one-way trip. In a bull run unprecedented in its scope and single-mindedness, all the major averages climbed virtually unimpeded. The Dow Jones Industrial Average (DJIA) rose from 2000 to nearly 8000, while the broader-based S&P averages turned in comparable performances. And never once did the averages drop 10 percent or more from a previous high, considered the threshold for a move signifying a fundamental change.

In October 1997 the market's extraordinary run finally came to an end when the DJIA fell from a high of 8170, on October 7, to 7161, on October 27, a more than 12 percent drop. Two things were notable about this plunge—what triggered it and what didn't.

First, what *didn't* cause the drop—a rise in interest rates. For more than 70 years prior to 1997, market declines greater than 10 percent were almost always preceded by interest rate hikes (though not every rise in rates was followed by a decline). This was true even for the crash of 1929, which followed several tightening moves by the Federal Reserve. It seemed to be an ironclad relationship—for the market to tumble significantly, thereby indicating a fundamental change in the United States economy, rates had to be rising.

In fact, the 1990s bull market already had survived a dramatic tightening of interest rates by the Federal Reserve, in 1994. Early that year, industrial commodity prices had begun to rise. Copper, for example, which had bottomed in the low 70s per pound toward the end of 1993, rose to over 90 cents a pound in the first part of 1994. Suddenly the economy seemed to be growing too fast and inflation seemed to be a threat. The Fed acted immediately and decisively and over the course of the year short-term interest rates more than doubled. The bond market, reacting as you'd expect, experienced one of its worst years of the century, with long-term yields rising from under 6 percent to nearly 8 percent. Stocks, though, held their course. The major averages stumbled a bit but never closed more than 10 percent below a previous high. Investors, rightly, were convinced that the long-term prospects for growth and stocks remained bright.

Now for what *did* cause the drop—the fact that several economies of Southeast Asia were experiencing difficulties. In earlier years, this fact probably would have passed totally unnoticed. After all, together these economies accounted for only a nominal share of the world's gross economic product. In fact, the country that started the ball rolling—Thailand—had an economy in 1997 that was valued at less than the market value of Microsoft or the sales of General Motors. Yet events in Thailand—specifically, a run on the country's currency—worried investors in the United States enough that they began to unload stocks. True, once Thailand began to crash and burn, three other South Asian economies—Malaysia, Indonesia, and South Korea—also were exposed as having severe financial woes. Still, the combined GNP of the four countries was just a drop in the economic bucket, and geographically, certainly, they were about as far removed from the United States as possible.

Let's move ahead to the market's second correction, in the summer of 1998. New worries had emerged—the biggest Asian economy of all, Japan, was floundering. The culprit was the previous year's consumption tax hike, which the Japanese had instituted in an effort to balance a deficit-ridden budget.

THE 10 PERCENT RULE

In October 1997, when for the first time in years stocks closed more than 10 percent below their highs, it was a clear tip-off that something major was going on. That's because one of the most reliable rules in the stock market is the "10 percent" rule, first formulated, as far as we know, by the redoubtable money manager Roy Neuberger. The rule states that if a stock goes down by more than 10 percent, it's probably time to get out (or, if you're short a stock, if it goes up more than 10 percent). Or at least take a good look at your position and make sure you have a good reason not to get out. The same goes for the market as a whole—moves of 10 percent or less probably don't mean a lot, but moves greater than that mean the market may be shifting gears and you need to take action.

The thinking is that moves of up to 10 percent can be random, but anything greater means you're probably dealing with a more fundamental change. This makes intuitive sense. To give an analogy, suppose you're a teacher and one of your students does much worse than expected on an exam. You'd take note of the fact but you wouldn't change your teaching methods or rewrite the test—it might just be that the student hadn't gotten enough sleep or some other one-time reason. Suppose, though, that two-thirds of the class did exceptionally poorly. You'd have to assume there was a more fundamental problem—you weren't teaching the material in a way that made sense or the exam was poorly drawn. It's similar with the stock market. Declines of a large enough nature don't occur without a fundamental cause. Why 10 percent? Because it has always worked in the past.

CURRENCY CONNECTIONS

The world's economies are more intertwined than ever before, and the most important link is through their currencies. Investors can trade and price most currencies relative to all other currencies. These relative prices are in constant flux. When Thailand, say, experiences economic difficulties, traders sell its currency, which declines in value. This puts pressure on Thailand to clean up its economic act, which may include taking measures such as cutting back on government subsidies and expenditures and encouraging bankruptcies of weak firms, as well as nearer-term measures such as raising short-term interest rates.

On the plus side, when its currency declines, a country will sell more goods abroad and attract more tourists. On the negative side, it becomes more expensive to buy the goods and services of other countries. Theoretically these distortions work themselves out naturally over time. The idea is that the economic reforms, undertaken to correct the financial imbalances that led to the weak currency in the first place, combined with a renewed surge of exports will revitalize the economy, which in turn will lead to a recovery in the currency.

But in a world where every country is competing with every other country, a weak currency in one can't be so neatly isolated. When the Thai currency weakened, it became easier to sell Thai goods to other countries. This put other Asian countries, which were offering the same sorts of goods as Thailand, at a sudden disadvantage. Their own economic problems, which probably could have been resolved fairly painlessly, rapidly worsened and their own currencies weakened. Soon they were facing major economic crises and suddenly the whole region, including the strong economies of China, Singapore, and Taiwan, were threatened: hence the "Asian flu" that gave the United States stock market the shakes in the fall of 1997 and again in the summer of 1998.

Once again, United States stocks reacted with another drop of more than 10 percent. Investors were convinced that weakness in Japan threatened United States growth—and this was true even though at its worst Japan's economy still was the second most productive in the world and Japan had a lower unemployment rate than the United States. Despite its banking problems, Japan still had trillions of dollars in savings to tap and many potential policy options in reserve to prevent a full-fledged collapse.

In other words, problems in a handful of small Asian economies, and problems that had fairly attainable solutions in a big Asian economy, temporarily brought the formerly unstoppable United States stock market to its knees and triggered a worldwide financial crisis. Clearly, this was a different world from any we had seen before in the postwar period.

Indeed, 20 years ago, economic problems in Southeast Asia weren't considered a big deal. In 1980, Korea was suffering through a recession—but it was barely mentioned in the financial pages in this country. Certainly no one thought to make any connection between that downturn and the economic problems the United States was facing from late 1979 through 1982, including high inflation and two recessions. Other than for the Middle East, the United States was relatively insulated from the ups and downs of other economies. Today nothing could be further from the truth.

UNITED STATES ACTIONS

The reaction of United States policymakers to both crises is highly instructive. When Thailand and other Southeast Asian economies hit the skids, the United States went into overdrive. Perhaps the clearest way of showing how seriously the United States, and in particular the Federal Reserve, viewed the Asian situation in late 1997 is through our chart "Money on the Move," which shows money supply growth in the 1990s. Apart from funds channeled through the International Monetary Fund, which loaned billions of dollars to the beleaguered

Asian economies, the most immediate adjustment we can make is through monetary policy. As you can see, once the Asian crisis started, the Fed jumped in and flooded the United States economy with money by allowing the money supply to grow very rapidly. The intent was to ensure that our economy would be strong enough to absorb any goods that Asia could sell. By early 1998 money growth had jumped from moderate levels to levels not seen since the early 1970s.

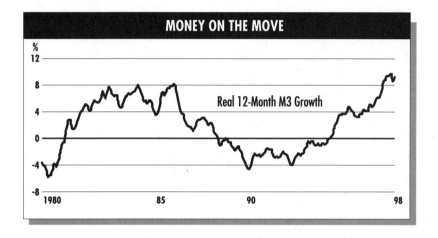

In essence, in the fall of 1997, the United States had de facto declared itself the consumer of last resort. There were risks to this approach. The surge in money growth was on a level seen in the past only when the Fed had been acting to bring the United States out of severe recession—in the early 1970s, in an attempt to jolt the economy out of the severe 1969–1970 recession; in the mid-1970s; and in 1982–1983. Never before had monetary policy changed so dramatically while the economy was running on all cylinders as in 1997. The risk was that this policy would lead to an overheating economy, thus generating inflationary pressures. Clearly the Fed thought it was a risk worth taking. The message was that not only do we live in a deeply interconnected world, but our future depends on us becoming even more interconnected.

The reaction of the United States in the summer of 1998 is equally revealing. Basically, we pulled out all stops to put pressure on Japan to reverse course and aggressively stimulate its economy—to get growth going again. Treasury Secretary Robert Rubin, one of the shrewdest Wall Street traders of his generation, virtually handed currency traders a gift on a platter by saying that the United States did not plan to intervene to stop the depreciation of the yen. The yen promptly sank like a stone, and markets around the world shuddered. Rubin's move, clearly calculated, smelled of desperation. The certain result was a weaker yen, and clearly this was Rubin's intent. Rubin had gambled that the Japanese, seeing the yen crumble, would take quick action to reverse their economic downslide.

The United States tried to pressure Japan in other ways as well. That summer, President Clinton and Secretary Rubin both visited Asia. The President, accompanied by an enormous retinue, traveled to China, where he spent considerable time, even managing to do a United States-like version of talk radio. Rubin went to several other Asian countries to discuss their economic concerns. What did Japan get? A visit by Undersecretary of the Treasury Larry Summers. This was an intentional slight that told Japan to get its act together or risk falling out of favor with the United States—perhaps losing its special relationship with the United States to its historical enemy, China.

Clearly the United States was willing to do whatever it could to get Japan to turn around. (It's worth noting that the United States actions came during an election campaign in Japan and no doubt played a role in the stunning defeat suffered by the ruling Liberal Democratic Party and the subsequent resignation of Japanese Premier Hashimoto.) Again, we were motivated by one critical reality: Over the past 15 years world economies have grown more interdependent than ever before, and more leveraged. United States investors feared that economic weakness in Asia would hurt profit growth of United States companies that sell their products there, and these fears caused United States stocks to plummet. United States policymakers jumped into the act because they couldn't afford to stay on the sidelines. They responded to a key emerging reality of the late 1990s—that in this inextricably interconnected world, a threat to growth anywhere is a threat to growth everywhere. And even more dire, if a worldwide slowdown ever started, there would be little anyone could do to keep it from turning into a worldwide economic catastrophe worse than in the 1930s.

In one sense this makes the world a more unstable, dangerous place. Paradoxically, though, it also makes it potentially safer. Because the consequences of a sharp slowdown in growth anywhere would be so deadly to economies everywhere, the result has been a new imperative for growth. Growth has become not just desirable but an absolute necessity, and the economic movers and shakers, such as the Federal Reserve, have become forced to make maintaining growth their first priority.

This new growth imperative is one of the most significant changes in the world over the past three decades. Combined with the slowdown in technological progress, it has become a key reality that will shape the financial markets for the foreseeable future.

GROWTH IN THE DEVELOPING WORLD

The nature of growth in developing countries makes them especially sensitive to any disruptions that could slow or derail that growth. One of the surest economic laws is that a developing economy will move from a predominantly agrarian focus to a predominantly manufacturing focus (and after that, presumably, to a service or information focus). The key transition is from agricultural to nonagricultural, for that is when it becomes clear just how essential rapid growth is for prosperity in a developing economy.

The chart titled "Farmer Facts" makes this clear. It looks at a broad range of countries from around the world and shows that economic prosperity, as measured by GNP per capita, is negatively correlated with the percentage of a country's workforce employed in

agriculture. There are no counterexamples—in no instance does high
prosperity go along with a high percentage of workers in agriculture.

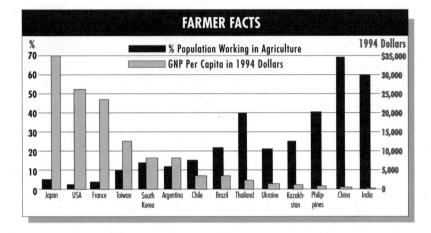

The move away from an agrarian economy doesn't come about
because a country suddenly decides to import its food. Quite the contrary—the impetus comes from the growing productivity of farmers.
As farmers become more productive, by definition fewer are needed
to produce the same amount of food. The ones that remain on the
farm, enjoying increased wealth as a result of their rising productivity, provide a consumer base for the country. There's a price, though.
The economy must generate enough jobs for those who leave the
farms and migrate to the cities. For a country like China, far and
away the largest and most important of the developing economies,
estimates are that growth must remain at 6 percent or higher to avoid
widescale unemployment.

The point is that a recession throughout Asia could easily lead to
enough social unrest to undermine the market economies that have
been established. Once a developing country begins to grow rapidly,
any backward step can lead to massive jumps in unemployment and
is a major risk.

In its own development, the United States was fortunate enough
to avoid disruptions in growth. It experienced nearly uninterrupted

growth between the end of the Civil War and the early 1890s. (According to most data, the recession of the 1870s did not significantly affect the growth in real per capita income.) During this period, per capita income, which at the beginning was at about the level in China today, more than doubled.

One message is that China, despite torrid growth of more than 9 percent a year between 1970 and 1996, still has plenty of room left for further growth, considering that in real terms its economy is about where the United States was a century ago. A second message, though, is that China had better continue to grow rapidly or it, and the whole world, may be facing major upheaval.

The same is true to some extent for all of Southeast Asia. Since 1970 growth in Southeast Asian economies has been on average more than twice as fast as in the developed world, even taking the slowdown in the late 1990s into account. For some of these countries, such as Taiwan and Singapore, per capita income is well above $10,000, the threshold for defining developing countries. Growth was tempered in 1998 but should resume in 1999 and accelerate thereafter. The message is that if these more prosperous countries managed to sustain such rapid growth, it's plausible that less prosperous ones like China, which are starting from a smaller base in terms of per capita incomes, can do the same.

And we need to pray that they will—again, because we're all in trouble if they can't. Let's get specific. Roughly 25 percent of the United States economy today is based on foreign imports or exports, compared to less than 10 percent 25 years ago. True, the big surge in foreign transactions between 1970 and the early 1980s resulted largely from increased oil prices. But since the 1980s, the continuing gains reflect, pure and simply, our growing dependence upon foreign countries as markets for our goods and services and as providers of goods and services to us. Economic problems abroad that result in a fall in foreign imports to the United States would mean higher prices for products we are bringing in from abroad or the necessity to do without those products if we can't make them here. A fall in exports means a loss of business for United States companies.

Suppose both United States exports and imports were to fall by 10 percent, which would bring the level of foreign transactions back to where they had been in 1993, and still much higher than for most of the postwar period. What would that 10 percent decline mean? Extremely rocky times. The fall in exports alone would mean a more than 1 percent fall in total sales, while the drop in imports would mean consumers would be paying more for about 10 percent of all goods purchased here, amounting, in effect, to a big tax increase. Because of the leveraged nature of the United States economy, which we discuss later, the overall result would almost certainly be a recession—if we're lucky. Even more probable, though, would be a full-fledged depression. The United States is in no position to permit even a relatively small step backward in the degree of involvement of foreign economies in United States economic life.

And it's not just the United States whose economic well-being has become increasingly dependent on other countries. Since the early 1980s, world trade has accounted for an ever greater portion of the world's gross economic output. In 1983, fewer than 1 in 10 economic transactions in the world were intercountry. Today the figure is less than 1 in 8, and it's falling rapidly.

In sum, developing countries have a lot more room for rapid growth—that's the good news. On the downside, though, interruptions to that growth are dangerous, because they would likely trigger widespread social unrest that could undermine the developing countries' market economies. Finally, the United States must and, it is hoped, will do whatever it can to keep growth in the developing world alive—because in our increasingly interdependent world, the United States has a vital stake in continued growth everywhere.

GROWTH AND THE DEVELOPED WORLD

The necessity for growth has become urgent not just in the developing world but in the developed world as well. Paul Samuelson, Nobel-prize-winning economist and author of one of the most successful textbooks of all time, *Economics,* once famously quipped that the stock market had forecast seven of the preceding four recessions. In other words, there were three times when the market had plummeted and the economy remained fine. But today, that no longer could happen. Today the United States economy is dependent as never before on the continued health of the stock market, which in turn is dependent upon continued economic growth. Any significant weakening in stocks would likely unleash a series of reactions that would bring the economy crashing down.

What makes the United States economy today so different from those of the past? The changes can be seen in four records the United States economy has been setting throughout the 1990s. First is our record dependence upon foreign economies, which we discussed previously. Second is our record dependence upon financial assets as opposed to real assets like real estate. Third are record debt levels, and in particular consumer debt levels. And fourth are record inequalities between rich and poor. Together these four records make continued economic growth essential. There is no longer a middle ground between growth and depression, because even a small stumble could start the whole economy unraveling.

Let's now look at the second point, our record dependence upon financial assets. Probably the most significant financial event in all of the 1990s was not the balancing of the budget or the passage of the Clinton tax program or megamergers between banks. It was a shift whereby, for the first time, the value of stocks in this country surpassed the value of real estate. (When the major newspapers picked up this story, it wasn't news to us—we'd been writing about it for more than a year.)

This was a highly significant change. Until the mid-1990s, the most valuable asset for most Americans was their home, and this provided much solace in times of economic stress. No matter how bad things got, most Americans could go to bed at night knowing that their chief asset was providing them with financial as well as physical shelter.

Look at our chart "Steady Homes, Shaky Stocks," which traces the median price of single-family homes over the past three plus decades. As it shows, in the postwar period prices have never declined in nominal terms. This has gotten many people through some pretty rocky times: times like the early 1970s, when high inflation and recession were bedfellows; times like the late 1970s, when buying gas for your car became a major challenge; times like the savings and loans crises of the late 1980s and early 1990s. The point is that through all kinds of crises, the average price of single-family homes continued to rise. Sometimes, as in the early 1970s, the rise was less than inflation. But still, even in the worst of times, the family home was a pretty reliable performer, always providing at least a fair measure of security. Homes and real estate have always acted as a dependable shock absorber against a bad economy.

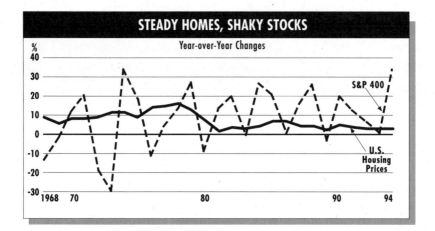

In the 1990s, though, with stocks replacing homes as Americans' most valuable asset, this was no longer true. By 1997, stocks represented more than 150 percent of the value of family homes, compared with about 50 percent in 1980. When people today want to get an idea of their approximate net worth, it no longer suffices to check with a friendly local realtor to get an estimate of the value of their home, as they might once have done. Rather, they need to look over their latest brokerage statements.

And for a long time, with stock prices appreciating steadily and rapidly, brokerage statements have also provided a lot of comfort. As long as stocks continue to rise, fine. The problem is that there is one stunning difference between stocks and homes: While home prices have always advanced pretty steadily regardless of economic conditions, stocks—which are an exceptionally accurate leading economic indicator—are highly leveraged to changes in the economy. Prior to every recession, at least in this century, stocks have fallen 20 percent or more, and sometimes they have dropped this much even without a recession waiting in the wings.

In the past, with stocks a relatively modest part of the country's overall assets, this was not catastrophic—people always had their homes. But today, a protracted decline in stocks would leave people with nothing to fall back on, and the results would be devastating.

Here's how it would work if economic growth were threatened. Stocks, as is their nature, would drop in anticipation of a weakening economy. As stocks dropped, consumers would see their most important asset shrink—and remember, a drop of, say, 20 percent in stocks, which would be in line with past bear markets, would easily dwarf the biggest decline those same consumers ever had experienced in home values. The natural reaction would be to cut back on spending. This, however, would further weaken the economy. Guess what this would do to the stock market—and so on and so on in a particularly vicious and devastating down cycle that truly could spin out of control.

The only way to prevent this cycle from ever getting started is to keep economic growth going. As with the developing world, growth has become necessary in the developed world because the consequences of a failure of growth are so grave.

DIVIDENDS STILL COUNT

Wait a minute, you might be protesting. Wouldn't stocks at some point hit support levels, as their lower prices created greater values? In the past that has been the case. Indeed, in the late 1970s, when the

Dow Jones Industrial Average was trading at about 800, if you can remember back to those primitive times, we had just started our first investment letter, *Investment Strategist.* In one of my first issues we wrote, with as much confidence as you ever can feel in this business, that downside risk in the market was minimal. Why were we so sure? Because the Dow was then yielding nearly 6 percent. The historical record showed that even during the absolute worst of times—in the 1930s, for example—the Dow never had yielded much more than that. In other words, there was reason to be confident that the yield on the Dow in the late 1970s represented a value that investors would be willing to pay for no matter how bad times became.

Prior to the 1990s, while 6 percent was about the most the Dow had ever yielded, 3 percent or so was the least. That record was shattered in the 1990s. In 1997–1998 stocks had been bid up to such high levels that the yield on the Dow dropped—almost unbelievably—to below 1.5 percent. This meant that the Dow had to fall 50 percent just to be yielding what previously had always been considered the upper boundary of yields. It would have to fall 75 percent before being valued, on a yield basis, as it had been at past bottoms. A 75 percent drop in the Dow would be equivalent to more than a year's worth of GNP and to about 30 percent of this country's entire wealth. It probably would mark the end of capitalism as we know it.

Possibly because these figures are so daunting, many Wall Streeters are arguing that dividends don't count any more. They say it's silly to value stocks in terms of yields because investors no longer buy stocks for their dividends but for their growth potential, and that therefore earnings should count a lot more than dividends. And in terms of earnings (that is, price to earnings ratios), the argument goes, stocks are less overvalued than when viewed in terms of dividends and yields.

Yes and no. P/Es may be less out of whack than dividends—though by many measures P/E's, especially for the broad-based S&P averages, reached record highs in 1997–1998. Still, as long as earnings continue to grow rapidly, you could argue that P/E valuations at least are not other-worldly.

But a second consideration is more important. A key difference between earnings and dividends is that earnings are far more sensitive to changes in the economy. Even during recessions most companies keep their dividends intact. But earnings can go into practically free fall. During the 1990 recession—which by historical standards was not particularly big—earnings dropped by more than 50 percent. The point is that if you are trying to assess how far the market could fall during bad times, P/Es are meaningless because earnings will likely be falling faster than the economy. Dividends or other variables such as book value are far more important in assessing downside risk because they are likely to remain constant.

Whatever measure of downside risk you use, risks are greater—and by a wide margin—than they ever have been before. And if the risks in stocks are at record levels, then so are the risks to the economy—and the risk that the stock market and the economy together could enter into a vicious pas de deux resulting in economic meltdown.

RECORD DEBT

Perhaps this sounds a bit extreme. But if anything we are *understating* the dangers of a falling stock market. Why? Because not only are consumers loaded with stocks, they also are loaded with debt. We've all been congratulating ourselves on our grand success in balancing the federal budget. But that achievement amounts to putting in one storm window while ignoring a gaping hole in another, and then congratulating ourselves on being ready for the cold. As the chart titled "Total Debt as % of GNP" shows, despite the balanced budget, debt in the United States as a percentage of GNP is higher than it has ever been, with one exception. That was in the early 1930s, just before massive amounts of debt were liquidated because of the Great Depression. But in modern times, debt has never been higher. And while the still very high level of government debt gets some of the blame for our debt-heavy country, the major culprit by far is consumer debt. Mortgage debt as a percentage of home values is also at a postwar high. One of the most remarkable economic statistics of the late 1990s is that after a nearly record period of economic growth, personal bankruptcies remain at or close to all-time highs. But this makes sense given the amount of debt in the economy.

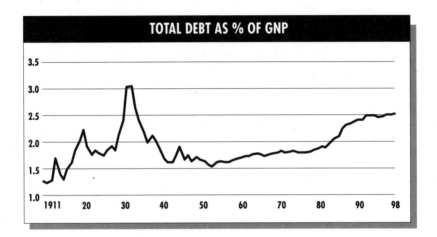

In and of itself, heavy debt is not a problem. It's the same for the country as a whole as for an individual. If you are making good money and expect to continue to do so, and to receive steady raises to boot, debt is no big deal. You'll use your rising income to service it and eventually pay it off. But what if your income starts to decline? You'd no doubt feel a tremendous sense of panic, and you might be driven into personal bankruptcy. Similarly, panic would grip a large number of consumers if suddenly their most important asset, the stock market, started to decline. Bankruptcies, already at postwar highs, would approach levels not seen since the Depression—and eventually could top even those levels.

Debt-heavy consumers wouldn't be the only ones pushed to the brink. The lenders to those consumers also would be in big trouble. Some of the country's biggest financial institutions also happen to be the biggest consumer creditors. In many cases these institutions have dramatically leveraged their balance sheets to make consumer loans.

Citicorp, now one-half of the world's largest financial conglomerate, is a striking example. Citicorp, which twice in relatively recent memory has been bankrupt by any accepted accounting definition of the term, would reach that point again if a recession were to hit. But this time the problems might be so huge that even the enormous resources of the Federal Reserve might not be enough to save the day. The problems that in the past nearly brought down the banking giant and many other banks as well were Third World loans in the early 1980s and real estate loans in the early 1990s. In both cases, although the problems were severe, they were still restricted to particular sectors of the economy, and in both cases highly stimulative Fed policy that dramatically lowered interest rates was a sufficient remedy. This time around, though, the problem would be more pervasive—the entire consumer base of our economy.

RECORD INEQUALITIES

One final factor will put further pressure on policymakers to keep opting for growth—record inequalities between rich and poor in this country. Our society is becoming increasingly fragmented, in large part the result of the fact that our economy—as we discuss in more detail in Chapter 4—has become predominantly service-oriented. In a service dominated economy, workers become increasingly divided into two groups. The first and by far the smaller group consists of those with special talents or abilities that enable them to contribute to quality. These include all the stars of our world—the celebrities, creative geniuses, and leading businesspeople. They can name their price. The second group consists of the vast majority of workers who do not have unique talents. They are expendable, easily replaced.

These widening inequalities mean that even when the economy is strong, most people don't participate in the good times as fully as they would have in the past, when the economy was less fractured. It's an utterly extraordinary fact that in 1998, for instance, despite a near record seven years of economic growth, personal bankruptcies and debt delinquencies were close to all-time highs. Clearly, the political as well as the economic mandate for growth will remain strong, even at the cost of rising inflation. The growing contingent of have-nots will be a potent political force that will put continual pressure on policymakers to keep revving growth up.

If growth fails, it would bring in its wake weak stocks, weak consumer spending, further weakness in stocks, weakened banks, still weaker stocks, panicked consumers, tottering banks, crashing stocks, crushed consumers, and defunct banks. What makes this picture truly scary is that we could be just one relatively small spark away from setting the whole forest ablaze. The only way to prevent this vicious circle from starting is to keep growth alive and well, which is why growth has become a necessity. We have to keep the plane, referred to earlier, aloft, because there won't be any soft landing.

THE INVESTMENT MESSAGE

Our highly leveraged, interdependent world requires continued economic growth as never before. This means investors will be playing to a whole new set of rules. Some of the consequences include the following.

Invest in companies that are leveraged to growth and inflation. The need to make growth the first priority will ultimately contribute to rising inflation. Policymakers won't be able to afford to let the economy take a breather even when growth is strong. As a result, wage pressures inevitably will emerge. At the same time, strong economic growth will increase the demand for energy and other natural resources. The only thing that would allow growth to push forward without causing inflation would be accelerating technological progress, but as we showed in Chapter 2, this isn't in the cards.

In the next section, and especially in Chapter 7, we describe a whole slew of investments that are leveraged to growth and inflation, and we tell you which other ones to avoid. Among the winners will be small (nontech) growth companies. They benefit because in times of rising inflation they can generate profit growth simply by raising prices. Because they start from a relatively small base, they can sustain more rapid growth than can a larger company—it's far easier to double profits from a one-million-dollar starting point than from a billion-dollar base. Thus, smaller companies can count on the fastest profit growth, which in turn should be rewarded by higher market multiples. They benefit all around.

Watch the policymakers. It's a scary but inescapable thought: Now more than ever, the stock market's health, and that of the economy in general, is dependent upon the decisions of a few key people. It's as if we're all on a tightrope but we're counting on Greenspan, Rubin, and other policymakers to do the walking for us. If they slip, we all fall. Right now all the indications are that they understand the necessity for growth and are willing to act accordingly, even if it means tolerating more inflation than they would like. As we noted, through monetary policy and other steps they acted to get Southeast Asia and Japan back in gear. But this will be an ongoing effort, and investors should pay close attention to the words and actions of our economic leaders and those elsewhere. If it ever appears that they have forsaken growth in favor of some other goal, get ready for the deluge.

Prepare for increased market turbulence and occasional sharp dips. Just because the world has become so dependent upon continued economic growth, any time growth appears threatened you can expect the market to react sharply, as in the summer of 1998. The downturns may be both abrupt and deep, and while we expect them to prove temporary, you should be prepared both mentally and in your portfolio to ride them out. In Chapter 9 we discuss some ways you can protect yourself against these scary interludes.

4

THE PRODUCTIVITY DEBATE

Despite what many economists claim, productivity in the United States has been slowing and will continue to slow, and technology can't reverse the trend. Why should this matter to investors? Because without productivity gains, economic growth is certain to be inflationary. For investors, it's one more reason to switch into the fast growers and other inflation beneficiaries we highlight in Part II.

Productivity probably seems like a fairly straightforward economic concept. At the most basic level, it means that you can produce more in less time. If one person makes a cabinet in one hour, and a second person in half an hour, the second person is twice as productive as the first. Economic theory tells us that when productivity is rising, you can pay workers more without causing prices to go up. That's because although you're shelling out more in wages, you're getting more of a product to sell, so your profits can rise in tandem with your rising costs.

So far so good. There's one stumbling block, though. This definition works only as long as you're talking about manufacturing, or about an economy that is predominantly manufacturing based. That's because it has to do with quantity—producing more of something in a given time or with given resources. The underlying premise is that more is better, and in a manufacturing-based economy, that is true.

Today, however, more than 75 percent of workers in the United States are in the services sector, including waiters, teachers, economists, computer programmers, sports stars, travel agents, and others. Service workers may perform such tasks as fixing a broken faucet or preparing a tax return, or they may be engaged in meeting a more subtle range of needs—the need to be entertained, educated, and in a variety of ways fulfilled.

In the services sector you no longer can assume that more is better. Instead, quality counts more than quantity, and being more productive means producing something of higher quality. That's because when it comes to services, you've moved beyond churning out the basic necessities and onto a higher plane where consumers have the luxury of being more discriminating. Only if something is of sufficient quality—in their minds—will they buy it. One book is not the same as any other book; what counts is the imagination of the author.

This has two important implications. First, as we discussed in Chapter 3, with the service sector dominating the economy, society has become increasingly fragmented into the few stars and the large supporting cast. The stars are those with the special talents to add to quality and thereby increase productivity. The supporting cast members at best can merely help to produce that quality more efficiently, but they can't add to value. The stars command respect and large salaries, while supporting cast members are faceless and interchangeable.

Take a sports franchise like the Chicago Bulls, for example. The team uses a variety of service workers, such as accountants, ticket sellers, travel agents and so on, who may help the team function more efficiently. But there is no doubt that in the recent past the real star of the team was Michael Jordan. He increased quality and productivity, because it's his presence that drew fans and generated revenues. Because of his unique talents, he earned millions of dollars a year, while the other workers earn tiny fractions of what he did. And when he decided to step down, the decision made headlines around the world, vying with the President's impeachment trial in terms of press coverage.

In Chapter 3 we discussed one aspect of this star/supporting cast dichotomy—such fragmentation creates pressure to keep economic growth going. But there's another implication as well that relates directly to productivity. When it comes to services, how do you evaluate improvements in quality, which are the basis for measuring increases in productivity? In the case of Michael Jordan and other sports figures, it's actually not that difficult: You can measure ticket receipts. Most service areas, though, are far murkier.

University professors are a good example of how tricky it is to try to measure productivity and quality in the services sector. It is a basic economic tenet that the more productive you are, the more you should earn. At the university level, however, the professors who by some standards might seem the most productive—the ones who teach the most classes—are rarely the highest paid. Instead, those doing research generally earn the biggest salaries. True, a researcher who makes a great discovery might end up being in some sense more productive than the teacher who directly reaches the greatest number of students. But by what criteria do you judge the research or compare its importance with that of educating students? Clearly there are no hard and fast answers when it comes to measuring productivity in the service sector.

So how do our policymakers decide if productivity is rising? It turns out that it comes down to a lot of subjective, and often political, judgments—judgments that happen to have a direct or indirect impact on us all, from the senior citizen dependent upon cost-of-living increases in Social Security to the investor trying to figure out future economic trends.

In recent years a somewhat curious thing has been happening. According to the actual reported data from businesses, overall productivity has risen just slightly—about 1.3 percent over the past decade. Productivity gains in the manufacturing sector have been brisker, coming in at around 4 percent. This obviously implies that productivity gains in the service sector—which are not reported directly—have been negative. Many economists and economic policymakers, though, aren't taking these figures at face value. Instead, they are arguing that productivity actually has been rising across the board, and far more strongly than the figures indicate.

In this chapter we try to cut through some of the confusion about productivity to show what's really going on in our economy. We show that while productivity has indeed been rising in the relatively small manufacturing sector, it has been falling in the far more significant service sector—to the extent that the overall reported gains in productivity probably have been overstated. Why should this matter to you as investors? Again, the key link is inflation. Without broad-based productivity gains, when economic growth starts to quicken—as our analysis from the previous chapter tells us it will—and wages to rise, there will be nothing to keep inflation in check.

EFFICIENCY VERSUS PRODUCTIVITY

One reason for some of the confusion over whether productivity has been rising is that people commonly mix up efficiency with productivity. In manufacturing, the two mean the same. If you can make something more efficiently, you can make more of it in a given amount of time, which is the definition of being more productive.

In the services sector, though, while technology may help increase efficiency, it can't increase productivity. In services, being more efficient means doing the same thing using fewer resources. It's a subtle but important distinction. You're performing a service more efficiently but you're not increasing output. That's important because while productivity can increase more or less indefinitely, generating sustainable noninflationary growth, efficiency has built-in limits. The support staff of the Chicago Bulls can contribute to increased efficiencies, but they can't increase output.

Another simple example is your genial corner bartender. A bartender's job is to pour drinks and possibly provide a sympathetic ear to morose or chatty customers. If a customer's personal limit is two vodkas and the bartender prepares them skillfully and in a friendly manner, he's doing his job just fine. But if he pours that same customer four drinks, he's not doing his job twice as well, or being twice as productive—he's just getting that person twice as drunk.

Now suppose the bar has been employing two bartenders to serve its capacity crowd of, say, a hundred customers a night. It turns out that one of the bartenders is particularly adept and can handle the entire crowd himself. The bar fires the other bartender and now has one bartender serving 100 customers rather than the 50 he previously served. The bar is saving money on the salary of the bartender it let go, and its profits should rise. It is serving drinks more efficiently. But productivity has not risen because it is still serving the same number of drinks—it hasn't increased output, which is what productivity is all about. (And meanwhile, one bartender is out of work, the unfortunate victim of downsizing.)

Can the bar hope to increase efficiencies further? Not really—it has downsized all it can. It can't cut down any further on its bartending crew, for it would have no one left. Increasing profits by increasing efficiencies has inherent limits.

In recent years, many large companies have managed to increase profit growth by virtue of downsizing and other efficiency-enhancing measures. But these measures are running their course—they can't continue indefinitely. In 1998, despite continued strong economic growth, profit margins for the big companies declined and profit growth slowed. Companies had simply run out of room to downsize further and had no ability left to effect additional efficiencies. Efficiency gains are not the same as productivity gains.

THE INTERNET AND EFFICIENCY

Wait a minute, you might be thinking—what about the Internet? Doesn't it have tremendous potential to help businesses operate more efficiently? After all, while the glory part of the Internet is consumer retailing, chat rooms, auctions, and so on, from a monetary point of view these are really small potatoes compared with business to business use of the net. And when companies use the net to carry out operations in a faster, cheaper, less laborious way than previously available, the result by definition is greater efficiency.

Some analysts estimate that business to business transactions on the net may reach as high as about $1.2 trillion by early next century. That's a massive figure, equivalent to more than 10 percent of the U.S. economy. But it means a bit less than you might think in terms of increased efficiency. Ball park estimates are that when a company uses the net to conduct business, it can save at most 25 percent compared to the costs of doing business over other channels. This means that the net offers roughly $400 billion in overall efficiency gains for the foreseeable future. While this is a big number, it is, to put it in some perspective, less than the capitalization of Microsoft and represents only a small portion of total U.S. economic activity.

Also, keep in mind that these savings will mean a loss of jobs for many people. Thus, to some extent they are zero sum—that is, the savings for business will be balanced by losses for workers. Overall, it will not add up to a sea change in the economy. Moreover, it is likely to be the final word on efficiency gains. Even efficiency gains via the net are within a few years of technological limits.

MOVING BEYOND HISTORY?

Confusion between efficiency and productivity is just one reason some economists have mistakenly assumed that productivity is rising. An even more basic but equally erroneous assumption is that technology and specifically the computer have led to qualitative improvements in the service sector.

Those who argue that there have been qualitative improvements generally reason as follows. They look at the economy and note that profit margins and return on equity have been rising throughout the 1990s, results that typically would imply gains in productivity. Moreover, while economic growth has been strong and steady, inflation has remained low. This could only happen, they assert, if productivity indeed has been increasing across the board, including in the service sector. Otherwise, growth would have been inflationary. Ergo, productivity *must* have been rising.

So how do they explain why these alleged productivity gains haven't shown up in the data? By arguing that these figures don't take into account improvements in quality that, they assert, must have been occurring. To explain what must lie behind these alleged improvements in quality, they point to technology, and in particular the computer.

Alan Greenspan, in testimony before Congress in the first quarter of 1998, went so far as to say that the economy may have "moved beyond history." He asserted, "Signs of a major technological transformation of the economy are all around us." In other words, productivity gains in the economy, though not apparent in the data, are so great that they suggest an economy that is better and more productive than any other before. Nearly every other Wall Street analyst has taken the same point of view, and the conventional wisdom now has it that it is technology that has allowed companies to raise profit margins to record levels—and that technology will continue to lead to further productivity gains, thereby helping to keep inflation low.

TECHNOLOGY AND QUALITY

Are they right? Has technology led to qualitative improvements, and hence productivity gains, in the service sector? Remember, this isn't just an academic debate—if technology can increase service sector productivity, it means inflation can remain low even as economic growth heats up and wages rise. And as we can't emphasize enough, inflation is pivotal to the shape of the financial markets.

THE EGALITARIAN COMPUTER

One simple way to test the theory that the computer is enhancing productivity in ways we aren't measuring is to compare the economic performance of small and large companies. A nice thing about the microcomputer is that it is egalitarian—affordable by big and small companies alike. In the great bull market of the 1990s, big companies have far outperformed small ones, reflecting their bigger profits. More of the larger companies are in manufacturing, and just because they are bigger they have had the luxury of downsizing—that is, achieving gains through increased efficiency.

Most of the smaller companies are in services. Because of their size, downsizing hasn't been an option—thus any efficiency gains would have to come from technological advancements. Small companies, in other words, are a good proxy for the service sector and constitute a laboratory of sorts for testing whether technology can lead to productivity gains in that sector. The fact that small companies have on average shown no profit gains in the 1990s is strong evidence that productivity in the service sector continues to decline and that computers can't help companies produce products that are qualitatively better and hence more profitable. By contrast, in the early 1990s, before the microcomputer revolution had taken firm hold, the very small companies were the profit leaders.

The inescapable conclusion is that the great majority of companies in this country are not producing goods more efficiently. When efficiency through downsizing is not an option, profits have to suffer because we can't produce higher-quality goods just through the use of computers.

PRODUCTIVITY AND THE COMPUTER

Several excellent books provide more theoretical explanations of why computers don't contribute to productivity increases in a service-heavy economy. One is Daniel E. Sichel's *The Computer Revolution.* One of his points is that computers are tools that may be used to improve quality but that by themselves don't contribute to quality. The ultimate provider of quality is always the unique human being. For instance, a person may use a computer to trade stocks. But if that person's portfolio outperforms another's, it's the person, not the computer, that deserves the credit. In part Sichel's reasoning has to do with a distinction he draws between societal and individual good. It may be true, for instance, that using a word processor may help an individual write a book. But it doesn't improve the value of that book to society.

Another insightful thinker is Stephen Roach, well-respected Morgan Stanley economist who was one of the first to distinguish between productivity and efficiency. In the early 1990s he was convinced that technology would lead to a productivity boom. Later in the decade, though, he changed his mind. Technology, he argued, was much better at increasing efficiencies than in increasing outputs.

The distinction between productivity and efficiency might become clearer if you consider the following. Look at the economy as revenues generated by a combination of labor and other factors. The biggest factor is wages. No matter how much technology contributes, you still have to pay workers. Moreover, if wages become too small relative to profits or dividends, workers will rebel. Unless technology can actually raise revenues, you eventually reach a point where further efficiencies no longer are possible. In other words, gains in efficiency change how the pie is distributed but don't affect the size of the pie.

To some extent the answer has to be subjective—a qualitative improvement to you might be just another blasted ATM to us. But the anecdotal evidence suggests that computers have *not* particularly increased the level of satisfaction with services in this country. The best statistical evidence points in the same direction. The University of Michigan, for example, over the past five years has carried out a respected survey that consistently has found that people feel quality has been declining. Let's quickly survey a few areas.

Medicine. It's indisputable that if you're feeling poorly today, doctors can perform an array of tests well beyond what they could have done in the past. Technology also has made possible early detection of various cancers, and sonograms are important in discovering potential problems in pregnancy. Still, it is far from clear that technology has improved medical care overall. As we noted earlier, life expectancies are increasing at a slowing rate. But there's more to medical care than that, and in many ways the very availability of more technology has compromised doctors' ability to maintain close one-on-one relationships with their patients. Today the assembly line view of medicine prevails, with patients treated more as a collection of parts than as individuals. Some people may say so what, the kindly family doctor of old often couldn't tell a colon from a comma. But as we'll discuss later, science has yet to disentangle the physiological from the psychological. A caring doctor may turn out to be just as important to one's health as a sophisticated battery of tests.

Real estate. Recently we learned from personal experience that word processors have simply made the process of signing a lease more time-consuming and costly. We were renegotiating the lease for our office, located in Rockefeller Center. The suite we occupied was roughly the same as it had been in the 1930s. The building's manager mentioned that leases in the 1930s were about six pages long. The lease would be presented to the prospective tenant, who would read it. If the tenant happened to have a relative who was a lawyer, the tenant might ask that person to look at it, too; otherwise, lawyers generally didn't get involved. The process was nearly cost free and took about half an hour. By contrast, the lease we were presented with ran to about 100 pages and we were given several copies, including one for our files and one for our lawyers, who were happy to charge us hefty fees to look it over. The availability of technology in the form of word processing has made such quantitative leaps easy. But there's no reason to believe the quality of the lease, or our satisfaction with it, has improved.

Law. Law offices have become computerized with a vengeance. Briefs are composed on word processors, and many firms are compiling large databases of court decisions. It seems unlikely, though, that briefs are better than in the past or that the quality of research has improved. A computer cannot make someone a smarter lawyer. Meanwhile, e-mail, fax machines, and other telecommunications advances have put greater demands on lawyers to give instant answers to clients, often at the expense of giving lawyers the time to think issues through before giving advice.

Finance. Today the electronic infrastructure enables us to make many more transactions than ever before. Only a few years ago a day in which 10 million shares traded would have been a big deal. In today's liquid and efficient markets, however, investors can trade virtually any time they want, and there have been days in which New York Stock Exchange (NYSE) volume exceeded 1 billion shares. A qualitative improvement? Not if you believe Warren Buffett, the most successful investor of our time or almost any time, who is well known for saying that his favorite holding period for a stock is forever.

Recent studies help document the downside to electronic trading. On July 23, 1998, *The New York Times* reported a speech in which John L. Steffens, vice chairman of Merrill Lynch, noted that people who trade over the Internet tend to make three to four times the number of trades as those who use traditional channels. Steffens then cited a study by economists at the University of California who had looked at the investment results for 60,000 households between 1991 and 1996. The most active traders gained 10 percent a year, while the least active were up 15 percent. "People are killing themselves by trading too much—there's no question," said Terry Odean, one of the authors of the study. Or as Steffens put it to his audience of mostly online traders, "The question is, are you interested in fun and games or investing? The two are very different."

Banking. Recently we were talking with a young associate about our ideas for this book, and he suggested the ATM as an example of how technology has moved us forward. These little money dispensers certainly are convenient, but even ignoring the sometimes outrageous fees you get charged for withdrawing your own money, are they really a qualitative improvement? Not according to someone like Stephen Pollan, who in his book *Die Broke* argues persuasively that the availability of ATM machines is one reason we're not saving enough for our retirement.

Taxes. Computers have made possible a phenomenal increase in the complexity of our tax codes, imposing an expensive and time-consuming burden on taxpayers. According to David Littmann, in an op-ed piece in *The Wall Street Journal* on November 12, 1998, the federal tax code has grown from 11,400 words in 1913 to 555 million words today. The previous year's Taxpayer Relief Act, which supposedly was designed to simplify the tax code, created 824 amendments and added 285 sections to the existing code. All in all they will require taxpayers to spend an additional 60 million hours a year preparing taxes.

There are other indications that when it comes to helping companies perform better, the computer isn't all it's cracked up to be. *The Wall Street Journal* in the spring of 1998 wrote about companies that are "de-engineering"—deciding not to install various computerized operations, or abandoning existing ones. Noting that about 50 percent of all tech projects fail to meet executives' expectations, it cited the experience of Howard Selland, president of Aeroquip Corp., a Maumee, Ohio automotive supplier. Selland acknowledged that his company had upgraded to Windows 95, at the cost of about $20,000 per employee, without ever trying to determine if the expense was justified. In fact, he said, it was clear most employees used just a bare fraction of the computing power available to them. Meanwhile, Chrysler Financial nixed a planned computerized system for getting information from its dealers. Instead, it took the radical step of adding a few clerks to talk to dealers over the phone. It found it could get nearly all the information it needed, and the operation took just 90 days to set up—compared with the millions of dollars and several years it would have required to set up a fully computerized system.

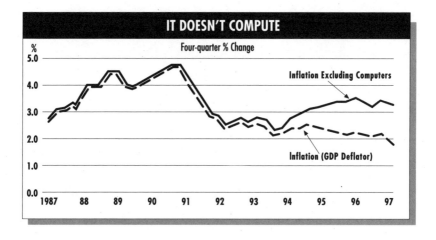

In sum, while it's indisputable that technology and the computer are infiltrating our society and economy, in area after area we'd argue that they aren't actually adding value to the services you receive. They aren't resulting in qualitative improvements, which means they aren't increasing productivity. And this, in turn, means they can't help keep inflation low.

EXPLAINING THE RECENT LOW INFLATION

If technology-fueled productivity gains don't explain the low inflation we've been enjoying, what does? There are several answers.

Inflation is actually higher than has been reported. Look at the chart titled "It Doesn't Compute," from the Economic Report of the President. It clearly shows that the only reason inflation has been falling rather than rising since 1994 is that computer prices—supposedly—have been falling. Let's look at that assumption more closely. It's true that you're likely to pay less for a computer today than a few years ago. But that drop in price doesn't account for the bulk of the sharp drop in computer prices as calculated by the government. Rather, the way the government looks at it, you're also getting a far more powerful machine today. In other words, you're paying less per calculation and less per unit of memory. And in the view of the Bureau of Labor Statistics—following the lead of the Boskin Commission, which was established to ferret out the extent, if any, to which the Consumer Price Index had been overstating inflation—this means computers have gotten much cheaper, even beyond any actual drop in price, and hence inflation is down.

But are you actually benefiting from this extra power? As we outlined previously, in instance after instance most of the evidence regarding quality of life issues suggests not. More is not necessarily better, and our greater computing power doesn't translate into greater productivity or efficiency. It's true we can build computers more efficiently— but what difference does this make if the additional computing power doesn't contribute anything worthwhile to the economy?

Here's an easily understood analogy. If $15,000 used to buy you a Plymouth, and now it buys you a Porsche, you might agree that prices had come down. Even though you're still spending the same $15,000, you're getting a lot more car. On the other hand, if even in your new car you can't ever go faster than 40 miles an hour because traffic conditions are as bad as ever, you might reasonably conclude that you haven't gained a thing.

Or, to look at it another way, suppose the tools a carpenter uses to build a cabinet keep getting cheaper—or suppose, rather, that he can get more tools for about the same amount of money he used to have to pay out for fewer tools. However, even with all his new tools, he still can't build a cabinet any faster than he used to. All the new tools help him to do is to build more new tools that are even cheaper. But regardless of how cheap the tools get, he still can't build any better.

It's the same with computers. We can build cheaper computers (i.e., more powerful computers for the same price) but it is circular reasoning to argue that inflation is falling rather than rising because of it. It's also relevant that, as we pointed out in Chapter 1, the era of rapid miniaturization, which has been behind the fall in computer prices, is ending. This means that even if in the past our ability to produce ever more powerful computers at no increase in price really was meaningful in terms of inflation, it won't continue.

Another point is that to the extent that lower computer prices have reduced inflation, they also have raised estimates of economic growth, because growth is calculated as a single number that includes both real growth and inflation. In other words, if no qualitative gains were imputed to greater computing power, then economic growth would have come in considerably slower. A substantial chunk of growth in the U.S. economy came from assuming that a dollar's worth of computing power in 1998 was worth a lot more—that is, added more to the economy—than a dollar's worth of computing power in any given earlier year. But as we have seen, there's no reason to think this is true, which means growth was probably slower than assumed. And if growth was slower, productivity would have been less as well, and inflation higher. Indeed, productivity—without assuming qualitative improvements in computers, which, again, is a circular argument—would have been zero or perhaps even negative for the five-year period 1994–1998. Thus even the meager reported gains in productivity are the result of the increased productivity in building computers, not the result of computers increasing productivity throughout the economy.

Some of the strongest evidence that inflation actually is higher than the government has chosen to report comes from looking at inflation-adjusted family incomes. In the 1950s, the typical family could get by very comfortably on one income. Today, though inflation-adjusted family incomes are higher than in the 1950s and early

1960s, it's only because two-income families have become the norm. Even if you argue that many women who today work outside the home do so because they want to, it is indisputable that they also have to if their families are to enjoy the same level of comfort as families a few decades back. This is a powerful argument that inflation has been dramatically understated. In other words, today's incomes, though higher in inflation-adjusted terms, do not buy as much as they used to. This is exactly contrary to the Boskin Commission's conclusions.

Wages have taken unusually long to rise in the current economic cycle. Another reason that inflation has managed to remain low is that in past economic cycles, wages rose much earlier into the expansion. The fact that this time they didn't is a byproduct of our increasingly interdependent world, where goods can be made as easily in one country as in another. What's relevant is that all good things eventually end, and in a world in which growth has become a necessity, we'll eventually run short of workers. When that happens, it's inevitable that wages will rise.

Asia's temporary downturn has helped dampen inflation. The crisis in Asia has also helped keep commodity prices low, but this won't last. In fact, while Asia's woes have kept prices down short term, over the longer term the net effect of the crisis almost certainly will be to raise prices. The reason is that the crisis has tied the Fed's hands. As a result, wages, which would be uptrended anyway, will rise even faster. Historically wages move in much steadier and longer trends than commodity prices. When they start to rise, it's hard to reverse direction. This will be especially true under current circumstances, when any attempts to slow down growth would have disastrous consequences. By contrast, trends in commodity prices can reverse abruptly.

THE INVESTMENT MESSAGE

Inflation, inflation, inflation. That's the heart of what the productivity debate is all about. Inflation has been held in check up to now by a rare combination of temporary factors. But these are in the process of gradually reversing. Only two things could short-circuit inflation at this point. The first—recession and deflation—would be both catastrophic and politically unacceptable, as we discussed in Chapter 3. The second—rising productivity—is simply not available, as we showed in this chapter.

Prepare to switch into inflation beneficiaries. Like the necessity for growth, the productivity debate points to rising levels of inflation. Without productivity gains, profit growth for companies will have to be generated by pricing power—the ability to raise prices—rather than through producing a product more cheaply. Again, the message is that investors should focus on investments leveraged to growth and inflation. In the next four chapters we offer a slew of possibilities.

Keep a close watch on productivity data. If it ever appears that productivity is rising, investments geared to inflation may lose some of their appeal. Be careful, though, because as we showed, the way productivity data are reported can be misleading. Don't be fooled by implicit claims that quality is improving when it isn't.

Watch computer prices. Both the prices of computers themselves as well as the stock market performance of the major computer companies will be revealing. As we pointed out, one of the major reasons that productivity has come in as positive at all and that inflation has remained as low as it has is that computer prices have been falling. But the limits to technology and in particular to further miniaturization suggest that at some point computer prices will begin to rise. When that happens, expect a chain reaction. Growth in computer sales will slow, inflation will rise, and productivity growth will slow even further. On a macro level inflation is leveraged to changes in computer prices. As for specific investments, computer stocks like Dell and Gateway, which have risen to fame and fortune on their marketing skills, will falter. Even the best marketing will not overcome higher prices.

Be even warier of high-flying Internet stocks. In talking earlier about efficiency and the Internet, we noted that the Internet might be expected to generate around $400 billion in efficiency savings over the foreseeable future. It's a relevant investment consideration to ask how much of this amount businesses might be willing to shell out to the providers of the Internet services they use. And while there are no hard and fast answers, typically businesses aren't willing to pay out more than 20 to 25 percent of savings to the providers of those savings. Let's say, though, that in this case businesses are willing to pay out as much as 50 percent. That puts an upper end of something like $200 billion on the potential revenues Internet companies can expect from the business world. Given that the total valuation of Internet companies in early 1999 far exceeded that figure, you know that something is out of whack. This is another good reason to be exceedingly wary of Internet stocks.

P A R T

CASHING IN

5

OIL STOCKS: READY TO IGNITE

One of the surest ways to cash in on the emerging trends we described in Part I will be to snap up the oils. Oil stocks have been in the doldrums, but they won't remain stuck there too much longer. Surging worldwide economic growth will mean a sharp increase in demand for energy. With technology unable to come up with meaningful alternatives, and as oil supplies become depleted, oil prices inevitably will rise. So will the stock prices of oil companies—along with the fortunes of those smart enough to invest in them in the early stages.

In 1998, oil stocks were an investor's worst nightmare. During that year, oil prices sank almost 50 percent, from about $20 a barrel to below $11. The major integrated oil companies—historically safe, defensive stocks with such illustrious names as Exxon, Mobil, and Royal Dutch—fell about 10 percent (falling oil prices, for the majors, have one offsetting positive in that they boost refining margins). Not only was this performance dismal in and of itself, it lagged that of the S&P 500—which in the same period gained 15 percent— by about 25 percentage points.

Investments *leveraged* to oil fared even worse. The drillers, for example, were catastrophes, dropping by more than 50 percent as the rental rate for drilling rigs collapsed. And these losses in the oil service stocks came despite the fact that rigs were in relatively short supply. In the 1980s sharply falling oil prices had meant that virtually every major rig company either had gone bankrupt or been forced to recapitalize its balance sheets. As a result no new rigs had been built for nearly a decade while many existing rigs were junked.

Nor was the carnage limited to United States oil investments. Entire economies of countries such as Venezuela and Russia, which are highly dependent upon oil, suffered massive damage, with the stock markets of both countries down more than 70 percent. Russia's economy suffered a nearly total collapse.

Nonetheless, we have no hesitancy in predicting that within the next few years oil shortages will develop, oil prices will rise sharply, and oil stocks will soar. In fact, if there is one group of stocks that every type of investor—conservative and aggressive alike—should own, it is oil stocks. For in the years ahead, oil stocks are likely to outperform, and very likely dramatically outperform, the market as a whole. The only thing that would stand in their way would be if we're wrong about growth—that is, if policymakers by acts of omission or commission take a wrong turn and trigger deflation. But barring that least-likely scenario, oil is a must-own investment. In this chapter we explain why oil prices are almost certain to rise and then discuss the best of specific energy investments.

RISING DEMAND

Energy, obviously, is essential to economic growth. To pinpoint just how essential, over the past half century the world's gross economic product has grown by a factor of five. During that period, demand for energy has increased by a factor of three. There are no signs that this historical relationship between demand for energy and economic growth is lessening—if anything, energy requirements per unit of growth are increasing. Over the past decade, the growth in energy demand per unit of gross world product has been slightly above levels of the early 1980s.

The biggest growth in demand for energy will come from the developing world, and in particular from giants China and India. Significantly, the developing world is still in the early stages of development, meaning there is tons more room for further industrialization—and hence a greater need for energy. China is nearly certain to use fossil fuels for more than 90 percent of its energy needs through at least the year 2025, as Thomas Drennen and Jon Erickson point out in the March 6, 1998 issue of *Science*. The reason is that hydroelectric, nuclear, and solar projects currently under consideration in China will at best be able to meet around 7 percent of the country's future energy needs. The story is likely to be similar in India, where hydroelectric projects are far less advanced than in China.

On a per capita basis, the developing world currently uses about one-third as much energy as the developed world. The implications are staggering, especially given the relative sizes of their populations. Assuming no dramatic improvements in energy efficiency—and also no population growth—a fully developed world would consume nearly three times as much energy as the world consumes today. By the year 2015, China alone will be importing nearly as much fossil fuel as we do in the United States today. And keep in mind that China, big as it is, still accounts for just a bit more than 20 percent of the developing world.

If the developed world were conserving energy to the same extent that the developing world is stoking its energy appetite, oil prices might have a prayer of holding steady. But just the reverse is true—conservation efforts have faltered, and demand for energy in the developed world is growing rapidly. In the United States, by far the world's largest consumer of energy, fossil fuel demand per unit of GNP has stopped falling. One major reason is our ongoing love affair with the automobile, and especially our newfound lust for large, gas-guzzling vehicles. It's a testament to the remarkably short memories of consumers, and the basic short-sightedness of the human race in general, that despite the energy scares of the 1970s and early 1980s, automobiles purchased in recent years actually consume on average more gasoline per mile than the vehicles of a decade ago. Moreover, because many of these new vehicles are light trucks whose life expectancy is longer than that of automobiles, the United States will be stuck with a large contingent of energy-inefficient vehicles for many years to come.

The bottom line is that per capita energy consumption in the United States has been rising steadily in the past decade and is now more than 10 percent higher than in 1985. Just as striking is that energy consumption per unit of gross national product in the United States is no lower today than in 1989. Energy consumption per unit of Gross World Product has been in a 50-year downtrend—but as we indicated previously, this downtrend has been decelerating recently. The evidence is strong that future economic growth will require at least as much energy per unit of growth as did growth in the past.

OIL PRICES: A SHORT-TERM DROP . . .

It's a fairly immutable law that whenever oil prices fall, the down-trend turns out to be temporary—more than that, any downturn inex-orably lays the groundwork for higher prices ahead. In 1998, oil prices dropped to decade lows, and in real terms to the lowest levels since the early 1970s, prior to the Arab oil embargo. The world rejoiced and went out and bought its sports utility vehicles. Instead, it should have been preparing for prices that will be higher than if they never had declined in the first place.

Three things contributed to the sharp fall in oil prices in 1998. We discuss these factors next.

An unusually warm winter. In 1997–1998 the densely populated East Coast of the United States experienced an exceptionally mild winter, which sharply curtailed consumption of home heating oil. We can't, of course, predict the weather in coming years with pinpoint accuracy. We do know, however, that weather patterns in the 1990s have been anomalous, and we also know that throughout the ages, warm spells have been followed by cold spells, which in turn have been followed by warm spells. Even if it's true that greenhouse warming means we're in a period of gradually rising temperatures, it's still the case that unusually warm periods—especially if caused by an El Nino—are often followed by unusually cold spells. For reasons that are not understood, El Ninos tend to be followed by La Ninas, which have the effect of causing temperatures to drop.

A slowdown in growth in Asia. The financial crises in Southeast Asia and Japan resulted in weaker than expected demand for energy from that region. But as we've discussed, this slowdown should prove temporary. In fact, the threat to growth in Asia in 1998 turned out to be a wakeup call that should end up spurring an acceleration of growth there and in the rest of the world. China has entered upon a trillion-dollar program to build infrastructure. At the same time, Japan, in efforts to spur its lagging growth and become more of a locomotive for all of Asia, in 1998 authorized well over $100 billion in spending and tax cuts, reversing previously entrenched policies geared toward reducing the government's deficit. The upshot of these and other actions is that growth for Asia as a whole should resume at a healthy clip before the next century.

A family quarrel within OPEC. In an effort to reestablish discipline within the cartel, Saudi Arabia jacked up its oil production so that OPEC as a whole was producing at about 90 percent of capacity, a much higher rate than normal. The Saudis' action was intended to convince Venezuela that nonadherence to OPEC quotas would inflict economic hardship on all cartel members. It had an immediate and dramatic impact on prices, because over the short-term oil is very responsive to even small changes in supply.

Suppose, for instance, that the world needs 72 million barrels of oil a day and that exactly that amount is being produced, at a selling price of $20 a barrel. Now suppose that production rises by just 3 percent. You might think that prices would drop by only about 3 percent, but you'd be wrong—they would drop considerably more. In fact, given that scenario, it would be more realistic to think that oil prices would fall to as low as $10 or $11 a barrel, which are the "marginal production costs"—the highest costs required to produce oil. Why is that? By way of analogy, imagine you're very hungry and go out to dinner to a fine steakhouse. You willingly pay $30 for a sirloin steak, which you consume with pleasure. Now you're not so hungry. Suppose the restaurant invited you to order a second steak. You'd probably decline at $30—it's just not worth that much to you anymore. You might, however, be willing to order one at a much lower price—maybe $15, maybe $10, bringing the average price per steak down to $20 or $22.50. The same principle applies to any commodity. Once demand has been satisfied, even a small increase in supply brings down the overall price by a disproportionate amount.

At the start of 1998 the world was producing oil at about 95 percent of capacity. This meant that virtually every oil-producing nation in the world was producing at full capacity. The one exception, an exceedingly important one, was Saudi Arabia. When the Saudis decided to produce about 1 million extra barrels a day, which came on top of a 1.7 million barrel per day drop in demand stemming from above-average temperatures and Asia's economic woes, the effects were dramatic. And this was true even though both the rise in production and the drop in demand were relatively minor. That's the nature of commodities, at least over the short term.

...AND A LONGER-TERM UPTREND

Longer term, the demand/supply situation for oil is about as tight as it can get. Just as production at 97 percent of worldwide capacity was enough to cause oil prices to plummet short term, production at 92 or 95 percent of capacity will eventually cause prices to spike upward, though there may be time lags because of inventories. Remember, too, that when oil prices drop even for short periods of time, it lays the groundwork for increased demand over the longer term. Just ask your neighbor, who probably owns a sport utility vehicle. In addition, the fact that the oil rig business has been bad will help boost oil prices in the future, because we've cut exploration activities.

Look back to the late 1970s and early 1980s. Oil prices spiked up. Yet the world was then producing at about 70 percent of capacity. The spike in those years resulted from a political crisis, including the Iran–Iraq war. This meant that potentially the problems could be solved through political or military means.

Today, however, the world's oil profile is very different, and there is no meaningful excess capacity. This means that the next crisis will not be susceptible to a political solution. The only real solution would be to come up with practical alternatives to oil or else to produce more oil. As we show later, neither of these alternatives is feasible.

The bottom line is that drops in oil prices are just interruptions in a long-term uptrend. There has never been less reason to be complacent about energy, and yet complacency never has been higher. As investors, your proper response is to bemoan the complacency—and then quickly take advantage of it by buying oil stocks while you can still get in on the ground floor.

OIL IS FINITE

One reason the price of oil is going to rise is that we are running out of the stuff. Look at oil production in the United States today and a generation ago. We're producing a lot less now than then. As the chart titled "U.S. Per Capita Energy Production vs. Energy Consumption" shows, since 1970 oil production per capita in the United States has declined by more than 30 percent, while total energy production per capita has dropped by more than 10 percent. Meanwhile, over the same nearly 30-year period, per capita energy consumption in the United States has risen. Up to now the gap between demand and supply has been made up by foreign sources, which today provide about 50 percent of United States energy needs. But foreign sources are no more unlimited than was the exceptional endowment of energy in the United States.

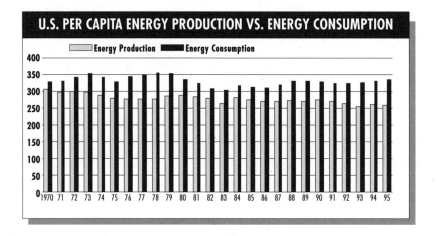

How much oil is left? According to most estimates, the world has about 1 trillion barrels of oil left to produce. At current rates of production, and assuming a growth in demand of about 2 percent a year—which may well be a conservative projection if economic growth comes on strong over the long term—this means that, theoretically, oil will run out in 40 to 50 years.

Actually, though, we probably have a lot less time left than that. The reason is something called Hubbert's law, after a geologist named M. King Hubbert, who wrote in the 1950s about the relationship between energy endowment and energy production. Hubbert posited that oil production from any big field peaks when about half the oil in the field has been exhausted. He proved remarkably prescient in forecasting that oil production in the United States would peak in the late 1960s.

What does his law suggest about future supplies of oil? It tells us that the key date is not when we've actually used up all the oil in the ground but rather when we've used half of what we started with. According to most estimates, the world will have consumed about 800 billion barrels of oil by the end of 1998. That is very close to the halfway mark of the world's estimated original oil endowment. It suggests that oil production will begin to drop off as early as 10 years from now, and certainly a lot sooner than 40 to 50 years. Nor will technology come to the rescue, extending the halfway point. Technology in the oil patch has been advancing, but it hasn't helped much, with oil production in the technologically sophisticated United States continuing to decline.

Maybe, you're thinking, we'll discover new oilfields that will keep the black gold flowing. Don't count on it. According to Colin Campbell and Jean Laherrere, writing in the March 1998 issue of *Scientific American*, during the 1990s, while oil companies were producing more than 20 billion barrels a year, they managed to discover on average only about 7 billion barrels of oil a year. The oil simply isn't there, and even the most advanced technology in the world can't find it if it doesn't exist. Moreover, even if we were to find a whole lot more than the 1 trillion barrels estimated to be left, it still wouldn't make much difference. That's because of the strong relationship between oil produced and oil consumed. If we had as much as 1.5 trillion barrels of oil remaining rather than 1 trillion, we would still reach the halfway point relatively quickly thanks to the resulting slightly faster growth in the demand for oil.

OTHER FOSSIL FUELS

Potential reserves from two other fossil fuels, natural gas and tar sands, are considerable—probably the equivalent of about 1 trillion barrels of oil. But this trillion will be much harder to use than the like amount of oil. The reason is that these other fossil fuels have to be converted into liquids before they can be used as an energy source. No matter what technology is used, this is an expensive and time-consuming process. It may extend the life span of fossil fuels but it will not prevent the price of oil from escalating relentlessly in the years ahead and at most will add less than a decade to the point at which total production of fossil fuels begins to decline.

Nor will another fossil fuel, coal, free us from our dependency on oil. Currently coal accounts for about 23 percent of the world's energy needs, down from over 25 percent in 1970. Moreover, coal as a percentage of fossil fuel use has been declining steadily since the 1950s. In the 1950s coal was used far more than all other fossil fuels combined. And if fossil fuels were used in proportion to their world-wide reserves, coal would still be our biggest source of energy, by a huge margin. We have enough coal to supply our energy needs for hundreds of years. There is more coal in the world than we know what to do with.

But once again, technological limits are the stumbling block. Coal is plentiful, but it's also dirty, and we haven't come up with ways to produce energy from it in a clean manner. Even with scrubbers, it emits far more pollutants than any other fossil fuel. The more rigorously we try to control pollutants, the more expensive it becomes to use coal and the less attractive it is as an alternative to oil. Even after oil prices have risen considerably, oil still could be more economical than coal.

FISSION, FUSION, CONFUSION: ALTERNATIVE ENERGIES

In the 1970s, in the midst of rising oil prices and long lines at the gas station, energy alternatives were all the rage—or at least they were talked about and in some cases even tried. But as oil prices fell, there was a collective loss of interest. In fact, *The New York Times* science writer Malcolm W. Browne, in a column in the spring of 1998, noted that he recently had been cleaning out his old files. What struck him was that the files from many years back that related to alternative energy sources were many inches thick, with ideas ranging from harvesting desert plants to harnessing ocean waves. In recent years, though, the files had grown barely at all. No one was sending out press releases touting exciting ideas for new sources of energy.

Can any of the old plans, or new ones, be implemented in time to prevent oil prices from rising? With technology hitting limits, the answer is an almost certain no. By the time anything resembling a viable energy alternative makes the scene, the price of oil is likely to be far higher than it is today.

Let's quickly look at some of the likeliest alternatives to fossil fuels.

Nuclear fission. Nuclear energy from fission—the breaking apart of the nucleus of an atom—was long expected to be the energy source most likely to replace fossil fuels for many uses. Between 1970 and the early 1990s, according to World Watch, a Washington-based nonprofit environmental group, nuclear energy capacity jumped about 20-fold worldwide, and by the end of that period nuclear power accounted for more than 6 percent of the world's energy needs. Since then, though, nuclear power has stagnated, with more nuclear plants being closed than commissioned. We can't count on nuclear energy to meet a significantly greater portion of our energy needs—thanks to a combination of technological limits and environmental concerns.

The chief limit stems from the basic laws of physics. The energy released in nuclear reactors and in nuclear waste comes from the so-called strong force, one of four basic forces in physics. By contrast, the world around us—trees, our bodies, automobiles, mountains—is held together by the electromagnetic force. The strong force is far more powerful than the electromagnetic force. In some form or another over the past 20 years we have been trying to contain the far more powerful strong force with materials bonded by the much weaker electromagnetic force.

Not surprisingly, we've run into problems. Three Mile Island and Chernobyl clearly illustrate the tremendous risks of nuclear reactors, and no one has figured out how to dispose of nuclear waste satisfactorily. As a result, use of nuclear energy is shrinking. Even France, the Western country most wedded to nuclear energy, has begun mothballing nuclear generators.

Nuclear fusion. While fission releases energy by breaking apart the nucleus of an atom, nuclear fusion generates energy by fusing nuclei together, producing not radioactive materials but innocuous water. It offers the hope of unlimited, clean energy—but unfortunately, we haven't figured out how to carry out fusion at a practical cost.

The dilemma is that while we know how to fuse particles and create energy, it requires energy to do so, and so far no one has managed to come up with a way of producing a net gain in energy. Once again an overreliance on computers has been less than fruitful. Computer simulations are being used to try to redesign fusion reactors bit by bit in an effort to squeeze out marginal improvements. This approach is unlikely to result in real breakthroughs—and for fusion ever to be a practical alternative, a genuine breakthrough, not marginal improvements, is probably essential.

The United States has sharply cut research funds for fusion. One reason is that the electricity produced by fusion reactors would be so expensive. T. Kenneth Fowler, author of *The Fusion Quest*, estimates that fusion reactors would generate electricity up to 63 percent more expensively than through fission. Even if we could figure out how to build fusion reactors that produce a net energy gain, the cost of that extra energy would be prohibitive.

Hydrogen. Carmaker BMW has on the drawing board plans for producing a hydrogen-powered car in the second decade of the next century. But a lot of obstacles will have to be overcome first, and that car may well remain on the drawing board. For at the rate things are going, hydrogen poses no threat to the current dominance of fossil fuels.

To use hydrogen for energy, you first have to break apart molecules that contain the element so as to liberate pure hydrogen. The most obvious source of hydrogen is water, each molecule of which consists of two hydrogen atoms and one oxygen atom. But to break the water molecules apart requires energy, and right now that means employing fossil fuels. As Rob Edwards, writing in *New Scientist* on November 23, 1996, notes, "Cracking water with electricity generated from fossil fuels makes no sense because any environmental gains from using hydrogen would be wiped out by pollution from the power plants." To which we can add, what good is an unlimited supply of hydrogen if the only way to get it is through dwindling supplies of fossil fuel?

Another approach is to try to use energy from solar cells to crack water molecules. However, technological progress in solar cells is proceeding slowly. Even supposed breakthroughs turn out to be less than meets the eye. In 1998, for instance, a seeming breakthrough was described in the April 17 issue of *Science*. A team headed by John Turner and Oscar Khaselev reported that it had developed a solar cell that separated hydrogen from water more efficiently than earlier versions. The story made headlines, with the media acting as if solar-powered cars were ready to sprint out onto the highway. In fact—as Turner himself noted—while his cell operated for 20 *hours*, a practical device would have to function for five to 20 *years*. Real breakthroughs are unlikely because, once again, researchers are taking the combinatorial approach—trying out large numbers of different combinations of materials in hope of finding one that works better. Without breakthroughs, there is no reason to doubt the conclusion of Allen Bard, an electrochemist at the University of Texas, that "a crossover to hydrogen might not be possible for 50 to 100 years." The key point is that if a hydrogen-powered world ever dawns, it will be well after fossil fuels have run out—or at least after fossil fuel prices have risen manyfold.

SPOTLIGHT ON STILLWATER

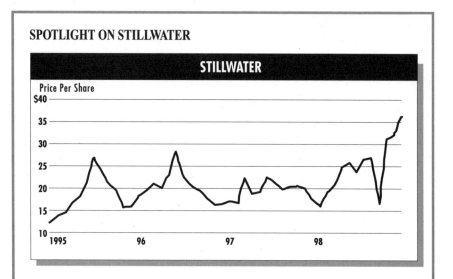

- Stillwater is the only North American producer of platinum group metals (PGMs) such as platinum and palladium.

- All other producers of PGMs are in politically volatile spots such as South Africa and Russia, giving Stillwater a monopoly-like position in a vital market.

- Despite depressed prices for PGMs, the company's revenues and earnings have grown thanks to increased production and better control over costs.

- A telling sign that PGMs are likely to be in short supply over the foreseeable future is that the company has negotiated the sale of a major chunk of its output through 2003 for a guaranteed minimum price. There is no upside cap on the price.

- Thus the company has a nearly guaranteed earnings stream over the next five years.

Fuel cells. Fuel cells, which are like batteries with an external energy source, have been looked at to replace the internal combustion engine in cars, but don't expect to see it happen soon. Technology and the combinatorial techniques favored by researchers haven't produced practical versions and aren't likely to do so. One big problem is cost. Fuel cells require platinum, palladium, or another platinum-related metal to serve as a catalyst, and these metals are prohibitively expensive. (Moreover, if we ever were to produce fuel cells on a large scale, the price of platinum and related metals would soar even higher in response to the rise in demand—in fact, we'd probably run out of platinum before we run out of fossil fuels.) Fuel cells also give off large amounts of waste heat. Finally, while fuel cells would power cars in a more energy-efficient way than the internal combustion engine, they would need fossil fuels as their energy source. Thus, even if fuel cells ever did become used in cars, they wouldn't wean us away from fossil fuels entirely when it comes to driving.

Wind and Solar Energy. How about wind or solar energy? There certainly is plenty of sun and wind in the world, and solar and wind energy might be quick fixes in parts of the developing world where big generating plants aren't feasible. It's unlikely, though, that we'll be able to figure out how to use these renewable energy sources efficiently enough to cut back on fossil fuels to any large extent. Again, technological limits come into play—specifically, limits in our ability to predict climate. To rely on energy from sun or wind you need to be able to count on stable climates. But as we noted earlier, our ability to forecast overall climatic trends is shaky. We could waste a lot of money—and a lot of precious land—by building expensive wind turbines and solar generating plants that end up being useless. At current prices of fossil fuels, solar and wind energy will be also-rans. At much higher prices for fossil fuels, they may become more interesting, but even in that case basic limitations in technology argue against their broad-based use.

ENERGY AND MASS PRODUCTION

MODEL T: PRICE VS. CUMULATIVE PRODUCTION		
Years	Cumulative Production (Units)	Price (1978 Dollars)
1909	15,741	$7,932
1910	50,021	7,209
1911	110,249	6,027
1912	298,247	4,746
1913	490,544	4,365
1914	753,552	4,418
1915	1,270,029	4,015
1916	1,999,160	3,627
1918	2,967,957	2,908
1920	4,406,236	2,675
1921	5,252,173	2,318
1923	8,028,992	2,304
1998		8,400*

*Assumes price of cheapest Ford is $20,000 in 1998 dollars.

Clearly a major sticking point for many alternative energies such as solar cells is cost. You might think that once demand for alternative energies increased enough, the costs would come down, as economies of scale took over. After all, computer prices fell many million-fold as more computers were produced. But this hope is misplaced. Unlike computers, most manufacturing processes do not benefit from multiplicative gains. Gains from economies of scale can be dramatic at first, but they run their course pretty quickly.

Look at the chart titled "Model T: Price vs. Cumulative Production." As you can see, when Henry Ford introduced mass production, costs declined sharply and then leveled off. That's

	LABORATORY PHOTOVOLTAIC CELL EFFICIENCIES 1978 THROUGH FEBRUARY 1994		
Year	Flat-plate Thin Films	Flat-plate Single Crystal Silcon Cells	High-efficiency Concentrator Cells
1978	5.0%	16.0%	23.1%
1979	6.0	16.7	23.4
1980	7.0	17.5	24.7
1981	7.6	18.1	24.7
1982	8.9	18.4	24.7
1983	10.1	18.6	25.0
1984	11.1	19.0	25.3
1985	11.1	20.4	25.7
1986	12.0	21.6	26.5
1987	12.9	22.0	28.3
1988	14.5	22.5	31.1
1989	14.6	23.0	31.8
1990	14.9	23.1	32.6
1991	15.6	23.1	32.6
1992	15.7	23.1	32.6
1993	15.8	23.1	32.6
1994	16.4	23.1	32.6

how it works with most items, and it has been true with solar cells. The chart titled "Laboratory Photovoltaic Cell Efficiencies" tracks the efficiency of different kinds of solar cells since 1978. As it shows, after big initial leaps, starting about a decade ago gains in the efficiency of solar cells became incremental, and over the past several years there even are indications that the cost of producing solar cells is increasing right along with the general inflation level.

CASHING IN: INVESTING IN THE OILS

It should be clear now why we are so confident that oil prices will soon begin a long-term uptrend. A relentless rise in demand coupled with a relentless decline in supply and no meaningful alternatives will translate into a relentless rise in prices. As a result, oil stocks should be among the core holdings in every investor's portfolio.

In fact, to put it even more strongly, in times of rising inflation and high oil prices, oil stocks are a *necessary* investment if you want to beat inflation. Look at the chart titled "Oil During Inflationary 1970s." As the chart shows, not only did energy stocks rise in those years of rising inflation, they far outperformed the major market averages. Oil stocks as a group rose an average of 14.2 percent a year. Domestic oil companies rose 19.2 percent a year. And oil service companies, the most leveraged group of energy stocks, gained 31 percent a year. Meanwhile the S&P 500 rose only 8.4 percent a year, and excluding energy stocks it rose just 7 percent a year—which was 1.1 percentage points below the inflation rate.

One other consideration further strengthens the case for U.S. energy stocks—the fact that investors will be awarding ever higher premiums to non–Middle Eastern oil suppliers. Currently the United States imports more than 50 percent of its oil. This figure

OIL DURING INFLATIONARY 1970s	
Oil Investments	Average Annual Return—1970s
Oil - The Commodity	26.40
All Oil Stocks	14.20
Oil Service Stocks	31.00
Domestic Oil Stocks	19.20
S&P 500	8.40
S&P 500 Excluding Energy Stocks	7.00

will rise in the years ahead as our demand for oil increases and our own production declines. Inevitably we will become ever more dependent upon the Middle East, for the simple reason that that's where the oil is. According to most estimates, oil production outside the Middle East will peak within the next five years. Keep in mind that it won't be just the United States that is becoming more dependent on Middle East oil—it will be every other oil importer as well, including China, Japan, and Germany. That will make us all more vulnerable than ever to political turmoil in the Middle East that could affect supply—and will be a further boost to domestic energy companies, both those that own the oil in the ground as well as those involved in trying to locate and produce whatever supplies remain outside the Middle East.

Which specific energy stocks should you invest in? Energy stocks are like a market unto themselves—there is an energy stock for every kind of investor, from the most conservative to the most aggressive. You can take your pick, because, as the aforementioned chart shows, when oil prices are rising there is no such thing as a bad oil stock—they all go up.

Next we discuss the ins and outs of the three major types of oil stocks: the majors, the drillers, and the diversified service companies.

The majors. The large and diversified energy companies listed in the chart titled "The Major Oils" are particularly well suited to conservative investors because they offer plenty of downside protection. They let you enjoy the fun of a bull market in oil without taking big risks. As we noted earlier, even when oil prices are falling, the majors can hang fairly tough by virtue of big "downstream" operations such as refining. Falling oil prices can even boost the profits from refined energy products such as gasoline. Most major oil companies also produce chemical products, and here, too, lower oil prices can be a boon, as petroleum tends to be a feedstock for those products. In the worst of times, the major oils earn plenty of money, while in the best of times their profits zoom and so do their stock prices.

THE MAJOR OILS								
Company	Current P/E	5-Yr. EPS Growth	Div Yield in %	5-Yr. Div. Growth	Ann. FY Sales (Mil.)	5-Yr. Sales Growth	Market Cap (Mil.)	5-Yr. Price Gain
British Petrol	20.3	17.3	2.8	21.7	71,700.00	8.6	82,440.00	25.4
Chevron	23.4	4.3	2.8	6.8	42,000.00	2.3	56,060.00	14.0
Exxon	25.0	10.6	2.2	2.8	137,200.00	4.5	181,440.00	19.0
Royal Dutch Pet	29.3	7.3	2.8	5.7	77,500.00	7.0	103,577.00	13.2
Texaco	21.9	11.4	3.2	2.9	46,700.00	6.0	30,135.00	12.5
Average	24.0	10.2	2.8	8.0	75020.00	5.7	90932.00	16.8
S&P 500 Averages	30.6	9.1	1.4	8.0	9817.00	11.8	18755.00	20.1

A further plus is that major oil companies have much better than average yields, typically more than twice that of the market. Moreover, they almost never cut their dividends. The only exception in modern times was Texaco in the late 1980s, when a legal battle with Penzoil forced the company temporarily to declare bankruptcy. This legal tactic was reversed within a year or so, and the dividend rose to its previous level within two years. The bottom line is that if you want totally reliable income—indeed, almost surely rising income—and a sure play on rising energy prices, the big oil companies are the right investments for you.

Oil service companies. The companies listed in the chart titled "Oil Service Companies" do the actual seismic work and drilling for the majors. They are a riskier but potentially more rewarding way to tap into an oil turnaround. Unlike the big oils, the service companies have no buffers. It's all or nothing—either they're running at full throttle or they're bad news.

First the risks. During the 1980s, as oil prices declined, oil service companies crashed and burned. The most leveraged among them, the offshore drillers, were decimated. Only one dedicated off-

Company	Current P/E	5-Yr. EPS Growth	Div Yield in %	5-Yr. Div. Growth	Ann. FY Sales (Mil.)	5-Yr. Sales Growth	Market Cap (Mil.)	5-Yr. Price Gain
OIL SERVICE COMPANIES								
Diamond Offshore	8.9	N/A	2.1	N/A	956.0	N/A	3,175.0	N/A
Halliburton	N/A	6.3	1.6	0.0	8,819.0	5.3	13,521.0	14.7
Helmerich Payne	10.1	28.0	1.6	2.6	518.0	12.2	883.0	4.8
Nabors	9.4	22.8	0.0	0.0	1,029.0	21.6	1,260.0	14.4
Rowan	5.0	41.0	0.0	0.0	695.0	17.6	822.0	2.9
Schlumberger	21.4	11.8	1.7	5.1	10,754.0	9.8	23,850.0	9.2
Average	25.7	22.0	1.2	1.5	3,795.0	13.3	7,252.0	9.2
S&P 500 Averages	30.6	9.1	1.4	8.0	9,817.0	11.8	18,755.0	20.1

shore driller, Rowan Co., survived the 1980s intact. All the others went bankrupt or were forced to recapitalize.

When times are good for the group, however, they are very good. In the 1970s, oil service companies gained more than 30 percent a year, totally overwhelming overall market performance. The offshore drillers did even better than the group as a whole.

You might conclude that oil service companies are simply a leveraged way of playing oil prices. That is, when oil prices are rising, these companies, with their relatively high fixed costs, see their stock prices soar as their fixed assets, such as drilling rigs, turn out an ever-growing revenue stream. When oil prices are falling, the situation is reversed; revenues dry up while the big fixed costs remain unchanged.

But it's a little more complicated. In the mid to late 1990s, oil prices alternated between weak and strong, yet the profits of the oil service companies remained positive—even in 1998, when oil prices fell to decade lows. True, the companies were disasters in the stock market, but in contrast to the 1980s they never had deficit earnings and they were able to survive. And earlier in the decade, when oil prices were somewhat higher but still far below all-time highs, profits for the drillers and other oil service companies rose at a furious pace.

What was the difference between the 1980s, when oil prices were low and the service companies went bankrupt, and the 1990s, when prices were low and the service companies hung in there? The key difference was the amount of worldwide oil capacity that was being used. In the 1980s, oil production rarely represented as much as 80 percent of total capacity. In the 1990s, however, oil production was almost never much less than 93 to 95 percent of total worldwide capacity. As a result, it was clear that regardless of existing low prices, it was essential to find more oil to meet future needs. We no longer could rely on our excess capacity to fill the gap.

Also, in the 1990s there was growing recognition that it would become increasingly hard to find new supplies of oil outside the Middle East. Thus despite low oil prices, oil companies began to place a growing value on securing new oil supplies for the future and were willing to pay fairly hefty prices for drilling and other services.

As oil prices begin a new uptrend and production begins to wane, the need for new oil supplies will become even more pressing. Oil companies will likely become close to frantic in bidding for oil services, and the oil drilling stocks will benefit in a big way. The best of them have the potential to increase severalfold. In fact, from their 1998 lows the group as a whole is likely to climb by as much as fivefold by the early 2000s.

Still, you can't ignore the ongoing risks, even in times of rising oil prices. As 1998 illustrated, the group is exceptionally volatile and you have to be in it for the long haul. Moreover, the group has commodity-like characteristics. There's not much to distinguish one company from another—one rig is about the same as another rig. So when the group gets hot, as inevitably it will, more rigs will be built. Large rigs can represent a hundred-million-dollar investment and can take several years to build. Historically the industry has tended to get ahead of itself by overbuilding. Thus, even if we're right and oil prices remain uptrended for the next generation, there still may be

SPOTLIGHT ON SCHLUMBERGER

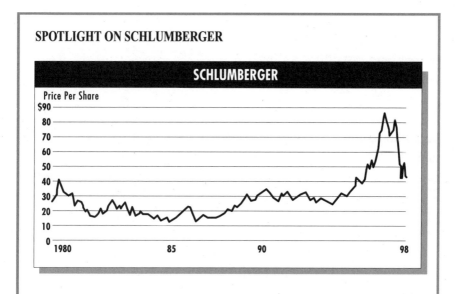

- By a wide margin Schlumberger is the most profitable and dominant oil service company in the world.

- Even in the worst of times Schlumberger spends nearly 5 percent of revenues on research and development, a far greater percentage and much greater absolute amount than any other oil service company.

- Revenues and earnings have grown at a relatively steady 10 plus percent rate throughout the 1990s.

- Revenues can continue to grow even when exploration activities are in a lull because the company's products are needed both to produce oil and to find new oil, and thus production revenues act as an offset.

- In the 1970s, when energy prices were rising, Schlumberger's earnings and stock price appreciated at an annualized rate of about 30 percent.

- In the coming decade as the need to find new oil becomes ever more pressing, profit and stock growth could become torrid once again.

times when a glut of rigs causes rig rental rates to sink. So the drillers' potential for outsized long-term payoffs is matched in part by risk and volatility. As investments, they are not for the weak in stomach.

Diversified oil service companies. These offer nearly as much potential as the drillers at less risk. The standout by far is Schlumberger, which we consider an essential stock for almost any portfolio. In an industry characterized by commodity-like plays, Schlumberger stands out as a true leader and franchise. It is the leader in many areas of oil services, including well logging, exploration, and even offshore drilling. There are few if any major exploration and production projects in the world in which Schlumberger's name does not figure prominently. Leveraged and sure gains make this great stock a must own for investors of all stripes.

6

FOOD STOCKS: THE NEED TO FEED

Strong economic growth, particularly in developing countries, will create a tremendous appetite not just for energy but for food as well, as populations move up the food chain and demand greater quantities of more protein-rich nourishment. Technological and natural limits will curtail our ability to expand the supply of food, and prices will rise. A variety of food-related companies will see both profits and share prices soar.

While we were working on this chapter, our youngest son, then nine years old, thoughtfully brought to our attention a book he owned called *Earth Search: A Kid's Geography Museum in a Book*. A collection of science exercises and experiments, it was designed to explain the natural world to elementary school age children.

And although it certainly was not intended to introduce young children to the joys of commodity trading, it might well have done so, for it contained a vivid exercise that helps explain why food prices are destined to rise. It began by asking the young reader to take an apple and imagine that it is the earth. The next step was to cut the apple into quarters, discarding (or eating) three of them, which the book explained represented the world's oceans. The remaining quarter represented all the land in the world. Our son, following instructions, then cut this quarter in half and put aside one of the halves, which the book explained represented land that is not habitable.

He now had one-eighth of an apple left, representing the portion of the earth where humans can live. However, very little of that remaining portion can be dedicated to growing food. In fact, three-quarters of that remaining one-eighth are given over to urban development, golf courses, and other human pursuits, or else is too rocky for growing food. This leaves just a relative sliver, one-thirty-second of the planet, seemingly suited for agriculture. But then the book instructed the reader to shave off the very top part of the skin from that one remaining sliver—a small, vulnerable-looking scraping. It is this minuscule part of the apple that contains sufficient soil for growing food and that bears the responsibility of meeting all the nutritional requirements of every human being on earth.

As this exercise suggests, the amount of land available for growing food is both finite and relatively small. The question is, will it be enough. And that, of course, depends on how much the demand for food will grow and how effectively we can raise yields on the land we have. The latter question leads once again to the issue of technology. If through technology we can boost food supplies sufficiently, a rise in demand won't be a problem. But if technology is stumped, then the world is likely to face chronic food shortages. As with oil, there are clear investment implications. Food prices will rise, adding to overall inflation, and companies that produce food or can increase food productivity will be stock market winners.

RISING DEMAND

It's almost certain that in coming years the planet will need to produce more food—lots more. The most obvious reason is continued population growth. Currently the world's population is growing by about 1.5 percent—or 70 million people—a year. At this rate in just 15 years we'll have added 1 billion people to the planet, most of them in developing countries. All these people will need to eat, and moreover, as life expectancies in these countries increase, they will need to eat longer.

But that's just one factor, and even if we were able to achieve zero population growth, demand for food would still grow. That's because as developing countries move up the income ladder, the expectations of their people about what they should eat also rise. Typically as countries become more developed and more urbanized and as their people have more disposable income, one of their first priorities is to eat better. Not only do they want to eat more, they begin to demand more concentrated forms of protein—meat in addition to grains.

This shift can be seen clearly in Hong Kong, for instance, which today is the world's largest per capita consumer of chicken and one of the largest per capita consumers of pork. More generally, the world's per capita consumption of meat has been growing steadily over the past half century. And in recent years, as world growth has accelerated, so has growth in per capita meat consumption. As incomes in the developing world continue to rise, this trend will accelerate further. This will put increasing pressure on food production, because producing meat, which requires growing grain for cattle or other animals to eat, is more wasteful of agricultural resources than is growing grain for direct human consumption.

INCREASING SUPPLY: THE PAST ISN'T PROLOGUE

Until the early 1980s, the amount of arable land in the world had been increasing every year for over 10,000 years, an awesomely sustained multi-millenium trend. But sometime in the first years of that decade, during the heyday of the Reagan years when greed and Wall Street reigned supreme, the amount of arable land in the world quietly peaked. In fact, over the past 18 years arable land has been eroding, thanks to the boom in industry; the paving over of farmland to make way for factories, cities, and parking lots; the demand for such amenities as golf courses, and so on. As a result, for the first time in recorded history we have become dependent solely upon rising food yields to meet the growing demand for food.

Can we meet this challenge? Optimists would say no problem. And one of the chief arguments they have going for them is recent history.

A FAMOUS BET

When it comes to the environment, sometimes the pessimists get carried away. In 1969, Paul Ehrlich, well-respected Stanford environmental scientist, proclaimed in his book *The Population Bomb* that the world was on the verge of an apocalyptic famine. The book contained such horror-inspiring assertions as, "Most of the people who are going to die in the greatest cataclysm in the history of man have already been born."

His work inspired a famous bet with one of the leading optimists of the period, the late Julian L. Simon, author of *The Ultimate Resource 2*, which basically proclaims that necessity is the mother of invention and that every problem in the world will be solved by human ingenuity. Simon confidently wagered that over the 1980s the prices of most basic commodities, such as copper and zinc, would decline. Simon won the bet, no sweat.

But being right for a decade or even longer doesn't mean you'll be right forever. Conversely, crying wolf when the wolf is elsewhere doesn't mean he'll never show up in your pasture. Simon won his bet, but over the longer term Ehrlich's pessimism may prove more prescient.

It's indisputable that in the past several decades science has been marvelously successful in improving food yields. Through the increased use of fertilizers, better irrigation, and a greater reliance on genetic breeding, food yields per unit of land rose impressively and steadily in the "green revolution" of the 1960s and 1970s—on average by 4 to 5 percent a year. As a result, while the world's population has been growing, so has the number of calories consumed per person. In 1969 nearly 60 percent of the planet had subsistence diets of less than 2200 calories a day. Today the figure has been reduced to 10 percent. The optimists argue that these trends will persist into the future.

The evidence, however, is that the pace of agricultural progress is letting up. On November 18, 1996, in an op-ed piece in *The Wall Street Journal*, leading optimist Julian Simon included a chart designed to show that per capita food consumption is in a clear uptrend and that therefore worries about running short of food are misplaced. In fact, though, his chart, which is similar to the chart titled "U.S. Grain Yield, Per Hectare, 1950–1997," suggested just the opposite. It's true that over the past 46 years the overall trend is up. More significant, however, is that it is an uptrend whose slope is declining. (For calculus buffs, the second derivative of the curve is

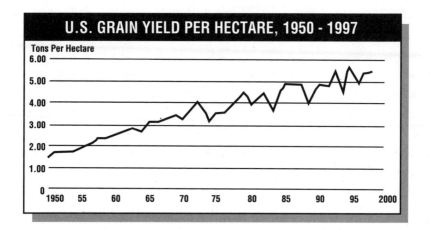

negative.) In other words, for whatever type of food you choose you find that yields per unit are increasing but at a diminishing rate.

Similarly, while both the World Bank and the United Nations' Food and Agricultural Organization have placed themselves in the optimists' camp, they are ignoring the most recent data. They both assume that the trendline defining the increases in yields between 1960 and 1990 will remain in effect indefinitely. But that's quite a leap of faith in that it ignores the downward blip between 1990 and 1997 when wheat yields, for example, barely increased at all.

The optimists would doubtless argue that this is merely a brief pause in an overall uptrend. But in fact there's lots of evidence that we're fast approaching some pretty firm limits in our ability to boost food yields. They include both physical limits and technological limits that stem from our imperfect understanding of the exceedingly complex processes through which Mother Nature makes our food. Let's quickly survey some of these limits—and then look at what they mean for investing in food stocks.

RUNNING LOW ON WATER

You can't grow food without fresh water, and there are limits to how much water is available in the world. One exhaustive analysis of this variable comes from scientist and author Joel Cohen, author of *How Many People Can the Earth Support?* He drew up various scenarios of how many calories the world can produce, all of them based in part on how much fresh water is available for growing crops. Next he correlated this with how many calories people consume today in various parts of the world and how many calories they can be expected to consume in the future. One of his points is that as people add more meat to their diet, as they probably will insist upon doing as economic development proceeds, a lot more water will be needed for growing food. The reason is that it takes about ten times more water to produce one calorie from meat as it does to produce one calorie from grain (thus, one calorie from meat is equivalent to ten "grain calories"). Not taking into account water losses in the growing process, Americans use up on average about 1000 cubic meters of water per person per year just for growing food. By contrast, the average person on an all-grain diet in a developing country uses up just 200 cubic meters of water a year.

Cohen concluded that the world probably has available somewhere between 9000 and 14,000 cubic kilometers of fresh water a year and that based on current grain yields this will allow us to produce somewhere between 2800 and 4200 grain calories per day per person. By comparison, current estimates are that the average American consumes about 10,000 grain calories per day.

The bottom line is that there is not much difference between what we theoretically can produce and what we actually consume. In other words, under current growing conditions and looking just at the amount of water available, there is very little excess food capacity in the world today. Another way of looking at it is that the amount of fresh water in the world will allow the planet to grow only enough grain to feed the current world's population about one-third as well as we eat in the United States today.

Moreover, Cohen's estimates of available water could prove optimistic because of water that is lost through pollution, which is one consequence of development and urban growth. Even in the United States, where pollution is less of a problem than in the developing world, the Environmental Protection Agency (EPA) has estimated that it will need to spend nearly $140 billion on infrastructure over the next generation just to assure enough safe drinking water. Worldwide the expense clearly will be in the trillions of dollars. The point is that not only do Cohen's estimates as they stand indicate that water will be a serious constraint on food, but his assumptions might turn out to be too sanguine.

TECHNOLOGICAL FIXES?

With arable land shrinking and water supplies approaching limits, the only hope for avoiding a food crunch is through technology. But the outlook is not promising.

Desalinization. If a limited amount of fresh water is a problem, it would be nice if desalinization—wringing fresh water from seawater—could make up the difference. But we're limited in our ability to do so by the fact that desalinization is a highly energy-intensive process. In the book *Nature's Services*, Sandra Postel and Stephen Carpenter explain that nature performs an almost incalculable service in delivering fresh water to land. The process of desalting water is accomplished in a complex fashion that is still not completely understood. What is known is that the sun's enormous energy is critical to the process. The only countries that can afford to attempt to mimic nature in this regard are those sitting on gobs of energy, both solar and fossil fuel—namely, the Persian Gulf states.

Thus, limited water dovetails with limits in energy and energy technology. Right now water from desalinization plants is far too expensive for widespread use. Joel Cohen calculates the cost of desalting ocean water to be about $1.50 a cubic meter, more than 30 times what farmers pay for water and about five times what city dwellers pay. In other words, inexpensive water above and beyond the hydrologic cycle is well beyond our current abilities.

If we could develop alternatives to fossil fuels, it would help a lot. But as we discussed in Chapter 5, such alternatives are not yet close to being meaningful realities. As a result, any large-scale attempt to create fresh water through existing desalinization technologies would require massive amounts of fossil fuel, which in turn would raise the price of oil. At best we'd be trading one constraint for another.

Moreover, using increased amounts of fossil fuels to create more fresh water could be self-defeating because it might—through increased greenhouse gas emissions—change the climate in unforeseen ways that might affect rainfall patterns. This, in turn, could affect fresh water supplies in ways far beyond what we could counter through desalinization. We might end up no better than when we started, or worse.

Biotechnology. There is a widespread assumption that the next great leap forward in agricultural productivity will come from progress in manipulating the genetic structure, or genome, of various crops. For example, if we could decipher the genome of wheat in any detail, we might be able to construct a new, improved combination of genes that would produce a much more fertile version of this grain, increasing food yields and circumventing limits in land and water.

However, success in this area is unlikely, and in fact, when it comes to increasing plant yields, biotechnology hasn't been able to add much to standard genetic breeding techniques based on Gregor Mendel's original observations in the nineteenth century. Why not? The answer has to do with the enormous complexity of basic biological processes and in particular photosynthesis, the magical process through which plants somehow mix together sunlight, carbon dioxide, and a hydrogen source such as water and turn them into oxygen and carbohydrates.

Basically, genetic plant breeders—the folks who simply mix and match seeds, as Mendel did—have already hit the jackpot, at least under normal photosynthetic processes. That is, they've succeeded in creating plants that are maxxed out in terms of how much of the product of photosynthesis goes toward the seed (i.e., the edible part). This means the only option left for increasing food yields further is somehow to improve the efficiency of photosynthesis itself. A plant more efficient at photosynthesis would do more with whatever time it had in the sun—creating more carbohydrates and giving off more oxygen. But while photosynthesis is something we've all studied in school, at a deep level no one understands it very well, and efforts to mimic it in the lab have not been successful. Without a far better understanding of photosynthesis, it's unlikely that we can improve upon it. What's required is a theory of life, which is something no computer can give birth to.

There's one more point. Suppose that by some miracle we actually could increase the efficiency of plant photosynthesis. We might end up regretting it. Photosynthesis not only makes food, it also helps regulate environmental processes such as the release of carbon dioxide and oxygen into the atmosphere. Given the limits of our understanding of climate, tampering with photosynthesis could backfire. It is truly tampering with life and risks triggering unforeseen and possibly unpleasant consequences.

COMPLICATED WHEAT

In Chapter 2 we noted the complexity of the human genome
and why it's unlikely that computer-led efforts to decipher it
will bear much fruit. You might think the wheat genome
would be a lot simpler. But it's not. I've asked dozens of intelligent and well-educated people to guess how many bases the
wheat genome might have, given that the human genome has
around 3 billion. No one came close to the right answer,
which is 16 billion. That's not a misprint. The wheat genome
has more than five times as many bases as the human
genome.

This means that from a genetic point of view, photosynthesis
may be as complex as, or even more complex than, human
intelligence. Attempting to make photosynthesis more efficient is akin to trying to model the human genome in such a
way as to produce more intelligent human beings. Logically
it's possible, but for all practical purposes it's impossible
unless we can gain a clear understanding not only of all the
interactions among genes but also of those between genes and
the environment. Those kinds of interactions are well beyond
the scope of any computer.

Nitrogen fixing. Nitrogen is essential to plant growth, and one way
to boost food production would be to increase the amount of nitrogen
available to plants. This might seem easy, given that nitrogen is the
most common element on the planet—in fact, it makes up nearly 80
percent of the atmosphere. The problem is that this nitrogen is useless to plants unless it can be "fixed," or separated from other elements. Nature does this through certain bacteria that convert
airborne nitrogen and hydrogen into ammonia, from which plants
can withdraw nitrogen. The plants could use more nitrogen still,
though, which is where nitrogen-based fertilizers come in.

Fertilizers contributed in a big way to the green revolution of the recent past. However, they have one huge drawback: They pollute, with big risks to water and soil. If we overuse them, we could destroy some of our fresh-water supplies, which would be self-defeating. (This is yet another example of trade-offs whose complexity defies our computer-based means of analysis.)

It would be great if biotechnology could come to the rescue by figuring out how to transplant the nitrogen-fixing bacteria directly onto the plant genome, which would eliminate the polluting effects of fertilizers as well as save farmers huge amounts of money. Biotechnology is unlikely to be successful in this, however. Gordon Conway, president of the Rockefeller Institute, sums of up some of the difficulties in *The Doubly Green Revolution*. "Although plants, animals, and bacteria share the same genetic code, they have different reading systems: the promoters, the number of genes read at a time, and the ways of handling the genetic message all differ. These are formidable obstacles and will take years of fundamental research before they are overcome."

Others have pointed out that even if we could solve the problem of nitrogen fixing, it might not help because it likely would divert the plant's available energy away from food production. In other words, a solution like nitrogen fixing can't be viewed in isolation—it is just one part of an immensely complicated equation that we are nowhere near to understanding. What we need is an all-encompassing theoretical approach. Our continued fascination with computer-driven combinatorial approaches won't get us there.

SOME MARGINAL SUCCESSES

While helpless to conquer the big problems, biotechnology has helped increase crop yields in a few marginal ways. The best-known success is the development of transgenic crops, which are resistant to pesticides and herbicides. The idea is that farmers can then use pest and weed control substances more freely, leading to a bigger harvest.

Not surprisingly, it's not that simple. The major concern with transgenic crops is the fear that they will pass on their engineered resistance to other organisms—in particular, to the pests and weeds the pesticides and herbicides were created to control. They could lead to the development of "superweeds" or "super pests" and the whole experiment would have backfired big time.

Another approach biotechnology is taking is to try to engineer changes in what are known as crops' "output variables"—that is, to change the final form of a crop to make it more nutritious or in some way more desirable. This could be anything from developing a lemon that is less tart to creating soybeans with less saturated fat. Perhaps this has some potential, but again it's not as clear-cut as you might think. One consideration is that if you manipulate one aspect of a crop, you might cause undesirable changes in other characteristics. Also, we can't be sure we know what a more desirable form of a food is. Remember the old Woody Allen movie *Sleeper,* which depicts a future in which ice cream is good for you? This might not be such a fantasy. For years we've all been told to cut back on saturated fats. Recently, however, we've learned that while such fats promote heart disease, they also seem to help prevent strokes. The point isn't that we should have bacon and eggs for breakfast every day—it's that we don't know as much about nutrition as we think.

Even forgetting about all these possible problems, on a best-case basis transgenic crops and manipulating output variables won't lead to a major leap forward in food yields. According to figures developed by Noble Laureate David Kendall, for instance, we might be able to get yields up an additional 25 percent in the developing world. That won't be enough to compensate for population growth and a rising demand for protein. The bottom line is that in the decades ahead we are facing food shortages, and food prices will rise.

CASHING IN: INVESTING IN FOOD STOCKS

What's the best way to cash in on rising food prices? Like energy, food is big business—in the aggregate. The United States spends nearly the same amount on food as it does on energy, more than half a trillion dollars a year, and both commodities obviously are vital to human welfare. But that's where the similarities end. The food industry is highly fragmented, consisting mostly of a collection of privately owned farms. If we're right about food prices, farms will be great investments over the next several decades but the only way to invest in them directly is to go out and buy one, not something most of us can do. Luckily, there are easier ways to participate in rising food prices.

Seed companies. As demand for food grows and prices rise, there will be tremendous interest in any product that can boost food productivity. The most direct play in this area is seed companies. Most of the big gains in productivity probably are behind us, as we explained previously. But this means that even small gains in productivity will be highly valued by the market. Moreover, as food prices rise, seed producers will find their prices and margins rising even if their seeds are not all that much more productive.

The world's largest seed producer is Pioneer Hi-Bred, which also is by a wide margin the leading producer of hybrid seed. These seeds, which are used extensively in the developed world, are more expensive than standard seeds and have been used only sparingly in the developing world. Thus, the potential untapped market is enormous, and Pioneer is assured of both growing revenues and margins— meaning leveraged gains in profits—for the foreseeable future.

Until recently, Pioneer was easily the standout pure food play and our top recommendation in this area. Now, however, while its prospects remain as bright as ever, it is being acquired by chemical giant DuPont, which up to now has owned 20 percent of Pioneer. With revenues of about $2 billion compared with nearly $25 billion for the parent, Pioneer simply will be too small a portion of the whole for us to consider switching our allegiance to DuPont as a food play.

However, it still will be possible to participate in a meaningful way in Pioneer's prospects. DuPont plans to issue a "tracking" stock that will reflect the performance of all its life science operations, including Pioneer as well as DuPont's other agricultural and pharmaceutical businesses. (A tracking stock is a separate stock a company issues to measure performance of a particular group of divisions. It is valued in line with the financial results of those divisions and makes it possible for investors to participate in one part of a company's operations without having to invest in the company as a whole.) The DuPont tracking stock still won't be as pure a food play as Pioneer was on its own, but its fortunes will be highly dependent on the fate of food prices and it should prove a good way to benefit from growing demand for food.

Still, keep in mind one caveat. Food, like oil, is a commodity and even though the long-term outlook is for growing scarcities and rising prices, there can be violent short-term fluctuations. Corn, which is Pioneer's most important seed, soared from about $1.50 a bushel in 1987 to well over $5.00 a bushel in 1995, only to fall to about $2.00 a bushel in 1998. As with all commodities, small changes in either supply or demand can translate into huge short-term price swings. In 1998 corn and other crops were affected by a variety of short-term factors—among them, the Asian crisis, which reduced the demand for grain; increased production stemming from remarkably good weather; and small increases in acreage. It is a tribute to Pioneer and a sign of its dominance within its market that earnings growth only slowed and did not turn negative. Still, because of its slowing earnings growth the stock disappointed investors in 1998 and ended the year with a loss in the face of big gains by most market averages. In short, while the DuPont tracking stock should fatten your portfolio over the long term, there can be some sickening short-term drops. Buy it with a view to the long term—pretty good advice in general—and you should end up a happy camper.

Another play on food is Tejon Ranch, the largest publicly traded landowner in the United States. The company owns about 270,000 contiguous acres in Southern California, which are devoted to agriculture and to oil and gas drilling. Over the past several years as commodity prices have fallen, Tejon has lost more than half its value.

Over the long term the stock should benefit from major uptrends in both food and energy prices.

Genetic engineering companies. While genetic engineering is a rel-atively small part of Pioneer Hi-Bred's operations, it's a big deal for Monsanto, which is the company that has staked the most in this area. We have mixed feelings about Monsanto, but as the leader in a high-profile area, it's a company that you'll be hearing more about and it's not one that can be ignored in any discussion of food plays. So far Monsanto's major accomplishments have been to produce crops that are resistant to pesticides. The company benefits twice over from this in that farmers buy both its genetically engineered transgenic seeds as well as greater quantities of the pesticides that Monsanto also sells. But as we noted previously, transgenic seeds carry environmental risks that could backfire in a big way, in partic-ular the risk of creating super weeds. So far this has not been a major problem but there are no guarantees, especially given the limits to our knowledge about how the genes of one plant interact with those of another. Transgenic seeds will probably come up with some suc-cesses, but there are definite drawbacks.

Perhaps our biggest beef with Monsanto, though, is not so much its focus on genetic engineering as the fact that it has overspent in its efforts to become dominant in this area. In 1998 Monsanto paid about 100 times earnings to buy DeKalb, which like Pioneer is a producer of hybrid seeds and which also is a leader in genetically engineered food crops. As with Pioneer, DeKalb's leading source of profits for the fore-seeable future will likely be in hybrid seeds. Pioneer, with a much stronger market position in hybrid seeds and a respectable position in genetic engineering, was trading at about 25 times earnings.

In short, barring an environmental disaster involving transgenic seeds, Monsanto will participate in the food boom and should be a good stock to own, but it is a distant second to the DuPont tracking stock, even though it's the company most likely to make headlines over the next several years. Buy some just to get some diversity among food investments, but concentrate on our other food-related choices.

Farm equipment companies. Increasing the productivity of land is just one part of the food equation. Another approach is to increase the productivity of farmers through improved farm equipment. We noted earlier that rising farm productivity is one of the engines of growth in the developing world. This trend will continue, and the latest farm equipment also will be in demand in the United States and other developed countries. Moreover, as with seed companies, the price of farm equipment will rise as food prices increase. Thus over the long term farm equipment manufacturers will benefit from both growing markets and higher profit margins.

But that's not all. Farm equipment companies, even more than seed producers, have traditionally been viewed and valued as cyclical companies because historically their fortunes tend to follow, with lags, the ups and downs of the food price cycle. And with farm equipment manufacturers the cycles can be even more dramatic because farm equipment is a major purchase that, in contrast to seeds, may often be postponed. As food prices rise, however, farm equipment companies will come to be viewed as more dynamic growth companies, which means they will command higher P/Es. Together with bigger markets and higher margins this should mean exceptional long-term gains for well-situated farm equipment stocks. Our favorite is the largest and most profitable company in the group, Deere Co.

Again, though, like any other food stock Deere will suffer occasional setbacks even in the midst of a powerful long-term uptrend. Moreover, Deere has a much more cyclical history than many of the stocks recommended in this book. In the mid-1980s, for instance, the company suffered outright losses. This history means that even a hint of a slowdown may well lead to investor panic. Thus in 1998 when demand for agricultural equipment began to moderate, Deere's stock price fell by over 50 percent despite the fact that the company will remain solidly profitable and indeed generate enough free cash flow in 1998 and 1999 to buy its own shares. Over the long term Deere—because of its low valuation and potential in the developing world, whose farmers currently can't afford expensive agricultural equipment—has the potential to generate manyfold gains. Another reason the company gets high marks is its exceptional balance sheet, which contains only modest debt.

Natural food companies. A more oblique way to play the future of food is through natural food companies, those that sell natural or organically owned foods. These companies could benefit significantly from a consumer backlash against foods that result from genetic tampering. Artificial means of increasing food yields engender a fair amount of distrust, possibly with good reason. Remember, mad cow disease resulted from efforts to "improve" cows by feeding them beef. If, as we expect, food shortages develop in the years ahead, efforts to increase food yields will intensify and may result in similar horror stories. Companies that shun artificially enhanced foods and specialize in organic foods will command ever greater premiums.

Our favorite is Whole Foods Market. It is the nation's largest operator of natural food supermarkets. Far more profitable than the typical supermarket chain, its growth in recent years has been spectacular. This is a much smaller company than most of our recommendations and therefore is somewhat riskier, not just because of its size but also because it will face competition from the larger food chains, which are likely to introduce or expand organic food sections. Still, as we explain in Chapter 7, as inflation heats up, small growth companies (as long as they are well situated and well managed) are likely to outperform bigger companies, and Whole Foods clearly fits the bill.

An even smaller dedicated organic food seller is Wild Oats. It features the same exceptional growth credentials as Whole Foods but because it is a smaller company is a riskier choice. Both Wild Oats and Whole Food have five-year growth rates above 20 percent and the promise of more of the same. Though both have above-average risks, they are exactly the kind of company that offers the potential for outsized gains in the more inflationary world we see developing through the early part of next century.

7

INFLATION PLAYS

All the trends now unfolding point to rising inflation over the next decade—not just in oil and food but across the board. We expect price increases to be gradual at first and then to accelerate, eventually reaching double-digit levels. Inflation will reconfigure the investment playing field. First and foremost it will benefit small, fast-growing companies, the same ones that have been most scorned of late. In addition, traditional inflation hedges such as gold and real estate will gain major appeal. Meanwhile, most of the safe big-cap stocks that have powered the market in recent years will suddenly find themselves at a disadvantage, penalized just for being big.

To all of us old-timers (first-generation baby boomers and older) it may seem amazing, but the fact is that many of today's investors have no idea what it's like to live in inflationary times. Inflation to them is as remote as the days of chamber pots and parlors lit by gas lamps. Thus, a little historical detour is probably in order.

Specifically, to get a general idea of what inflationary times are like—and thus of what the financial markets will look like in the years ahead—it pays to revisit the period between 1966 and 1980. During those years, inflation rose from less than 2 percent at the start to nearly 15 percent by the end.

How did stocks take it? The chart titled "Relative Strength of Small Caps: Rising Inflation" compares the performance of big-cap and small-cap stocks during those years, and the difference was dramatic. Small-cap stocks—represented by the smallest one-fifth of New York Stock Exchange stocks—gained more than 14 percent a year on average. This was more than twice the average annual return of big-cap stocks, as measured by the S&P 500, and more than twice the inflation rate. And these are just the averages. Some small stocks soared 40-fold between 1973 and 1980.

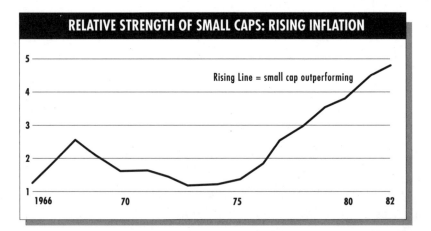

In the six inflationary years between the summer of 1976 and the summer of 1982, small stocks gained nearly 25 percent a year on average. If you had bought a representative group, you would have quadrupled your money in six years. Meanwhile, the big-cap stocks lost half their value in real terms.

What happens when inflation calms down? Look at the chart titled "Relative Strength of Small Caps: Low Inflation," which shows market action from 1994 through 1998, when inflation was ebbing. The smallest one-fifth of New York Stock Exchange stocks averaged a gain of just 7.6 percent a year. By contrast, the big S&P 500 stock average rose 20.5 percent a year.

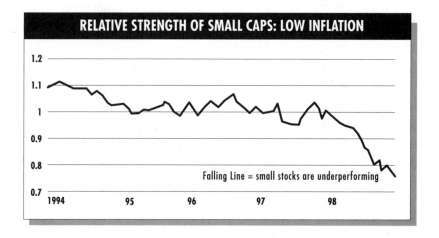

The conclusion is clear: Inflation benefits small-cap stocks. Stable prices benefit big-cap stocks. As inflation starts to pick up, it will be essential to switch into small-cap issues. They will be your basic vehicles for making inflation work in your favor.

SMALL-CAP DYNAMOS

What is the connection between small cap stocks and inflation? It's growth—during times of inflation, small-cap stocks have the potential to grow far more quickly than big-cap stocks. That's critical because when prices are rising at a rapid clip, investors become obsessed with growth. The reason is that the only way to keep up with inflation is to invest in assets that appreciate faster than prices are increasing. Thus, during periods of inflation investors seek out companies that can sustain rapid earnings growth. They will take a chance on smaller companies because sticking with bigger ones means they will barely keep up with inflation, if at all.

Moreover, in periods of inflation, the P/Es of most companies come down. With P/Es falling, the only way a stock can advance is if earnings growth accelerates.

Let's look at these relationships a little more closely to see why this is true. In times of fast growth and rising inflation—and remember, inflation comes about because the economy is growing strongly—conditions are less competitive and less cutthroat. There's enough to go around for everyone, and the emphasis is on generating higher sales, not on taking market share away from others. The size of the pie is constantly expanding.

During these times, one of the key concepts is pricing power. When inflation takes hold, all companies can generate growth merely by raising prices. But this helps the little guys more than the big guys, because they are starting from a smaller earnings base. If you're starting with $1 million in sales, it's not that much of a stretch to get to $2 million, generating 100 percent growth. If you're starting from a $1 billion base, though, to double your sales you need to tack on another $1 billion, and that's a lot harder to come by. In recognition of the superior growth prospects of smaller companies during inflationary times, investors may even bid up their P/Es, while the P/Es of larger stocks are coming down.

When the economy is less supercharged and inflation settles down, companies suddenly find themselves in a much more competitive environment. Everyone is scrabbling for the same customers and the same dollars, and you can't generate growth simply by raising prices. Under these circumstances, bigger companies have the edge because they have the resources to market their products most widely and forcefully. These greater resources also mean they can cut prices if they wish, out-muscling the competition.

By the summer of 1998, the relative valuations of small and large companies were very similar to what they were in the summer of 1976, when inflation still was low. That is, the average P/E of small stocks was roughly equal to that of the big stocks. This shows what little regard investors had for small stocks, because typically smaller growth issues should have higher P/Es. It's an anomaly that in the past has signaled the start of a long period of strong relative stock market performance by small stocks.

As inflation begins to creep up, even conservative investors should trade some of their blue chips for a selection of small growth stocks—it will be the only way to keep up. The blue chips, far from being the safe and profitable havens of the recent past, will be the dogs of the market. If you stick with them, you're almost certain to find your investments under water, in real and sometimes even in nominal terms. (A few blue chip exceptions are presented in Chapter 8.)

There are risks, however, and they are unavoidable, simply because the new era we are entering is inherently more volatile and risky. As long as growth remains strong, the small stocks will outperform. But periods of rapid inflationary growth tend to be erratic. In the past, they have been interrupted from time to time by recessionary interludes, usually triggered by rising interest rates. During these interruptions, the smaller stocks come down most sharply and you can see your gains evaporate quickly. During the recessionary sell-off of 1972–1974, for instance, the smallest one-fifth of the New York Stock Exchange lost nearly 50 percent of its value. The big stocks were down about 35 percent. In today's world, where growth is a necessity, we are likely to avoid serious recessions, but even periods of slowing growth may lead to worry and market turbulence.

Big companies can weather such downturns with more grace because of their entrenched market positions and larger bank accounts, which give them a cushion. Smaller companies typically have fewer resources to fall back on. If they can't grow, they may be forced out of business altogether.

Can you time these downturns so as to protect your gains in small growth stocks? One rule of thumb worked quite well during the turbulent 1970s. It was to buy small stocks whenever the annual rate of growth in the Consumer Price Index rose above 7 percent, and sell when the index fell below 4.5 percent. These numbers are not hard and fast, however, and may not apply to all markets. The general point remains true, however—the higher inflation goes, the more committed you should be to small growth stocks. When inflation is falling, you'll maximize your gains by ditching the small stocks temporarily until inflation picks up again.

But during periods of overall inflationary growth, even if you stick with the small stocks through any downturns, you'll still do better than if you had put your money into big stocks, as long as you've picked reasonably well-grounded companies that aren't going to disappear altogether. Remember, the years between 1966 and 1981 included periods of downturn and still the small stocks outperformed.

GO FOR QUALITY: THE BEST OF THE SMALL

More turbulent times lie ahead, and even the best investments, the ones that over the long term will make you tons of money, may experience sharp drops before coming back. That will be unnerving, but what you really want to avoid is investing in small growth companies that *never* come back—that aren't strong enough to survive the inevitable slower-growth interludes. The way to do this is to pick quality. We've pinpointed several criteria for picking the best of the small. These criteria are not infallible, but they help cut down on risk, protecting you against the biggest disappointments.

Earnings that have risen for at least ten years (or, if a newer issue, for as long as the stock has been publicly traded). Stocks with good stories but no earnings record are unknown quantities. They could turn out to be wildly profitable, but if expectations fall short there is nothing to cushion their fall.

A solid balance sheet—debt of 20 percent or less of total capital. This gives the company room to cut costs during an economic downturn, while companies with higher debt might be forced to curtail expansion plans dramatically if sales growth suddenly slows.

Free cash flow. This is the money left over after the company pays all its expenses, including interest on loans and construction costs. This cash can be used to repurchase stock, boost dividends, acquire other companies, or conduct other activities that benefit shareholders.

Operating margins that are close to all-time highs. This indicates that the company is dominant within a profitable niche.

Relatively low P/Es. Specifically, we'd suggest companies whose annual earnings growth for the past five years has been no more than 50 percent lower than their P/Es.

GET READY FOR GOLD

Another must-have investment in times of inflation is gold, the best known and best beloved of all inflation hedges. Few investments have been more disappointing in recent years than gold. Between the summer of 1996 and the summer of 1998, the metal lost 30 percent of its value. The average gold stock did even worse, declining by about 50 percent. In fact, gold and gold stocks have sunk to decade lows. But don't let all this bad news faze you. Once inflation gets going again, gold and gold stocks will make up their losses in a hurry.

Gold had two strikes against it in the 1990s and particularly in the latter half of the decade. First, of course, was low inflation. Second, during these years paper assets reigned supreme. In particular, 1995–1998 was the era of the dollar. Gold, that traditional safe haven against economic and political uncertainty, yielded pride of place to the greenback.

This made sense. When you hold gold, you are investing in an asset that loses money if it stays at the same price. For one thing, you have to pay something to store the gold. You're also foregoing the interest you could have earned on the cash you spent to purchase the gold.

By contrast, in the 1990s dollar-based assets were a powerful double play. That's because not only did the dollar rise in value but so did the assets most commonly bought with dollars—stocks and bonds. This favorable situation for the dollar, however, rested on one foundation—noninflationary growth in the U.S. economy.

SPOTLIGHT ON NEWMONT

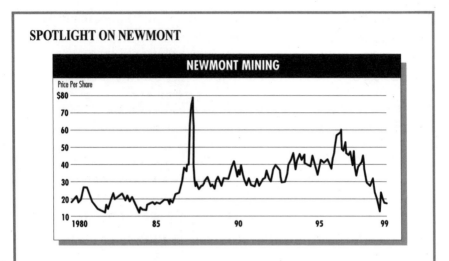

- Newmont is one of the largest gold mines in the world and the largest North American mine that does not hedge its gold portfolio. Hedging is a technique for selling gold in the commodity markets so as to lessen risk in the event of falling gold prices. Not hedging makes Newmont a purer play on changes in gold.

- Though the stock price has been extremely volatile over the past 15 years, Newmont in recent years has been steadily increasing production and reducing costs. Unlike most gold mines, Newmont has remained profitable for the past 15 years. Book value has risen steadily over the past decade despite a downtrend in gold.

- Newmont is a relatively low-cost producer, a major reason it has stayed consistently profitable despite low gold prices. There is a basic relationship between production costs and risks. The higher the production costs, the higher the risks and potential rewards. Thus Newmont is one of the least risky of the major gold mines.

- Smaller gold mines such as Echo Bay TVX and Homes-take are North American mines with higher production costs than Newmont. Both risks and upside potential will be somewhat greater for these.

The picture will turn around once inflation starts to pick up. Not only will the big blue chips fall, so will bonds. The dollar and other currencies are more likely to erode your wealth than to increase it. Gold, though, will make up for lost time with a vengeance.

What's so special about gold? Why is it the one metal that investors always come back to in the end? Indeed, why is it that despite its dismal performance over the past decade or so gold remains part of the reserve assets of every central bank in Western Europe, and probably always will? One reason is that gold is truly a noble metal, as it has been dubbed. It has unique properties. No metal is more beautiful or more flexible or more resistant to corrosion. Bankers know that unlike any other currency, gold is money that will always be accepted anywhere. "As good as gold" is a phrase that still means something.

Gold's character has made it uniquely able to hold its value over the long term. Go back over any fairly long period of time. In early 1934, for instance, gold was fixed at $35 an ounce. By mid-1998 it was selling at $290 an ounce. That more than eightfold gain in price roughly matched inflation for the same period.

One reason gold occupies such a special place is the very fact that it doesn't have many industrial or medical uses. Where it does have practical applications, there are cheaper substitutes. As a result, gold will never fall out of favor just because a better alternative is found. This isn't true of commodities that are used for industrial purposes. When they become too expensive, there is an incentive to use less costly substitutes. But gold is irreplaceable.

How high will gold go? Between the mid-1970s and 1980, as inflation reached double-digit levels, gold climbed from a low of $100 to a high of more than $800 an ounce. While the value of U.S. dollars and other currencies rapidly lost ground in real terms, gold held its own and gained speculative value as well.

The potential for inflation over the next decade is as great as or even greater than in the 1970s. This means that gold could rapidly come back to $800 an ounce and even to $1000 or higher. A buy and hold strategy for gold should make you a big winner. But if you're willing to be more active, getting in and out at selected moments, you're likely to do even better.

That's because while over the long haul gold slightly outperforms inflation, during short spurts its gains are phenomenal—100 percent or more. These big upward thrusts come when investors are most worried about future inflation. The peak of $800 an ounce, for example, came after 15 years of relentless price increases, when it seemed as if inflation would never end. Later run-ups in gold, in 1989 and 1990, were preceded by sharp upturns in inflation. These turned out to be temporary, but investors were spooked. In contrast, for much of the time gold has run in place, often lagging behind inflation.

The key to making it big with gold, therefore, is to buy when inflationary expectations are highest. How do you pinpoint these moments? The best way is to watch the trend in real (that is, inflation-adjusted) interest rates. Real rates are the difference between actual interest rates and inflation. If bonds are yielding 7 percent, for instance, and inflation is 3 percent, real interest rates are 4 percent.

When real interest rates are positive, which is most of the time, you make money in real terms just by putting it in an interest-bearing instrument such as a government bond. Suppose you have $10,000 to invest and real rates are 4 percent. You buy government bonds with your $10,000 and a year later you'll be 4 percent ahead of inflation. You've made money in real terms. When real rates are high, buying bonds makes sense. But it makes no sense to buy gold, because gold doesn't pay you a return—it just sits there.

When real rates are positive, gold must not only keep up with inflation, it must keep up with real rates as well. This rarely happens. As a result, when real rates are positive, gold is a poor investment. Historically, real rates usually are positive, which is why gold is generally a back burner investment.

But if real rates turn negative—which happens only in periods of rapid increases in inflation—gold suddenly moves into a starring role. It becomes a far better investment than bonds or other interest-earning investments. That's because if you buy bonds when real rates are negative, you wind up getting back less, in real terms, than you originally invested.

Suppose, for instance, inflation is 10 percent and interest rates are 7 percent. Real interest rates are negative. Now suppose you have $10,000, which is the cost of a new car. But instead of buying the car, you put the money in the bank. After one year, you have $10,700. That may sound good. But with inflation at 10 percent, the same car now costs $11,000 and you no longer can afford it. When real rates are negative, the worst thing you can do with your money is to lend it out to a bank or other borrower.

The best rule for timing purchases of gold is to wait for real interest rates to turn negative. In those periods, gold goes wild. The more you buy, the better.

Look at the chart titled "Real Rates and Gold," which shows clearly that the big gains in gold have always come when real rates were negative. In fact, since gold was decontrolled, it has multiplied its value five-and-a-half-fold during the total time in which real rates were negative. No other investment comes close.

Most of the time, though, real rates are positive. That, of course, makes sense, because lenders aren't crazy—they'd have no incentive to lend money if they'd end up losing in real terms. What causes real rates to turn negative? High inflation is the key. In the mid-1990s, real interest rates have averaged a relatively high 4 percent. But given the mandate for growth, eventually that number will fall, as the U.S. government becomes increasingly willing to pump money into the system in order to stimulate growth. It will take a lot of money to keep growth uptrended. The more that's added to the system, the more rates will fall and inflation will rise. That means negative real interest rates and sharply higher inflationary expectations—and much higher gold prices.

So wait for real interest rates to turn negative. The easiest way to tell when this is happening is to subtract the most recent 12-month rate of increase in the Consumer Price Index—listed in most financial newspapers—from the current interest rate paid on 30-year U.S. Treasury bonds. If the number is a negative, get into gold.

	REAL RATES AND GOLD		
Year	Average Gold	Real Rates*	% Change in Gold
1972	$59	0.01	
1973	96	-7.70	62.71%
1974	160	-13.56	66.67
1975	161	4.73	0.63
1976	125	4.20	-22.36
1977	148	2.23	18.40
1978	194	-0.47	31.08
1979	308	A.19	58.76
1980	613	0.08	99.03
1981	460	8.44	-24.96
1982	376	9.59	-18.26
1983	424	10.30	12.77
1984	361	10.16	-14.86
1985	318	9.79	-11.91
1986	368	12.19	15.72
1987	478	5.20	29.89
1988	438	5.33	-8.37
1989	383	4.83	-12.56
1990	385	3.27	0.52
1991	363	10.92	-5.71
1992	345	6.75	-4.96
1993	362	5.96	4.93
1994	385	5.77	6.35
1995	400	3.25	3.90
1996	385	4.99	-3.75
1997	320	6.85	-16.88
1998	290	8.90	-9.38

*AM bond yields minus Producer Prices.

GOLD INVESTMENTS

Exactly which gold investments should you buy? The safest and simplest one is gold itself—gold bullion, which comes in bars and in coins. When you buy the metal itself, you're guaranteed to keep pace with gold's moves. The worst that can happen to you—assuming you haven't borrowed in order to buy gold and that you stick with established dealers and brokers, avoiding the scam artists who sometimes emerge—is that gold may languish. But your investment can't go down more than gold itself.

During past bull markets in gold, no gold-related investment appreciated more in value than gold itself. During the inflationary 1970s, for instance, precious metals (gold and silver) rose at about 33 percent a year, while gold stocks gained 28 percent a year. Between 1966 and 1981, bullion gained 23 percent versus 16 percent for gold stocks. So once real rates turn negative, gold itself is likely to make the biggest gains.

The trade-off, though, is that gold bullion doesn't earn a return. By contrast gold mining stocks—though somewhat riskier—offer the possibility of rising profits even if the price of gold itself stays flat. With a well-run gold mine, revenues can rise because gold prices keep up with inflation and because improved efficiencies tend to cut the costs of digging up additional deposits. Costs over time rise more slowly than inflation. That's a recipe for long-term profit growth.

In picking specific gold stocks, the most solid investments are far and away the companies presented in our chart titled "North American Gold Mines." Most of them are reliable operations that are pro-

NORTH AMERICAN GOLD MINES								
Company	Current P/E	5-Yr. EPS Growth	Div Yield in %	5-Yr. Div. Growth	Ann. FY Sales (Mil.)	5-Yr. Sales Growth	Market Cap (Mil.)	5-Yr. Price Gain
Barrick Gold	24.3	-13.4	1.0	17.1	1294	13.2	7065	-5.4
Battlemountain Gold	N/A	-10.4	1.2	0.0	345	16.9	990	-12.2
Echo Bay Mines	N/A	-98.9	0.0	-43.8	305	-1.3	281	-29.4
Homestake Mining	N/A	-66.7	1.0	-8.6	724	1.5	2059	-10.4
Newmont Mining	27.9	-3.0	0.7	-27.4	1628	14.1	3031	-13.8
Average	26.1	-38.5	0.8	-12.5	859	8.9	2685	-14.2
S&P 500 Averages	30.6	9.1	1.4	8.0	9817	11.8	18755	20.1

ducing increasing amounts of gold at steady and sometimes falling costs. They should all be big winners as inflation picks up.

Major South African gold stocks also are attractive in the sense that they are prolific producers with tremendous reserves. The major drawback, though, is political uncertainty in this still potentially volatile country. If political unrest comes to the fore, these investments could be negatively affected.

During the gold bull market of 1986–1987, the Vancouver Stock Exchange was the home of countless "penny" gold stocks that shot up furiously. Unfortunately, once the boom ended in the stock market crash of October 1987, most of them crashed and burned. A wildly speculative market in small gold mines will likely reemerge during the next gold boom. We'd avoid these stocks altogether, unless you're willing to risk losing your investment and can take the time to research the stocks you're buying.

One other way to invest in gold stocks is through one of the no-load mutual funds that specialize in precious metals. These may underperform the best individual stocks, but they offer the advantage of instant diversification. Two favorites are Vanguard Specialized Gold and Precious Metals and Midas Fund.

The most leveraged way to invest in rising gold is through commodity futures and options contracts. This is for risk takers only. Also, because gold's price can fluctuate wildly over the short term, gold futures are not the way to cash in on a long-term bull market in gold. But for aggressive traders willing to lose a large portion of their investment, they offer the potential for quick and hefty gains.

REAL ESTATE

In the 1990s real estate and stocks traded places. Stocks became more important in terms of the country's total wealth, and real estate took a back seat. As inflation reemerges and the big blue chips falter, homes once again will become consumers' primary asset. And in general, real estate will be a time-proven way to play higher inflation. It has one advantage in particular over other inflation hedges: Even if inflation fails to rise as much as we expect, real estate still can be a winner. During the noninflationary 1990s, home values continued to increase in both real and nominal terms. Virtually any real estate investment did well—just not as well as stocks.

A return to an inflationary environment will cause a turnaround. Real estate will easily outperform big-cap stocks, though it will lag other inflation hedges such as small stocks and gold. In the 1970s, for instance, broad measures of real estate values outperformed inflation by about two percentage points a year, compared with negative real returns from big-cap stocks. While these gains may sound anemic next to those chalked up by small stocks and gold, the good thing is that they entailed very little risk. Indeed, in nominal terms real estate almost never goes down. Even in the hideous bear market of 1973–1974, when many small stocks fell by more than 50 percent and even energy stocks got pounded, real estate rose in value, at least in nominal terms. While the returns may not be outsized, their reliability in all sorts of economic weather may offer considerable comfort.

The problem with investing in real estate is that it's not all that practical. You can't just go around buying up houses or apartment buildings, and who'd want to manage them, anyway. Fortunately, there's an easier way—through real estate investment trusts, known as REITs. These are professionally managed pools of real estate traded on major stock exchanges. Management buys, builds, manages, operates, rents, and sells properties. REITs are ideal for income investors since they're required to pay out almost all of their annual profits in dividends. And because REITs own a diversified bunch of properties, they're generally pretty secure even if one property turns out to be a lemon.

REITs were created by the Real Estate Investment Trust Act of 1960. They must meet certain legal requirements—for instance, in addition to distributing at least 95 percent of otherwise taxable net income as dividends, they are not allowed to engage in short-term speculative buying and selling of real estate. They are managed by a board of directors or trustees, and must have at least 100 shareholders, with no five shareholders owning more than 50 percent of the shares. At least 75 percent of their gross income must come from real estate in the form of rents, mortgage interest, or capital gains from the selling of real estate.

The result is a tightly managed pool of properties generating above-average income for shareholders. Well-run REITs have increased their dividends and earnings consistently. There are three basic types. The great majority are equity REITs, which manage and own a combination of residential, commercial, industrial, and developing properties. A far smaller number are mortgage REITs, which own pools of property loans, and there also are a few hybrids, which own a combination of the two.

High dividends have made REITs somewhat interest rate-sensitive in the eyes of Wall Street, where some money managers trade them as virtual bond substitutes. The profits of mortgage REITs in particular are very sensitive to interest rate swings.

But for equity REITs, long-term returns have historically corresponded much more closely to stocks than to bonds, both in terms of actual gains and volatility. That's because they actually own individual properties. Just as with individual homeowners, faster growth and higher inflation appreciate the value of their properties, increase the rents they can charge, and erode the value of the debt they borrowed to buy them. This ability to profit from growth will dramatically boost the worth of equity REITs in coming years, even as inflation devastates bond investors and mortgage REIT owners as well.

As a group, the value of equity REITs rose throughout the inflationary 1970s, beating inflation by about four percentage points a year. REITs outperformed other real estate investments as well. There is plenty of room for similar success as inflation heats up in the next decade and beyond.

REITs do have pitfalls, however, and selectivity is as crucial here as anywhere. The biggest risk is economic slowdown, when real estate prices come down. Equity REITs with mostly retail properties, such as shopping centers and malls, are particularly vulnerable. A regional slump can hurt REITs whose properties are concentrated in a geographical area particularly hard hit by an economic downturn. Highly leveraged REITs carry the most risk, since they have less margin for error.

In picking a REIT, the most important thing to look for is top-flight management that has proven itself over the long haul in both up and down markets. A consistent record of dividend increases over the past 15 years, or at least no cuts, is one good sign. So are steadily rising profit margins.

Another plus is diversification, both among different parts of the country and among different types of properties. A REIT with properties in more than one geographical region has some protection if a downturn strikes one area particularly hard. And a mix of residential, commercial, and industrial properties allows a REIT to benefit from both the relative security of apartment rents and the faster growth of retail and other commercial rents. But don't be dogmatic. A REIT that concentrates in one type of property—for example, retail— might be a fine investment as long as management has proven its ability to perform in all types of markets.

In addition, look for REITs whose real estate portfolio has high occupancy rates. A REIT can't make money if it isn't getting rents. An occupancy rate of 95 percent is considered excellent. Low debt is another plus. Debt should be no more than 50 percent of capital. If not burdened by debt, a REIT has much more flexibility to expand in bull markets and to snap up bargains in bad times. Low debt gives it the wherewithal to cut rents in bad times and take other actions to get through.

Finally, look for low payout ratios based on funds from operations (FFO) with potential for growth. FFO takes the unique aspects of owning property into account, making it the most important measure of a REIT's profitability. The lower the FFO payout ratio (percentage of FFO paid out in annual dividends), the more a REIT can increase its payout over the long haul. FFO payout ratios under 70 percent are preferable.

8

BIG STOCKS THAT WILL BUCK THE TREND

While inflation will hurt most of the big blue chips, a few will thrive. They will offer the best of all worlds—strong growth and stock market gains plus the peace of mind that comes from investing in established companies. What distinguishes these giants from the ordinary big company? Among other things, they all dominate their markets. Moreover, they all have a major international presence, meaning they are sure to benefit in a big way from worldwide economic growth. These safe giants should be part of every investor's portfolio.

Now that we've done our best to pound it into your head that small stocks will rule the roost, we're going to look at the exceptions to the rule—big stocks that will put money into your pockets even as inflation rises. These are all companies known as "franchises," a term that basically means that they have near total control over their markets and as a result can sell just about anything.

Being a franchise is a wonderful position for a company to be in—almost as good as owning Boardwalk and Park Place in Monopoly. (Actually, Monopoly itself is a pretty good illustration of a franchise.) Franchises are known quantities that consumers have faith in. They sell products that are indispensable, desired, and in many cases consumed on a regular, even daily, basis. They can steadily extend their reach to new markets, and they also can successfully introduce new products with relative ease, because consumers will readily give new offerings the benefit of the doubt. If it's Disney, let's take the whole family. If it's Coke, it's got to taste good. You get the idea.

Not just any franchise will do, however. To be truly sterling investments in the increasingly turbulent times that await us, they must be worldwide operations run by exceedingly savvy marketers who know how to make the right decisions to capitalize upon their products' appeal and to reach out to ever wider areas. These companies will be winners even under inflation because they have considerable control over pricing and because they will benefit from strong worldwide growth. As underdeveloped nations become ever more urbanized, they not only will want more meat in their diet, as we discussed earlier, they also will want a Coke to drink along with it.

Next we look at four types of franchises—a one-of-a-kind super-investment; consumer franchises; drug franchises; and—somewhat of an oxymoron—technology franchises.

THE GREATEST OF THEM ALL: BERKSHIRE HATHAWAY

We can't hide it. We do have a favorite stock, we're in love with it now, and we expect to love it forever. It's a franchise, it's unique, and it's something we think every investor should own. In fact, if you could buy only one stock, this would be it, hands down. It's Berkshire Hathaway, the investment vehicle of super investor Warren Buffett, and it's a world unto itself.

Berkshire sports some pretty amazing statistics. For starters, it has returned investors an average of 25 percent a year from 1965 through 1998. That's an extraordinary number. It means that a dollar invested in Berkshire in 1965 would be worth $1,500. If you had invested just $1,000 with Buffett in 1965, it would have turned into more than $1,500,000. Moreover, these outsized returns have defied the maxim that great gains entail great risks. Berkshire's performance has been relentlessly consistent and the fund hasn't chalked up a negative year in all that time.

It's fitting and no coincidence that this great franchise rode to fame and fortune almost purely on the strength of carefully selected franchises in which it bought shares. Buffett has shied away from tech stocks, story stocks, and other iffy types of investments that promise short-term glory. Instead, in selecting investments for his fund, he has looked for overriding value and been guided by two basic insights. The first is that individuals are comfortable with the known and far less comfortable with the unknown. In other words, they will always tend to veer toward known products with known brand names. Second, if you want a great investment, you need to find a company with superior management. Put these two insights together and you come up with worldwide franchises like Coca-Cola, Disney, and Gillette, and with United States and local franchises like Freddie Mac and the *Washington Post*. These are all companies that have products with great public acceptance and management with a knack for making the most of this convenient fact.

But what turned Berkshire Hathaway into a true franchise was its 1997 acquisition of General Re, the giant reinsurance company. In one quick stroke this transformed Berkshire from a top-of-the-line investment fund into an equally top-of-the-line operating company positioned to dominate within its field. That's because the synergies between the two companies—Berkshire's huge capital assets and General Re's position as the leading reinsurer—gave the combined entity an unassailably huge edge over any rival.

Reinsurers are companies that insure other insurance companies. For instance, a regular insurance company might insure a shipping company against storms at sea. The insurer then might worry that if storms really came and it had to pay up, it would lose more than it can afford. So it goes to a reinsurer like General Re and pays it to assume some of the risk. Besides good management, a reinsurer's greatest asset is capital. The greater the capital base, the greater the risks the company can take and the greater the long-term payoffs. By joining forces with Berkshire Hathaway, General Re became part of a company whose equity base is one of the largest in the world. Only Dutch giant petroleum producer Royal Dutch and the incipient combo of Mobil and Exxon have more equity than Berkshire Hathaway does. And certainly no insurance company anywhere in the world can match Berkshire when it comes to the resource that counts most—capital.

By acquiring General Re, Berkshire not only became a dominant operating company, it became one with a P/E substantially less than that of other worldwide franchises. It also became inflation-proof in that reinsurers, like other major franchises, can pass inflation on to their customers. In other words, Berkshire had become the kind of operating company that Buffett would buy in a heartbeat—except that instead of buying it, he built it.

Berkshire has one other signal advantage besides those already discussed—it actually might benefit from technological limits. We've touched upon limits to our ability to predict and/or control the weather, and in Chapter 10 we argue that weather disasters such as floods and hurricanes are likely to become more frequent. If they do, the capital of smaller reinsurers will become depleted, while the best capitalized—and Berkshire stands head and shoulders above the rest—will be able to name their price.

To determine Berkshire's earnings as an operating company, you need to add the earnings from Berkshire's stake in its stock market investments such as Coke to the earnings from its operating companies, of which General Re, of course, is by far the biggest. In mid-1997 Berkshire was trading at about 35 times earnings. This was much less than the multiple of its major investments. Berkshire is one of the cheapest and deepest franchises in the world and is a must holding in virtually all portfolios.

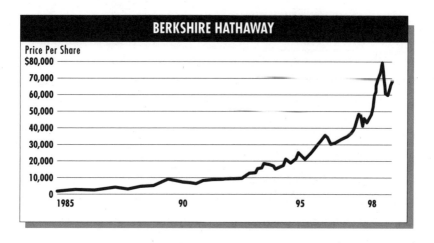

BUFFETT AND BERKSHIRE

You might have one concern about Berkshire—is it too dependent upon one person, i.e., Warren Buffett? Not to worry. Buffett's formidable investment skills are just icing on the cake. Even if Buffett were to renounce capitalism and become a monk, Berkshire would still be the cheapest big cap stock around. Remember, because of its capital base and collection of exceptional managers, Berkshire is almost sure to end up as the world's dominant reinsurance company. Dominant reinsurers can easily earn 15 percent on their equity. This means that at 2400 for its B shares, Berkshire is trading at about 11 times its underlying earnings power compared with a multiple of about 30 for the S&P 500. Moreover, the company's underlying earnings power should grow by at least 15 percent a year. In other words, Berkshire is growing about twice as fast as the S&P 500; has steadier prospects, superior management, and less debt; and is much cheaper. You just can't ask for more.

Note that there are two classes of Berkshire stock. For practical purposes there is no difference other than the price of the shares. In early 1999, for instance, the A shares were selling at about 72,000, while the B shares sold at about 2400. We realize that in absolute terms either one is pretty pricey. But even if all you can afford is one share, forget any odd lot qualms you may normally have and go for it.

By the way, brokers hate Berkshire Hathaway. Commissions often are based on the number of shares purchased, and obviously with Berkshire that figure will be low. Moreover, this is not a stock to trade short term, it's one to hold onto for life. No wonder that until very recently not a single major brokerage house has followed it. Ask your broker for information on this compelling value and you're likely to get a terse reply. Ask about a high-flying Internet retailer and you're likely to get an enthusiastic reaction and reams of research. Forget about your broker's feelings and buy as much Berkshire as you can.

CONSUMER FRANCHISES

Now that we've covered the most extraordinary franchise of them all, on to the merely great. The chart titled "Consumer Franchises" presents some salient characteristics of our three top picks in this category: Coca-Cola, Disney, and Gillette. These are all quintessential household names, companies whose products every reader probably drinks, watches, uses, or at least rubs up against every day or every week. When you look at all they have going for them, it's not surprising that Buffett has major stakes in all three—a fact that also tells us these companies must meet his nonnegotiable criterion of great management.

From the point of view of thriving in the inflationary times that lie ahead, the key point is that all three of these major consumer franchises are capable of rapid and sustained long-term growth, the only way to survive during inflation. Their stellar earnings growth will more than compensate for the fact that as inflation takes over, P/Es

CONSUMER FRANCHISES						
Company	Ticker Symbol	Current P/E	5-Yr. EPS Growth	5-Yr. Sales Growth	Ann FY Sales	Market Cap
Coco-Cola	KO	42.9	14.3	8.0	18,868	15,9763
Disney	DIS	40.4	9.7	22.0	22,976	73,829
Gillette	G	41.0	12.1	14.3	10,062	58,238
Average		41.4	12.0	14.8	17,302	97,277
S&P 500 Averages	SP 500	32.7	9.0	12.3	9,726	20,189

will be getting downsized. As a result, their share prices should be strong even as most big blue chips are floundering.

Note that the very fact that we have been able to select only three consumer franchises as good investments for the next ten years is testimony to just how difficult these years may be. These three all have the following critical ingredients in common, accounting for their special status.

They dominate their markets. Coke, for instance, with a return on equity of nearly 50 percent, totally eclipses all other soft drink makers.

Their markets are worldwide in scope. Not only does each of these three companies dominate its market, but each through worldwide distribution networks and name recognition dominates a market many times bigger than the company's existing sales base. To obtain the kind of growth needed to flourish in the stock market in the years ahead, it's not enough to dominate a market limited to the United States or even the Western world. Rather, a company must have products that appeal to people around the world. Each of these companies has established brand names and products that are affordable by a broad range of consumers around the globe. That's essential, because these already are huge companies. Coke, for instance, has annual revenues of more than $20 billion. For most companies it would be hard to generate significant growth off such a large base. But viewed in the light of a potential market of more than 5 billion consumers around the globe, even these outsized revenues suddenly seem rather modest. Coke is a behemoth, but it is one with the potential to become more of one. A combination of growing markets and the ability to raise prices ensures Coke of steady growth for perhaps the next 50 or more years.

Each has exceptional management with a big stake in the company's future. One good indication of superior management, for instance, is a company that has high profitability relative to other companies in the same industry.

Each has demonstrated the ability to market new products. Disney, for example, has established itself as a major presence on the Internet. Gillette has successfully broadened its line to include batteries. Coke is selling soft drinks other than Coke in many foreign markets.

Each offers downside protection. All three companies sell products that consumers consider close to essential, regardless of the economy. Even during the depression of the 1930s, men continued to shave, the demand for entertainment remained strong—was probably more important than ever—and the country continued to consume soft drinks. Thus all three of these companies will survive any deflationary interludes in better fashion than companies with more marginal products.

DRUG FRANCHISES

What product was the hottest sensation of the 1990s? Hands down it was Viagra, the drug introduced by Pfizer in 1998. This small, diamond-shaped blue pill, intended to help men sustain erections by increasing blood flow to the penis, became an instant household name and a runaway success. Within the first week of its release, doctors had written out nearly 40,000 prescriptions. The drug made the cover of *Time* and many other magazines and was the topic of early morning and late night TV talk shows. Although Viagra was not intended to help men get erections in the first place, it is clear that many men who besieged their doctors for a prescription were hoping it would do just that. According to a lot of anecdotal evidence, it apparently succeeded with a lot of those men. Moreover, although the drug had been tested only in men, a lot of women wanted it too. Not surprisingly, Pfizer's stock soared, rising from 60 in September 1997 to 120 in April 1998. (We recommended it at 80, knowing Viagra was about to be released and anticipating its monster success.)

You might think that Viagra was a technological breakthrough and that the investment lesson—contrary to all we've been telling you—is to look for technologically exciting products and invest in the companies that make them. But none of that is the case. Rather, the message is that innovation is secondary, marketing is king, and the big drug companies are genuine franchises that should be able to sustain steady growth in the years ahead, making them prime candidates for any investor's portfolio. Let's see why this is so by looking at what Viagra really tells us.

Marketing is still key. Remember how in Chapter 2 we compared the performance of Pfizer with that of the biotech group and concluded that as technology slows, you should focus on big established companies with superior marketing? Viagra's success merely confirms that. Viagra is less of a miracle drug than you might think. We're not saying it doesn't work—apparently it does what it's supposed to do for a large number of men. But it works for a combination of reasons that illustrates just why it's so essential to keep your focus squarely on big established companies that are marketing powerhouses.

The drug companies, which make up a $100-billion-dollar industry, spend a ton of money on advertising their products and on cultivating doctors. According to Linda Marsa, author of *Prescription for Profits*, the U.S. advertising budget for drug companies is about $10 billion annually, or about $13,000 per doctor. That's a lot more than the companies spend on research. It's enough to ensure that their products will gain wide acceptance among doctors and consumers

THE PLACEBO EFFECT

Our oldest son did a simple test of placebos as his eighth-grade science fair project. He took two groups of classmates and had them shoot free throws in the gym. Then he gave identical types of chocolate, scrunched into pill-like form, to each group. He told the first group it was plain chocolate. He told the second group it was chocolate that contained a harmless, tasteless drug identical to one that Larry Bird gave his Indiana Pacers to make them better free throw shooters. Each group then shot another around of free throws. The first group showed no improvement. The second group improved dramatically. In fact, one boy in that group, an excellent student, asked if he could get the drug at exam time because he said it helped him concentrate.

The placebo effect has been well documented. Placebos have been used, for instance, by dentists to alleviate severe pain and even reduce swelling. According to an article in the January 27, 1996 issue of *New Scientist*, British researchers succeeded in using an unplugged ultrasound unit to reduce swollen jaws by about 35 percent. The best-known placebo study took place in the late 1950s. At the time a standard procedure for treating angina was an operation that involved the ligation of internal mammary arteries. In one study, the procedure was performed on 13 patients, ten of whom improved. Five other patients, however, were told they were getting the full procedure but in reality were simply given an incision on their chest. All five improved.

Perhaps the best stab at explaining why placebos work comes from the pioneering work of Neil Miller, who about 30 years ago showed that people can condition their autonomic nervous systems, learning to vary such responses as blood pressure. We have more control over what goes on in our own bodies than you might think.

But aren't drugs tested against placebos? Yes—but most of
these tests are less conclusive than you might assume. The
reason is that most drugs do have some readily identifiable
effects. For instance, Viagra can create a bluish tinge to one's
vision and minor headaches. A patient who notices such side
effects—even though they are totally unrelated to the underlying symptom—may assume the drug is working, which in
turn will actually cause it to work. Pfizer tested Viagra against
placebos, but unless the placebos caused exactly the same
side effects, it wasn't a fair test. It's almost impossible to create perfect placebos (i.e., substances that perfectly mirror all
the side effects of a drug without containing the active ingre-
dient under study).

alike. And it's important in explaining why their drugs might end up
actually doing some of the things they're designed to do.

The placebo effect kicker. As we said, Viagra apparently works, and
so do a lot of other drugs promoted by the big drug companies. Why
doesn't that mean that innovation is what's critical and that the drug
companies will succeed only to the extent that they can keep developing exciting new products? Because any physiological effects
these drugs have are only one factor in how well they work. The other
factor has to do with whether a patient believes the drugs will
work—something known as the placebo effect. And it seems clear
that all the money drug companies spend to advertise and create public good will for their drugs and to promote them with doctors actually helps to make those drugs work better.

   In other words, if a doctor is convinced that a drug works, and if
the doctor conveys that belief to the patient, it very likely will work.
At the very least it has a greater chance of working than if it didn't
have all those positive recommendations going for it. Most of today's
popular drugs do work some of the time—that is, on some people
some of the time to some degree. For only a few drugs, though, is

there any evidence that on a consistent basis they work better and with fewer side effects than alternative and probably less expensive medicines. For most of them, the placebo effect is a key element in their effectiveness.

All of which merely buttresses the case for investing in the major drug companies. They are the ones that can afford the marketing that will keep belief in their products high. The placebo effect helps explain why the giant drug companies can count on sustained earnings and stock market profits. It is an additional, and very powerful, reason to invest in these companies that supplements all the other arguments in their favor.

There's nothing new under the sun. One other drug, in particular, has made headlines in the 1990s, and that's Eli Lilly's antidepressant Prozac. Millions of people now take it and swear by it, but what's interesting is that there is nothing really new about it. Drugs that increase serotonin, as Prozac and competing drugs do, have been around for more than 30 years. Moreover, no one knows for sure why these drugs work (that is, why increasing levels of serotonin in the system alleviates depression). In the last 35 plus years we haven't come any closer to understanding the neurophysiological workings of these medications. But as long as doctors and patients believe in them, they will be effective—and generate huge profits for the drug companies that make them. Walter Brown, a psychiatrist at Brown University, perhaps best sums up the success of Prozac and similar drugs by noting a dictum from an earlier century: "Use new drugs quickly, while they still work." He goes on to note that "as the drug's novelty fades and its side effects and limitations become more apparent, it becomes less effective."

Again, the message is that when it comes to drugs, technological innovation is less significant than a complex mixture of the placebo effect and marketing.

The top ten drugs. It's completely relevant and logical that of today's ten best-selling drugs, at least nine treat conditions that are clearly psychologically related (i.e., that are known to be related to stress and similar factors). Two of the drugs are for ulcers, three treat depression, three treat high blood pressure, and one treats high cholesterol. The point is that in today's world people are avid for medications that can help alleviate symptoms related to stressful lives. It makes sense to think that these conditions would be particularly susceptible to the power of suggestion that is the basis for the effectiveness of placebos. The tenth, Epogen, is used to treat anemia.

A steady stream of new diseases. A related point that also bodes well for the drug companies and for those who invest in them is that in today's world, as the past half century has shown, we never have to fear running out of diseases. Many new diseases are now common that didn't exist a century ago, such as inflammatory bowel disease, and many conditions are now being defined as diseases that require treatment. As Roy Porter noted in his tour de force book *The Greatest Benefit to Mankind: A Medical History of Humanity from Antiquity to Present*, medicine has begun to "fix its gaze on a morass of deep-seated and widespread dysfunctions hitherto hardly appreciated . . . backward children . . . office workers with ulcers . . . depression . . . . The health threats facing modern society [have] more to do with physiological and psychological maladies." It is exactly with these kinds of ailments that the placebo effect is most effective—and the giant drug companies are superbly positioned to deliver drugs to help the poor suffering consumer.

Which big drugs. The chart titled "Major Drug Stocks" presents the four best major drug companies: Pfizer, Bristol-Myers, Merck, and Schering-Plough. They all benefit from all the factors discussed previously, and they all qualify as among those highly desirable franchises whose earnings should grow faster than inflation.

In sum, in an age of technological limits and even in the face of rising inflation, the big drug companies are franchises and wonderful investments. They really have it all. They are marketing giants that don't have to rely upon technological breakthroughs to get them by. In fact, they benefit from technological limits because they don't have to worry that some upstart will come along with better products to challenge their dominion. They can rest assured that the drugs they bring to market will be successful because they have the resources to make sure they succeed and because the placebo effect will do the rest.

MAJOR DRUG STOCKS								
Company	Current P/E	5-Yr. EPS Growth	Div. Yield in %	5-Yr. Div. Growth	Ann FY Sales (Mil.)	5-Yr. Sales Growth	Market Cap (Mil.)	5-yr Price Gain
Bristol-Meyers	36.2	9.2	1.4	1.5	16,701	8.3	124,329	32.4
Merck	35.1	12.1	1.5	12.6	23,637	17.1	173,347	35.3
Pfizer	63.1	18.7	0.7	11.7	12,504	11.5	149,091	46.4
Schering-Plough	50.9	14.9	0.8	12.8	6,778	9.5	84,502	44.9
Average	46.3	13.7	1.1	9.7	14,905	11.6	132,817	39.8
S&P500	30.6	9.1	1.4	8	9,817	11.8	18,755	20.1

TECHNOLOGY FRANCHISES

While we're on the subject of franchises, it's worth returning to those few technology companies that can be considered franchises, such as Microsoft and Cisco. In the purest sense any technology company, almost by definition, is the opposite of a franchise, in that technology represents the pursuit of the latest idea, a gamble on something new and changing, not devotion to the familiar and timeless. The idea is that technology is always racing to replace itself, so obsolescence goes with the territory. But in a time of technological slowdown, a tech company that gains an edge on the competition can gain a stranglehold akin to Coke's dominance in the soft drink market. Just like any other franchise, Microsoft trades on its familiar name, basically upgrading its tried-and-true models and seeking ever broader markets. It dominates the field, which gives it pricing power, and it has a worldwide reach.

Still, as we indicated in Chapter 1, even the most established tech companies are not quite as attractive as investments as the best of the big consumer companies. One reason we discussed earlier was that the products of consumer companies need constantly to be replenished, from razor blades to soft drinks. A few other considerations are relevant as well.

One problem comes back to the issue of our almost knee-jerk tendency to deify technology, to see in it our salvation and to extend to it time and again the benefit of the doubt. Many of us in today's world are skeptics about most things, which is why we may be less than surprised to learn, say, that a politician's word, or a minister's for that matter, isn't the Gospel truth. But when it comes to technology, we want to be believers. As a result, investors are often ready to believe that technology has the answers and are willing to pay other-worldly prices for the stock of any company that seems to have stumbled upon an exciting new technology. The problem is that while the stock may skyrocket temporarily, nearly always technology's limitations will bring the stock back down to earth, often to just a fraction of what most people paid for it.

A possible example in the making is EntreMed, a small biotech company. In the spring of 1998, *The New York Times* carried a story about cancer researcher Judah Folkman, reporting that he had found proteins that seemed to be effective in starving tumors in mice. EntreMed was licensed to try to synthesize these crucial proteins. In a virtual instant, the stock of EntreMed shot up sevenfold—even though Folkman's work had been reported in various journals for at least a year prior to the *Times'* story, even though many cures that have worked with mice have struck out in humans, and even though there was no reliable process for making the proteins. The point is that it is inconceivable that anything other than a tech company could have climbed so fast and so furiously on such little tangible evidence of potential success. The stock's gains are vivid testimony to our willingness to worship anything with a tech label and to assume without question that tech will have the answers.

A related point helps explain our basic preference—and Buffett's—for a stock like Coke or Disney over even a tech juggernaut like Microsoft. It's that in our eagerness to embrace new technology, to believe that technology is always marching onward and upward, we assume that any technological change is meaningful and moves us further ahead. Meanwhile, we indulgently overlook any downside, from evidence that cell phones cause cancer to growing piles of nuclear waste, imagining that any ancillary problems either won't prove important or that we can deal with them later. We like to think of technology as being a matter of scientific advances, but in reality it is often nothing more than a question of jumping onto the bandwagon of the latest fad. A good example is the audio revolution that occurred when CDs replaced vinyl records. CDs are certainly more convenient, but audiophiles now freely concede that they simply don't reproduce music as faithfully as vinyl did. If you want to hear music the way it was meant to be heard, CDs are a second-rate technology. Yet CDs were latched onto as the best thing since sliced bread (a technological innovation nowhere near as tasty or nutritious as handmade loaves).

Another example on which the jury is still out is the microcomputer. It has been embraced as a vital cog in our civilization even though there is no evidence that it either increases productivity or better educates our children. Yet we buy blindly into the proposition that every child should have a computer, while schools race to find new ways to incorporate computers into teaching. Beyond any philosophical questions this raises, it suggests that even intrepid marketers of tech like Microsoft are particularly vulnerable to changes in fashion. They may someday lose out to a product that is not necessarily technologically superior but that simply is new. Unlike Coke, the microcomputer, just because it is a technological product, may not have timeless appeal. As a result, the managers of tech companies probably need to be even more skilled at marketing than the managers of any other type of company—no misjudgments will be tolerated.

If computer-related franchises offer less timeless appeal than more general consumer franchises, they are less attractive than drug franchises as well, for one additional reason. There is a legislated time gap between the development of new drugs and their introduction into the marketplace. All new drugs must go through a lengthy testing and approval process before getting patent protection. This window usually lasting several years allows drug companies to establish treatments without fear that another product will come along that is perceived to be better. For this reason drug companies with the best marketing capabilities are nearly assured a constant flow of hit products. In other words, the big drug companies have even less to fear from smaller rivals than the leading computer companies do.

INVESTMENT STORIES TO LIVE BY

Even franchises can miss the mark, especially when technology is involved. We'll conclude this chapter with two cautionary investment tales that illustrate two of our major points—the hyperimportance of skillful management in tech companies and the pitfalls of yielding to the spell of tech without an awareness of its limits.

First in line is a quick case study of IBM, the premier tech company of the 1960s and 1970s, which despite overwhelming resources, an established name, and a technological preeminence that has yet to be overtaken managed to lose its position as the leader in the computer field.

In 1972 IBM was the king of technology and indeed of all stocks. Though the company did not have the biggest revenue base, it was far and away valued the most highly. Investors were willing to pay up for IBM because they were so confident of its future. And this made a lot of sense. IBM was the leader of computer technology and in a position to maintain its dominance—just as Microsoft is today.

Why did it fail to do so, getting overtaken by Intel and Microsoft? Not because these companies came up with superior technologies. Indeed, one indication of just how dominant IBM was—and still could be—is the fact that microcomputers today fall into two categories. Macs, made by Apple, represent just 5 percent of worldwide sales. The rest, still known as IBM compatibles, represent nearly 95 percent of sales. The term *IBM compatible* stems from the fact that in the early days of the PC, IBM set the standard—and, in fact, totally dominated the PC business. Moreover, it was at least as expert as Intel at turning out microprocessors. Even to this day, in fact, IBM may maintain an edge in this technology, and it was IBM, not Intel, that discovered how to use copper instead of aluminum as a conductor on integrated circuits.

No, IBM fell from grace because of abysmally short-sighted marketing and business decisions. In the early 1980s IBM owned a big chunk of Intel and could have bought the rest for a relative pittance. But instead of foreseeing the potential in the PC market, IBM, in its first miscalculation, not only didn't buy more but sold its existing stake in Intel—which today far surpasses IBM in market capitalization. And it did so despite full knowledge about the likely advances in miniaturization that lay ahead. Why didn't IBM want to hold onto its stake in this emerging technology? Because, in its second big miscalculation, it made a commitment in the mid-1980s to continue focusing on its mainframe business rather than going whole hog into PCs, which it feared would cannibalize its mainframe sales. This was a marketing decision pure and simple, and in retrospect it probably was one of the worst decisions any company has ever made.

Adding insult to injury in this tale of mismanagement, in the early 1980s, if IBM could have bought Intel for a pittance, it could have bought Microsoft for cab fare. Microsoft got its start because IBM licensed it. And as in the hardware area, IBM went on to develop software that most computer experts considered better than Microsoft's. Again, though, marketing and management decisions undermined superior technology, as Microsoft beat it to the punch with aggressive marketing. The result is that Windows and not OS2 has become a household name.

The moral of IBM's flight from dominance is that for tech companies in particular, marketing and management are key. In investing in tech companies, don't get sidetracked by technological comparisons—and be on the alert for any signs that management is losing its touch.

Our second cautionary tale has to do with another former leader, AT&T. If IBM erred by refusing to recognize the importance of the personal computer revolution, AT&T erred by overestimating the significance of a new technology, cellular phones—proving that the deification of technology can be the downfall of big companies as well as small ones.

AT&T was once one of the greatest franchises in this country's history. In 1993, the company—which a decade earlier had been stripped of its Baby Bells, reducing the formerly undisputed king of telecommunications to just another long-distance operator—made a dramatic bid to regain its hegemony over the entire telephone industry. It offered around $12 billion to take over the world's leading cellular phone operator, McCaw Cellular. The deal went through, putting AT&T in control of what was assumed at the time would become the dominant telecommunications technology of the late twentieth century, wireless phones.

AT&T's action scared the dickens out of the telecommunications world, which was of one mind about the ultimate effect of the takeover—namely, that it would once again catapult AT&T to the top of the telecommunications heap, enabling it to rule a worldwide wireless network that inevitably would overtake the wireline operations of the various Baby Bells. Ronald Stowe, a senior official of Pacific Telesis Group, bemoaned, "AT&T is going to roll over everybody on the highway." Edward Whitacre, chairman of Southwestern Bell Corp., echoed this sentiment, predicting that "the AT&T of 1993 will look like the AT&T of 1983." Underlying these pronouncements was a faith in technological progress and the belief that it always pays to jump aboard the technological bandwagon. As the chief telecommunications analyst at Paine Webber put it, "They didn't want to make the same mistake Western Union did last century when it passed up the chance to [acquire] all of AT&T for a relative pittance." In other words, it was seen as manifest destiny that wireless communications would replace wireline communications, and AT&T was given a lot of credit for its foresight in recognizing this fact.

THE NIFTY FIFTY OF YESTERYEAR

Here's one parting thought on technology and franchises and on why only the right big companies will flourish in an inflationary period. Let's revisit for a moment the early 1970s, the era of the so-called nifty fifty—some fifty large, well-established growth stocks that investors viewed as one-decision stocks, the decision being to buy. In those years before inflation had come on strong they were assumed to be invulnerable to economic and even market vicissitudes, and for a while they were. Despite high P/Es, they continued to climb even as smaller stocks faltered, just as the big blue chips have done in the late 1990s.

By the mid-1970s, however, with inflation running rampant, the game was up. Many of the fifty were down as much as 70 percent from their 1972 highs. For most of them, it took a decade to recover from the ravages of the 1970s, and some of them never recovered. The great bull market of the 1990s carried many large companies to new highs. But even by the summer of 1997, most of the nifty fifty from 25 years earlier were still badly trailing the overall market. It's instructive to look at the 19 stocks of the 50 that did manage to outperform the market in the ensuing 25 years. Not one of them was a technology stock. Six of them, though, were drug stocks.

The point is that it will take a very special kind of big company to survive and thrive in the coming era. The few that do have to be able to count on growth strong enough to more than cancel out the effect of falling P/Es, and that means they have to possess the characteristics of the franchises described in this chapter. The more timeless the product, the better. Go for marketing, not research, and look to the quality of management, not to the degrees of the people in white coats. Look for companies that are dominant in their markets and whose markets are worldwide in scope. Follow these guidelines and you should enjoy some nifty results in your own portfolio in the years ahead.

Four years later, in 1997, revenues from cellular operations amounted to just 7 percent of total AT&T revenues. AT&T was struggling in the increasingly competitive long-distance telephone industry, with profits stagnating and its stock price lagging. Cellular phone stocks, which had soared when AT&T announced its deal for McCaw, had been among the worst market performers during the great bull market of the 1990s. It had become clear that in the United States, at least, cellular communications would be nothing more than a niche market—a profitable niche, maybe, but still just a niche. Recognition of this disappointing fact drove AT&T to attempt to merge with Southwestern Bell. Ironically, the plans called for Southwestern chairman Whitacre, who four years earlier had panicked that AT&T would dominate the telecommunications world, to become chairman of the combined company. Eventually, regulatory authorities nixed the proposed merger. But the fact remained: Cellular technology was not about to replace older, wireline technology.

Our point is that underlying AT&T's bid for McCaw, and industry reaction to that bid, was unbridled faith in technology. The assumption was that wireless communication, just because it was new, would overtake the older wireline technology. The assumption also was that any problems with wireless—the inconvenient fact, say, that it is all but useless in hilly areas—would be ironed out and that people would sign up for the new technology en masse. In fact, though, the problems have not been resolved. Transmitting electromagnetic signals in the protected environment of a wire or cable is inherently superior to beaming powerful signals through the air. Technology could no more advance wireless technology past wireline than it could somehow transform aluminum into a better conductor of electricity than copper. AT&T's performance is a clear warning to investors that rosy expectations about the potential of new technological products are more likely than not to meet with disappointment.

P A R T

HEDGING YOUR BETS

9

DEFLATION
DODGES

Everything we've recommended thus far is based on one critical assumption—the most-likely scenario of rising inflation. But there is no way to rule out that something will go amiss; in particular, that at some point policymakers will do something, or not do something, that brings on the opposite of inflation—deflation. In that case, all our inflation plays will go out the window and we'll be facing a very different and far grimmer world. It's not likely to happen, but no one can afford to ignore the possibility entirely. In this chapter we tell you how to tell if deflation is coming and recommend essential deflation hedges—the investments that will keep you afloat in case something goes wrong.

Many readers undoubtedly remember Stanley Kubrick's brilliant movie *Dr. Strangelove*, in which a mad and power-crazed general launched a nuclear attack that no one else wanted. The chilling point was that the prevailing theory of mutual nuclear deterrence, upon which the survival of the entire world depended, was based upon faith that all the world's leaders were in full possession of their senses and would act sanely and logically at all times.

Somewhat the same situation prevails today with respect to a deflationary meltdown. It can, should, and probably will be averted, but it requires all key policymakers to act rationally and intelligently. It depends upon them recognizing the highly leveraged nature of our economy, the sharply increased interdependence of economies around the world, and the resulting overriding necessity for growth. If they do, they will go for growth and realize that rising inflation is an acceptable price to pay, given the pain and suffering that would result if growth failed. But if ever they retreat from this recognition, deflation would ensue. And under current circumstances of faltering productivity growth, deflation would be a true disaster, bringing on all the horrific consequences we outlined in Chapter 3.

We consider some deflation insurance a must for every investor. Like insurance of any kind, you buy hoping you'll never need it. But the peace of mind it brings, the knowledge that you have some shelter in case of a storm, is worth whatever you pay.

READING THE FED

As we described earlier, in 1997 and 1998 the stock market declined more than 10 percent, finally interrupting the bull's long undisturbed reign. The downturns took place against the background of economic problems in Asia, which investors viewed as posing threats to growth in the United States and elsewhere. In contrast to market corrections of the past, there had been no rises in interest rates to trigger the declines. It is no coincidence, though, that both declines began almost immediately after Fed Chairman Greenspan intimated that he was *considering* interest rate rises to squelch incipient inflation. The mere threat of such rises in the face of weakness in Asia caused the market to panic, and in both cases Greenspan backed down.

In fact, in the second instance, 1998, the Fed not only backed down, it staged one of the most dramatic policy reversals in the history of economic policymaking. It went from warning about an overheating economy in midsummer to aggressively *lowering* interest rates in autumn. By one key measure, money supply growth, the Fed during the fall of 1998 went on an inflationary tear. And all this while the economy was showing no visible signs of recession.

The Fed's actions during 1998 were a first. Never before had the Fed aggressively lowered interest rates during an economic expansion. Never before had it let the stock market dictate economic policy. Clearly the Fed was very conscious of what a failure to keep growth going would mean. It responded to the potential for a vicious circle in which declining stocks would lead to a declining economy, which in turn would lead to further weakness in stocks. In a highly leveraged and interconnected world, those interactions could throw the world's economy into a black hole from which it might never emerge.

In 1998, however, breaking with tradition even as dramatically as the Fed did was relatively easy. That's because weakness in Asian economies and the still bloated worldwide oil inventories were keeping commodity prices very low. Moreover, until the Fed acted aggressively the dollar had been relatively strong, which depressed the prices of foreign goods. In other words, the Fed could be pretty sure that any inflationary pressures its actions engendered in the American economy would be offset by continued weakness in commodity prices and imported goods.

But it won't always be that easy. There will come a time when slowing profit growth, which characterized the economy in 1998 and which inevitably will come again because of slowing productivity growth, will lead to market weakness without a compensatory dampening of inflation. Then the Fed and other policymakers will face a more difficult decision. What are they likely to do then?

Given the alternatives, opting for growth and inflation would seem a no-brainer. And there are welcome signs that policymakers know this. Several major policymakers—among them, the head of the New York Federal Reserve, Treasury Secretary Robert Rubin, and the chief finance minister of Japan—went on record as saying that events in the summer of 1998 constituted the worst economic crisis of the postwar era. That's a pretty amazing statement. It means, in effect, that they were saying that the possibility of deflation was a more severe concern than such crises as the Arab oil embargo and double-digit levels of inflation in the 1970s or the savings and loans debacle in the 1980s.

Suppose, however, that policymakers lose this perspective or that something else goes wrong. Would there be any advance signs, any warning, before deflation and depression were upon us? This is one case where it's hard to draw conclusions based on history, because today's world is so different from at any previous time. In the last depression there was a clear warning, and it wasn't the 1929 stock market crash. Rather, the crash, in retrospect, was basically a plea for monetary help to keep the economy going. In 1930 the stock market staged one of the strongest and most intense rallies of the century, rising about 50 percent in just a few months. If you had been focusing on the market alone, you might have concluded that all was well—even as the bottom was falling out of the economy.

In those years, a far better clue than the stock market to the dark days that lay ahead was shrinking money supply. Money supply began contracting in 1929 and the contraction accelerated in 1930, a clear sign that something was terribly amiss. But in today's world, where events unfold so quickly, once the money supply starts contracting it may well be too late to take steps to protect yourself. Contracting money supply would confirm the onset of a deflationary spiral, but it probably would lag, not lead, the downturn in the economy.

Probably the best conclusion from 1998 is that there are two key signs to look for. The first is a market decline in excess of 10 percent. The second, which is harder to quantify, is any indication that policymakers appear content to wait on the sidelines as the market drops rather than take decisive action in the form of loosening credit. In other words, if you see that policymakers are complacent and willing to let a market slide go by unchecked, it would be a powerful sign to put extra money into the deflationary hedges we describe in this chapter. The fact that the world can change so quickly, however, means that it's important to establish some positions in these deflation hedges right from the start. If you wait too long, it could be too late.

IS DEFLATION EVER GOOD?

There is a theory going around that maybe deflation wouldn't be so bad after all. The U.S. post–Civil War years generally are cited as an example of deflation that is acceptable. Between 1875 and 1892, GNP grew at a torrid annualized rate of nearly 6 percent, while prices were in a steady downtrend. Deflation indeed can coincide with exceptional prosperity—but not under current circumstances. In today's world, deflation wouldn't be a matter of rising demand and gently falling prices. It would involve plummeting demand and a downward spiral in prices.

What accounts for the difference? One critical factor is the amount of debt in the economy. In the nineteenth century the United States economy wasn't leveraged. Stocks were a nominal fraction of GNP, and consumer debt was virtually nonexistent. Thus falling prices did not automatically mean a dramatic fall in asset values that would sharply raise consumer debt to equity ratios and lead to plunging money supply. Rather, falling prices could just as easily mean rising real incomes, as long as incomes did not fall as fast as prices were falling. And incomes did not fall as fast as prices because in the latter part of the nineteenth century productivity was on a tear. By some estimates, productivity was growing at an annualized rate of over 3 percent. This was possible because in those days the economy was made up almost entirely of farming and manufacturing, and the service sector was a minuscule and meaningless portion of overall economic activity. In contrast to the 1930s, money supply in those years remained in a fairly steady uptrend.

Today's situation is very different. As we discussed in Chapter 3, the economy is highly leveraged to the stock market, and consumer debt is high. And as we showed in Chapter 4, in our increasingly services-dominated economy, productivity growth since the 1970s has averaged just a touch above a paltry 1 percent a year, and even that is probably an overestimation. Even more important, technological limits ensure that productivity growth will not speed up in the future. Under these conditions, there is no way that deflation can be painless.

Even so-called benign signs of deflation such as falling commodity prices can't be considered as really benign. In the 1870s and 1880s falling commodity prices were a good thing, again because they were matched by incomes that were falling less rapidly. But that era is totally different from today's, as the experience of 1998 clearly shows. Today sharply falling commodity prices are invariably a sign of severe economic distress somewhere in the world, usually in the countries that are major producers of those commodities. When oil prices fell in 1998, the Russian economy collapsed, contributing in a big way to the severe economic crisis that faced us that fall. Severe economic stress anywhere today will quickly spread to the world at large.

In today's world, for all practical purposes deflation and depression are interchangeable terms. If anyone tells you that deflation can be good, quickly change the topic to something that person knows something about.

DEFLATION HEDGES

During deflation there are just two assets that do well: cash and bonds. With deflation lurking in the background as an economic sword of Damocles, it's important for all investors to have one or the other on hand. Moreover, as we've noted before, in coming years the markets will become more turbulent than in the recent past. Even if deflation never happens, there likely will be times when it appears as if we're shifting gears in its direction. During these moments your deflation hedges will provide a cushion against setbacks in your other investments as well as welcome peace of mind.

Cash. Even if interest rates are zero, the value of cash increases because with prices declining, you can buy more with your money. Note that when we refer to cash we aren't talking about money stashed in your mattress (though that will appreciate relative to falling prices, too), but money invested in very short-term money market accounts. And preferably money market accounts that either are fully ensured by the government or that invest only in government securities. That's because even ostensibly very safe companies can entail some risks when deflation/depression sets in. Some cash is vital insurance against deflation. Keep in mind, though, that the value of cash will erode once deflation recedes and inflation returns.

Straight bonds. The chart titled "Depression: Winners and Losers" shows how various investments fared during the depression of the early 1930s, and as you can see, the best investment by far was bonds. Keep in mind, too, that during deflationary periods, with prices declining, any gains you rack up are actually understated. If your bonds go up by 7 percent and inflation is negative 8 percent, you are 15 percent to the good. Thus a gain from bonds is a double play:

DEPRESSION: WINNERS AND LOSERS		
Assets	Nominal Return 7/29 to 4/33 (inf low)*	Nominal Return 7/29 to 6/32 (stk low)+
Stocks (S&P 500)	-23.67%	-44.12%
Small Stocks	-33.07	-53.13
Intermediate Bonds	4.99	4.40
Long-Term Bonds (Govt)	5.26	4.55
Long-Term Bonds (Corp)	5.04	2.97
Gold/Silver	-19.80	-19.80
Cash (T-Bills)	1.75	2.28
CPI	-8.08	-7.80

*To low point in inflation; +To stock market low.

Not only do you gain from the capital appreciation of your investment, but whatever dollars you have invested in them go up in value just because of deflation.

Zero coupon bonds. In the 1930s, bonds were pretty simple. They paid coupons, which determined their yields. In today's more sophisticated world, you can go regular bonds one better, by buying zero coupon bonds. These are bonds that don't pay coupons. You buy them at a discount to par and they are guaranteed to mature at par. For instance, if you invest $3000 in a zero coupon bond that has a maturity of 30 years, you are guaranteed to get back $10,000 when the bond becomes due.

Much of the time that might not be particularly attractive. If prices are rising, you won't have made that much in real terms and in fact you might actually lose money. But in deflationary times, it's a great deal—in fact it's the best investment you can make. The point is that zero coupon bonds are far more leveraged to changes in interest rates than are straight coupon-paying bonds. Typically, in deflationary times your gains from zero coupons will be about 50 percent higher than the gains from straight bonds.

Here's why. Roughly speaking, when interest rates change, straight bonds change in price so that the income reflects the change in yield. Suppose, for example, a bond pays a coupon equivalent to $100 a year. If interest rates are 10 percent, then the bond will trade at 1000. If interest rates go down to 9 percent, then the bond will go up to a price so that its yield is approximately 9 percent, which in this case would be approximately $1111 (if you divide 10 into 1111 you come up with about 9 percent).

With zeros, however, an interest rate change will have a greater effect on the price. That's because when interest rates change, the price of the zero has to reflect all future imputed interest rate payments. The difference between the zero's current price and the price at maturity is the value of all interest payments. Thus a change in interest rates is from the point of view of a zero coupon bond a change in all future interest payments.

Because zeros are much more sensitive to interest rate changes than are straight bonds, they are a better hedge against a deflationary environment, which by definition is one in which rates are falling. Moreover, the longer the duration of the zero, the greater the sensitivity. For example, if the zero matures in 20 years, it will move more for given changes in interest rates than a zero that matures in 15 years.

The relative rates of return of zeros with different maturities and of straight bonds are shown in the chart titled "Bond Returns." Note that in the chart we use the American Century mutual funds as a proxy for zeros. And this is exactly how we would recommend that you buy zeros. This is an excellent family of funds offering a wide range of maturities, and you won't have to worry about bid and ask spreads and sometimes hideously high commissions.

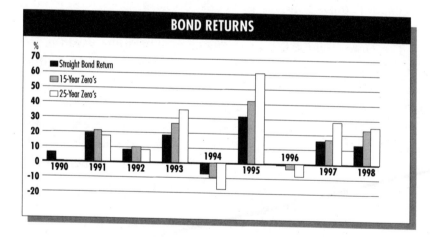

Stocks. Are there any stocks that provide a hedge against deflation and depression? In the 1930s gold shares had a great run. But that was because in those years the price of gold was fixed, and any price that was fixed was rising rapidly in real terms. Today, obviously, that would not be the case. Gold also was one of the few investments that did well in the terrible bear market of 1973–1974. But this bear market, far from being a deflationary event, occurred during a time of high inflation. Thus, there is no real evidence for believing that in today's world gold stocks will be a safe haven in the case of deflation/depression.

It's likely that deflation/depression will result in massive dislocations, which will lead to anomalies such as fixed prices for certain commodities or government work projects, with a positive effect on certain industries. But predicting which ones is next to impossible, and generally speaking most stocks will feel the ravages of deflation.

Your best bet is to try to find stocks that because of their particular characteristics have a stake in the investments that do flourish during deflationary times—that is, bonds. The one group that springs to mind is insurance companies. They are required to have large capital bases to back up the risks they take in their operations. Typically this capital consists mostly of bonds, because bonds tend to be less volatile and more dependable than stocks.

The largest and safest insurance company in the world is Berkshire Hathaway, which we discussed in Chapter 8 as a splendiferous example of big cap stocks that can buck the inflationary trend. This multipurpose investment can also give you some protection against deflation. With it you get the twofold comfort of a company whose earnings will likely continue to rise and whose book value, which will consist of a lot of bonds, also is likely to rise. Other insurance companies are pretty decent deflation hedges as well. CNA Corp. gets high marks for being headed by the fiscally ultraconservative Tisches, who in the event of a depression are likely not only to have a ton of bonds but will probably hold put options on the market as well.

10

ENVIRONMENTAL INSURANCE

In Chapter 9 we urged you to protect yourself against an economic accident that might trigger deflation/depression. Here we recommend buying some insurance against an accident of another sort, an environmental disaster. As economic growth accelerates, inevitably it will place further stress on our planet, raising the odds of a major environmental jolt. Technology will be helpless to step into the breach. As a result, companies that in various ways help repair or preserve essential environmental functions will see a sharp rise in value.

In recent years stocks with an environmental tie-in have been about as fashionable among investors as bell bottoms and love beads. Wall Street's prevailing attitude seems to be that the environment will take care of itself and that environmentally related companies are strictly for tender-hearted, fuzzy-brained idealists who care more about doing good than doing well.

But the idealists may end up with the last laugh—and the biggest profits. At some point it will become clear not just to charter Greenpeace members but to all of us that the earth and all its wonders are unique and irreplaceable. As a result, forest products companies, natural gas producers, and other companies that in some way help protect the environment will gain new respect. These are stocks that virtually all investors should own both because of their potential for outsized growth and because they provide critical insurance against environmental catastrophe.

In large part the case for these companies rests on a familiar theme—the complexity of the natural world. In earlier chapters we noted the complexity of individual organisms such as viruses and bacteria and of the individual genomes of humans and wheat. All our technological tools, from our fastest supercomputers on down, are insufficient to plumb the depths of these microscopic entities.

But their complexity pales next to that of the earth itself and the complexity of interactions between living organisms and the earth. It's not just that we don't have clear answers when it comes to understanding the many processes that have kept life going for so long. It's that we can barely begin to phrase the right questions.

This has several implications. For one thing, it means that we don't have the ability to predict or control the impact that continued economic activity will have on key life-sustaining processes of our natural world. Greenhouse warming is an obvious example of the kind of damage we may inflict, and there almost certainly will be other and possibly more severe problems in the future.

Second, once we do trigger an environmental crisis there will be no simple way to fix things. We'll be flying blind. The earth's complexity precludes any simple answers. Probably the only thing we can do will be to try to restore the status quo ante. Efforts to do so in all likelihood will boost the fortunes of a small handful of environment-related companies, which suddenly will be seen as saviors.

THE EARTH'S COMPLEXITY

The earth performs a wide range of activities that we take for granted but that we have never been able to duplicate or understand in any satisfactory way. Take something as basic and common as the earth's salt regulation. It's a question you may never have thought to ask—why the ocean is as salty as it is and no saltier. Complex interactions between the environment and living organisms have kept the salt content of the oceans within a narrow range that is consistent with life, and they have done so for eons. We take this balancing act for granted, but it is no easy trick—we have no idea how nature does it, and we would be utterly unable to duplicate it if for any reason nature ran amok.

James Lovelock, author of *The Ages of Gaia: A Biography of Our Living Earth*, describes the difficulty as follows: "Problems of salt regulation exceed in difficulty anything humankind has so far done in the way of planetary engineering. . . . It would have required the building of vast limestone reefs to trap salt in evaporite lagoons. The sheer magnitude of these reefs would dwarf any conceivable human construction. . . . The balance of erosion and formation seems always to have kept enough salt sequestered in evaporite beds to keep the oceans fresh and fit for life."

An equally remarkable balancing act is the earth's atmosphere. It exists in the form it does, with its constituents of oxygen, nitrogen, and trace gases, because of complex interactions among the earth's organic and inorganic substances. Somehow these interactions manage always to result in an oxygen ratio of about 21 percent relative to the rest of the atmosphere. This is just enough to support life yet below the level at which an excess of oxygen would lead to widespread fires that would stamp life out. Again, we have no idea how nature achieves this.

The evolution of species is another process whose complexity we have yet to penetrate. We've all studied Darwinism in school and probably assume that by now it's accepted as valid by everyone but the extreme fundamentalist right. In fact, though, Darwin's observations and conclusions add up to an outline of a theory rather than a comprehensive explanation. There is a lot we still don't know and we probably have just scratched the surface in attempting to account for the diversity of species on this planet.

For instance, as we noted in Chapter 2, the whole idea that organisms develop by chance mutations—a basic tenet of Darwinism—is possible logically but so improbable that in practical terms it might be considered nearly impossible.

Here's why. One way to look at evolution is as an intricate dance between DNA and proteins. Proteins make DNA, which in turn makes proteins. Let's ignore the question of which came first and look just at proteins, which are sequences of 20 different amino acids. As we noted before, the number of potential proteins is virtually incalculable, which is why such an eminent scientist as Nobel Laureate Francis Crick believes that the development of the right proteins—those that can make DNA—could not have occurred through mere chance.

Thinking in terms of the sheer numbers of potential proteins is one way to conceptualize why it is so unlikely that proteins developed through chance combinations. An even more dramatic approach is to think in terms of weight rather than numbers. Steven Rose draws this out in his book *Lifelines: Biology Beyond Determinism*. He notes, "A modest protein . . . containing combinations of only 12 of the naturally occurring amino acids could exist in 10 to the 300th possible forms, and if only one molecule of each existed the total mass would be around 10 to the 280th grams—compare this with the entire universe, which one estimate puts at 'only' 10 to the 55th grams!"

In other words, all the possible protein molecules that could result from one relatively modest amino acid chain would weigh as much as the product of five entire universes—each one with trillions of stars and who knows how much dark matter. Given this fact, how likely is it that the right proteins occurred through environmental trial and error?

THE GAIAN APPROACH

Probably the closest that science has come in the past 30 years to making any sort of stab at conceptualizing the earth's complexity is known as the theory of Gaia. It was first expounded in the 1970s by James Lovelock, author of *The Ages of Gaia: A Biography of Our Living Earth*, and has been further advocated by, among others, environmental theorist Lynn Margulis. Proponents of this theory argue that the planet and all its inhabitants make up a highly complex self-adaptive system, called Gaia after the ancient Greeks' earth goddess. As Lovelock puts it, "The biosphere is a self-regulating entity with the capacity to keep our planet healthy by controlling the physical and chemical environment."

The Gaian hypothesis is a provocative approach that, whether you buy it fully or not, at least makes an effort to come to grips with the multidimensional mysteries of the natural world. And there is considerable evidence that Gaians are onto something.

A decade ago, most scientists ridiculed Gaian thinking. They viewed it as new age, newfangled mysticism that implied that the earth was a sentient creature. That conclusion itself, however, was a clear indication of the limits of our understanding.

Today, while still far from mainstream within the scientific community, Gaian thinking commands more serious attention and respect. For instance, it recently was the subject of a major review in the ultrarespectable periodical *Nature*. Writing in the July 30, 1998 issue, Timothy Lenton, a British professor of environmental sciences, acknowledged the earth's complexity and science's inability to understand it at any deep level. "When asked to explain how planetary self-regulation could have arisen, we are in much the same position as Darwin when asked how the eye could have evolved. We see a complex phenomenon and have only the beginnings of a theory with which to tackle the puzzle."

The Gaian approach doesn't provide us with instantly usable answers. But it does suggest how little we know, in truth, about many of the forces that govern our lives and upon which we are as dependent today as were primitive humans eons ago.

Moreover, proteins are uncommonly complex in their arrangement—another thing that argues against their having randomly occurred. Here's how Michael Denton describes them in his book *Nature's Destiny: How the Laws of Biology Reveal Purpose in the Universe.* "It is immediately obvious even to someone without any previous experience in molecular biology that the arrangement of the atoms in a protein is unlike any ordinary machine built or conceived by man, or indeed unlike any ordinary object of common experience with which we are familiar. On superficial observation one is immediately struck by the apparent illogic of the design and the lack of any obvious modularity or regularity. The sheer chaos of the arrangement of the atoms conveys an almost eerie, otherworldly impression."

The problems are equally great when it comes to Darwinian explanations of not just of how life was created initially but of how life has continued to evolve. Darwin postulated that life evolves through chance mutations in DNA. But what are the odds that a chance mutation will lead to the exact protein that would result in an organism that is better adapted to its environment? Essentially the odds are zero. There must be more to it—but we have no idea what it might be.

NATURE'S AMAZING TRICK

Some scientists try to account for the development of proteins—without going so far as to endorse Crick's view that
they must have come from an alien civilization—by arguing
that their development was not purely random. Steven Rosc,
for example, in his book *Lifelines,* notes that "certain
sequences [of amino acids] are preferred in that they fall into
appropriate three-dimensional configurations . . . suggesting
they conform to least-energy configurations."

Unfortunately, however, this tack doesn't get us far. The folding of two-dimensional amino acid strings into three-dimensional protein molecules takes us to the problem of protein
folding, and here again, the inadequacy of relying on the computer for answers is clear. According to John Barrow, author
of *Impossibility: The Limits of Science and the Science of
Limits*, it would take a computer 10 to the 27th years to calculate the proper way of folding a simple chain of amino acids.
John Casti uses the far larger number of 10 to the 127th years
to calculate minimal energy configurations for a relatively
simple chain of amino acids. Yet nature has put together
sequences of amino acids that somehow fold naturally within
about a second.

GOETHE AND THE BIOSPHERE

The central point is that the earth and all its processes remain an
enigma. As Tyler Volk, a New York University professor and a Gaian
proponent, put it in a *New York Times* interview in 1998, "If you want
to worship mystery, studying the global metabolism is a great way to
go." And this bears directly upon our ability ever to pick up the slack
if the earth for any reason were to fall down on the job.

Every day, in a ceaseless and seemingly effortless rhythm, the
earth performs a myriad of activities and processes that are essential

to our life here. It has been doing so for as long as we know. The question is—what if human activities eventually put too much stress on the earth's continuing ability to carry out its work as effectively as it has up to now? What would we do then? The complexity of the earth, its essential mystery, suggests that we would be powerless to come up with meaningful fixes—more, that anything we try to do might backfire.

This point is made eloquently by Eisuke Sakakibara, a top official in Japan's Ministry of Finance, in an article that appeared in the October/November 1995 issue of *Foreign Affairs*. In fact, it was this article that, more than anything else, first started us thinking about technological limits and their implications. The article lays out several compelling arguments relating to whether or not technology will be able to cope with the environmental problems that economic growth will bring. Sakakibara notes, "Because natural science tries to understand vast systems from only minute observations, it will never be able to assess accurately the impact of human activity on the environment, much less solve environmental problems through technological innovation. . . . The progressivists' confidence in human competence and technology can properly be termed a myth because there is no logical reason to believe that someday the savior will come down to earth in the form of technological innovation and for some reason reverse all the problems that past progress has wrought."

Nor is Sakakibara alone in noting the problems that can occur when our activities have an impact on natural patterns. The Swiss economist Hans Christoph Binswanger is well known for his interpretations of Goethe's epic poem "Faust" in terms of modern economics. In a July 31, 1998 commentary in *Science*, he notes, "With great insight Goethe tells us that the intervention into the natural environment that this [human progress] demands may have unforeseen consequences because nature reacts to its own laws, which humans can never entirely predict."

If you think we're straying too far into the realms of poetry, one recent example perfectly underscores the earth's complexity and our lack of understanding of it—the ambitious multi-hundred-million-dollar biosphere that was constructed in Oracle, Arizona in the early 1990s. This was conceived as a self-contained ecological system capable of supporting human life. It was an attempt to create a miniature earth, affording scientists a chance to study how human activities, ecology, and the environment all interact.

The experiment was a colossal failure. When the humans left the biosphere at the end of two years, about the only life remaining within it were cockroaches and certain very robust ants. Joel Cohen and David Tilman sum up the results in an article in the November 15, 1996 issue of *Science*: "The management of Biosphere 2 encountered numerous unexpected problems and surprises, even though almost unlimited energy and technology were available to support Biosphere 2 from the outside." They concluded, "The major retrospective conclusion that can be drawn is simple. At present there is no demonstrated alternative to maintaining the viability of Earth. No one yet knows how to engineer systems that provide humans with the life-supporting services that natural ecosystems produce for free."

PUTTING A PRICE ON NATURE

All of this provides the background for understanding why it is almost inevitable that environmentally related companies and stocks will eventually see their value go up—why eventually investors will realize their importance. It's because there is no substitute for the environment. Its processes are too complex for us to understand and duplicate, and, furthermore, that complexity suggests that at some point human activity will inadvertently trigger some sort of environmental disaster. Then, if not sooner, we will begin bidding up environmental companies accordingly.

But how can we assess the monetary value of environmental services? In total, and in the final analysis, nature's services are beyond price, because without them we simply couldn't exist. Clean water, photosynthesizing plants, an oxygen-containing atmosphere—putting a price on any of these implies that there might be a point at which they would become too expensive for us to bother with them, and that is nonsense.

Still, particular services, such as desalination, can be assigned an approximate value. Also, even if the total value of a particular service is incalculable, its marginal value can still be estimated. For example, we can estimate what a hectare of forest land produces in terms of medicines, waste services, raw materials, and even climate regulation. We then can multiply the marginal value of that hectare by the total number of hectares of forest land in the world. Of course, the resulting figure would of necessity be a vast understatement—the value of forests in sum is infinite in that without them, life would vanish.

One well-known effort to quantify natural services was carried out by Robert Costanza and others, with the results published in the May 15, 1997 issue of *Nature*. Costanza and his associates concluded that the yearly economic value of the world's ecosystem is approximately $33 trillion (in 1994 dollars), or nearly twice the size of the gross world product of about $18 trillion.

Obviously, most of this $33 trillion is not money actually spent on environmental services. Rather, it is an estimate of their value relative to services that are directly expensed in the actual economy. In other words, even though we don't pay for desalination, we still can estimate the cost of removing salt from the ocean. The authors note, "A large part of the contributions to human welfare by ecosystem services are of a purely public goods nature. They accrue directly to humans without passing through the money economy at all. In many cases people are not even aware of them. Examples include clean air and water, soil formation, climate regulation, waste treatment, aesthetic values, and good health."

For investors, the key question is at what point the services rendered by the ecosystem enter the real economy. Clearly, if the assumptions in the preceding paragraphs are anywhere close to accurate, the economic and investment potential of environmental services is enormous—far greater than that of any other possible investment. And the answer is implied in the preceding quotation itself. Such services enter the real economy when we become aware of their value—which may occur when we are suddenly at risk of losing them and realize we'd better act swiftly to protect them.

It's like the husband who has long taken for granted all the jobs done by a stay-at-home wife and mom. If she ever decides to leave, and suddenly he has to pay someone else to do all the work she was doing, it's likely to be a revelation. He'd have to pay someone to clean, cook, drive the kids, be his social secretary, and more. He might well conclude he should have appreciated her more when he had the chance.

Today, environmentally related companies, as we noted earlier, are likewise unappreciated, and it likely will take a major environmental crisis or scare to get us to appreciate their value. For example, a sudden and dramatic change in weather patterns around the world might do the trick. All at once we'd likely be clamoring for someone, anyone, to take action. And any companies that seem to provide services or products that are directly or indirectly good for the environment, that might get the environment back on track, would suddenly be seen as immensely important. Such companies would finally get the respect they deserve—something they have been conspicuously lacking.

INVESTING IN THE ENVIRONMENT

Four groups are likely to benefit most from weather-related and other environmental disasters.

Forest products companies. These stocks have been shunned of late by investors—so much so that by summer 1998 the group was valued at historically low levels. Under the right conditions they will rebound sharply.

The biggest and the best of the group is easily Weyerhaeuser, North America's largest forest products company and landowner. In the summer of 1998 it was trading at only about 1.5 times book value. Even at the bottom of the 1974 bear market, Weyerhaeuser traded at more than twice book value. In other words, a bull market that lasted nearly 25 years and saw the Dow Jones Industrial Average soar from the 500s to just under 10,000 passed this company by.

But this indifference isn't going to last. Weyerhaeuser is exactly the kind of company that will be pushed to the forefront in the event of an environmental crisis, as it suddenly dawns on investors that forests possess unique ecological worth.

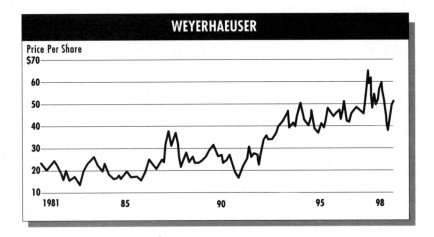

We may not be at that point yet, but we are getting closer. The world already has been experiencing alarming bouts of unusual and severe weather, and more may be on the way. In the summer of 1998, for instance, the southwestern United States suffered through terrible droughts that led to widespread fires and some deaths. This was bad enough. But if similar droughts had occurred in the farm belt, it would have been even worse.

That same summer, China experienced severe flooding, the worst in more than 40 years. All in all, 1998 was the warmest year on record for the earth as a whole. One major cause was El Nino, the warm ocean current off the coast of Peru. That was followed in turn by a cold water current known as La Nina. Its effects can be equally devastating—for instance, La Nina may have been behind the floods in China.

So far, the general reaction to recent weather extremes has been complacency. It's telling that although it is widely accepted that a major cause has been the burning of fossil fuels, which leads to greenhouse warming, the Kyoto accords, which seek to do something about greenhouse warming, have been ignored. No country is even close to establishing baselines for greenhouse emissions, much less having a plan in place to reduce them.

One reason for this ho-hum attitude is the consensus that worldwide temperatures will rise only gradually. After all, if it's only going to be two to five degrees warmer, on average, over the next century, what's the big deal? But the consensus could prove wrong. There is abundant scientific evidence that dramatic changes in weather can occur abruptly. In the past, worldwide temperatures have risen by several degrees in a matter of years, not decades or centuries. Moreover, even the recent relatively small rise in temperature may be more harmful than is appreciated. A recent study in *Science* notes that a major chunk of the Antarctica ice sheet may have begun to collapse. A full collapse could raise sea levels by more than 15 feet. Good-by New York!

We're not that pessimistic, and we expect New York to hang around. But one reason is that we trust that as the potential dangers become more evident, governments will take action. Given technological limits, their options might be narrow. One thing that they could do, though, is to make a big push to preserve forest lands. It is known that forests play an important role in recycling the basic components of our atmosphere—withdrawing carbon dioxide and returning oxygen. Any environmental crisis that had a negative impact on world economies would suddenly give these forest lands new visibility and highlight their importance to us—we would become aware of the value that they really have possessed all along.

Under these circumstances, the government probably would start to pay Weyerhaeuser and other forest owners not to cut down their forests. The authors of the *Nature* article referred to previously assigned a value of $141 per hectare of forest land for climate control and a total ecological value of more than $900 per hectare. This would be a reasonable starting point. Depending on the severity of the crisis these figures could turn out to be conservative.

The point is that eventually some sort of environmental crisis is likely, especially as economic development quickens. Companies that will suddenly be perceived as friends of the environment will quickly win newfound respect. Weyerhaeuser is an excellent example and is a steal at its current low valuation. Moreover, the values suggested in the *Nature* article almost certainly understate the ultimate value of forest lands because they take into account just the marginal value of land. But forests also provide biodiversity, which will come to be increasingly valued. One important lesson from the failure of Biosphere 2 is that biodiversity is essential to sustained life. If we lose too many plant and animal species, including thousands about whose roles we haven't a clue, we are putting the entire planet at risk.

Natural gas companies. Another group that will benefit from weather extremes and the stricter environmental regulations that are likely to result is natural gas companies. Reflecting low prices for natural gas, these stocks currently are trading at historical lows—but this won't last. One of the most painless ways to curb greenhouse gases is to substitute natural gas for oil. (Although natural gas is a fossil fuel, when burned it emits far fewer greenhouse gases than oil.) Efforts to encourage the use of natural gas will further spur the already heady growth of two major players in this area—Duke Energy and Enron. Together these companies control about 30 percent of the distribution of natural gas in the United States.

One of Duke's particular strengths is that it is able to use its stable of regulated businesses—including one of the best managed utilities in the country, located in the fast-growing Carolinas—and a leading interstate pipeline business to provide cash, infrastructure, and management for its burgeoning unregulated businesses. For example, the company's pipelines and management expertise provide the wherewithal for operating gas-based utilities in many parts of the country. As deregulation of utilities proceeds, Duke's presence as a nationwide provider of gas-based utility services should increase dramatically. Duke's earnings and dividends are currently growing by about 6 to 7 percent per year. As the deregulated businesses continue to grow, earnings growth will accelerate and eventually should reach more than 15 percent a year.

Enron is one of the most diversified and best positioned gas-based energy companies in the world. Its pipelines provide about 18 percent of the natural gas in the United States, while its 53 percent stake in Enron Oil and Gas provides additional leverage to both gas production and pricing. With its own source of gas production and transmission, Enron has a vertically integrated position in deregulated utility markets, giving it a major cost advantage.

Moreover, not only will Enron benefit from the increased emphasis on natural gas and the growing deregulation of utilities, it also is a play on the likely scarcity of another commodity, water. The company's recently announced acquisition of British-based Wessex Water, a worldwide water service company, will provide an immediate boost to earnings. More important, the acquisition should add several percentage points to long-term growth, which should climb to at least 15 percent. The company is currently trading at one of the lowest relative valuations in at least the past five years, with investors giving it no credit for the fast-growing potential of its stakes in either water or gas.

Environmental measuring companies. As environmental concerns heat up, so will pressures to measure and assess environmental damage and change. Thermo Electron is the leading provider of such measuring systems. Through multiple subsidiaries, including Thermotrex, the company also provides many other leading edge technologies. Because of the company's small stake in Asia, the stock by late 1998 had fallen out of favor with Wall Street and was selling at a deep discount to its underlying assets and at a historically low multiple of operating earnings. With more than $2 billion in cash and free cash flow that amounts to nearly $2.00 a share, the company plans to make a major acquisition and to acquire its own shares aggressively. Five- and ten-year growth rates have been approximately 20 percent, and more of the same is likely for the future, especially if environmental concerns pick up.

Alternative energy-related companies. Other companies that will benefit from increased environmental awareness will be those that provide products that directly reduce pollution or that offer alternatives to fossil fuels. One company that fits both of those bills is Stillwater Mining, which we mentioned in Chapter 5. Stillwater is the only major producer of platinum group metals (PGMs) outside Russia and South Africa. PGMs are a critical component of catalytic converters, which eliminate pollutants from car engines and thus are vital in reducing pollution. They also are used in fuel cells, which can help reduce our dependence on fossil fuels. Currently demand for platinum is growing at a 5 percent yearly rate, while growth in demand for palladium is somewhat higher. Growth in demand for both metals will accelerate sharply as environmental concerns mount. Significant is that worldwide demand for PGMs far exceeds worldwide production. Moreover, Stillwater is the only politically secure source for these metals. Based on current prices for PGMs, Stillwater's underlying assets are worth well in excess of $40 a share—a figure that will rise rapidly as the prices of PGMs climb.

Reinsurance companies. One final environmental play, our old friend Berkshire Hathaway, might seem at first blush an odd choice in this category. How does a reinsurance company—which, through its merger with General Re, Berkshire is becoming—benefit from environmental worries? Handsomely. Unusual weather such as powerful hurricanes causes insurance claims to climb and depletes the capital in the insurance industry. The end result is that well-capitalized insurers—and Berkshire Hathaway by a wide margin is the best capitalized—are then positioned to raise rates sharply.

Environmental stocks won't rise immediately. They have been undervalued for a while and probably will remain so a while longer. But in an era of worldwide development and technological limits, they offer essential protection against an environmental crisis, the odds of which are increasing. Any moves in these stocks are likely to be both sudden and, because they are coming from such depressed levels, substantial—and downside risk is low.

INVESTMENT WRAP-UP

11

MODEL PORTFOLIOS FOR THE MILLENNIUM

Energy, food, small cap, franchises, gold, zero coupons, the environment—in preceding chapters we've tossed out a whole hatful of investment ideas. Here we pull them together into sensible combinations designed to meet your individual needs. How much of each group and stock should you buy to take advantage of the inflationary surges that probably lie ahead? And how much protection against deflation and deflationary scares do you need to ride out the downward lurches that will almost certainly punctuate the market's upswings? In this chapter we present six model portfolios, variously geared toward both more cautious and more aggressive investors with anywhere from $50,000 to $2 million available to invest.

One thing is certain. If even half of what we've said about the pressures for growth and the limits of technology is right, the ideal portfolio for the millennium will look a lot different from the ideal portfolio of the past decade and a half. In fact, one of the ways in which you'd be guaranteed *not* to do well would be to persist with what has worked best in the recent past.

The past 15 years have been truly a unique period from an investment standpoint. Not only was this by any measure the longest and most powerful bull market ever—it also was the longest period of time this century in which small-cap stocks underperformed big-cap stocks.

During this exceptional period, the ideal portfolio was a broad-based mix of big-cap stocks. In fact, only a handful of mutual funds managed to outperform the completely passive index funds. Not surprisingly, one of the top-performing funds during these 15 years was the Vanguard 500, a fund designed to mimic the S&P 500. What an era! It was one in which the passive investor in the safest, biggest companies could easily outperform the vast majority of professionals—in which active was out and passive in—in which you could perpetually eat your cake and have it too.

Yes, it was a good era, and now it's gone, so forget about it. From now on you will have to work harder for your money. You will have to bear with periods of great market turbulence and not get panicked out of investments that over the long term will make you money. You will have to hold onto certain investments for no reason other than that they provide essential insurance against dramatic economic turnarounds. And at times you also may have to be flexible enough to move in and out of investments more quickly than in the recent past.

The period that bears the closest resemblance, though not a perfect one, to our forecast for the years ahead is the 1970s. That decade was marked by rapid growth and rising and ultimately very high inflation. The chart titled "Best of the 70s" shows how various investments performed during those years. Not surprisingly, stocks leveraged to growth, such as the oils and oil drillers, did splendidly. But the big-cap stocks—those that have been so marvelous over the past 15 years—were complete duds. In fact, if during the 1970s you had parked your money in those big-cap stocks, you would have lost money. Clearly,

BEST OF THE 70'S		
	The 1970s Annualized Returns	
	Nominal	**Real**
Stocks (S&P 500)	8.40%	0.30%
Stocks (ex energy)	7.00	−1.10
Small Stocks	17.50	9.40
Long Bonds (Govt)	3.90	−4.20
Oil	26.40	18.30
Oil Stocks	14.20	6.10
Oil Service	31.00	22.90
Domestic Oil	19.20	11.10
Real Estate	10.10	2.00
Equity REITs	12.10	4.00
Commodities	11.00	2.90
Gold/Silver	33.10	25.00
Gold Stocks	28.00	19.90
Cash (T-Bills)	6.80	−1.30
CPI	8.10	

Source: Leeb Investment Advisors

there is no one investment map that is good for all seasons. In this chapter we try to get as specific as possible in guiding you into preparing for the coming, more wintry season that we now are entering.

AGGRESSIVE VERSUS CONSERVATIVE

To help you sort out your choices, we've developed six model portfolios for the coming years geared toward six different types and levels of investors. Obviously, there are close similarities, but the emphasis and allocations are somewhat different depending on how much money is at stake and what your particular goals are.

We started by looking at three sample portfolios in terms of size—$50,000, $500,000, and $2 million. For each of these three levels we imagined two different types of investor—one more conservative, one more aggressive—and showed exactly how we might suggest allocating the amount of money available.

How do you know whether a more conservative or more aggressive portfolio is appropriate for you? As a loose rule of thumb, if you're within 15 years of retirement, you probably should veer toward more conservative allocations. While of course you want to see your investments appreciate, it makes sense for your primary concern to be the conservation of capital—you're less likely to be in a position to take the somewhat larger risks associated with more aggressive allocations.

More aggressive investors tend to be younger and concerned more with the growth potential of their investments than with conserving capital. If their investments dip temporarily, they will have time to get back into the game. Don't get us wrong, though—when we say aggressive, we don't mean reckless. Even our more aggressive portfolios contain plenty of insurance against bouts of deflation, because in the volatile years that lie ahead, no investor can afford to be utterly blasé about the risks. Still, if you're in a position to ride out some of the bumps, we'd suggest going with the more aggressive allocations—they represent a more forthright bet on inflationary growth, and you'll maximize the gains during inflationary surges.

Still, in deciding which portfolios suit you, age and logic aren't the only factors. Some people are constitutionally conservative, and if you're one of them, regardless of your age, don't push it—stick with your comfort level. I once knew a fairly young and well-heeled investor who just couldn't bear to see any one of his stocks go down, even when he knew logically that the selloff was almost certainly short term and represented a golden opportunity to amass more. Instead, he invariably would sell out his entire position—he just couldn't help himself. What's really ironic is that this particular individual was a broker (not mine).

SMALL PORTFOLIO – CONSERVATIVE

Deflation Hedges		Percent
Straight Bonds	$6,000.00	12%
Zoro Coupon Bonds	$5,000.00	10
Berkshire Hathaway	$5,000.00	10
Duke Energy		0
Franchises		
Coke	$4,000.00	8%
Gillette	$4,000.00	8
Disney	$2,000.00	4
Pfizer	$1,500.00	3
Merck	$1,500.00	3
Berkshire Hathaway	$4,000.00	8
Inflation Hedges		
Small Stocks	$3,000.00	6%
REITs	$2,000.00	4
Gold &Gold Stocks	$2,000.00	4
Energy Service Cos	$1,500.00	3
Large Energy Stocks	$3,500.00	7
Food Stocks	$2,000.00	4
Environment		
Berkshire Hathaway	$3,000.00	6%
Enron	$0.00	0
Thermo Electron	$0.00	0
Total	**$50,000.00**	**100%**
Total Deflation	$16,000.00	32
Total Franchises	$17,000.00	34
Total Inflation	$14,000.00	28
Total Environmental	$3,000.00	6
Total Berk	$16,000.00	32

SMALL PORTFOLIO – AGGRESSIVE

Deflation Hedges		Percent
Straight Bonds	$2,000.00	4%
Zero Coupon Bonds	$4,000.00	8
Berkshire Hathaway	$4,000.00	8
Duke Energy	$2,000.00	4
Franchises		
Coke	$4,000.00	8%
Gillette	$4,000.00	8
Disney	$2,000.00	4
Pfizer	$1,500.00	3
Merck	$1,500.00	3
Berkshire Hathaway	$4,000.00	8
Inflation Hedges		
Small Stocks	$5,000.00	10%
REITs	$2,500.00	5
Gold &Gold Stocks	$2,500.00	5
Energy Service Cos	$3,000.00	6
Large Energy Stocks	$3,000.00	6
Food Stocks	$2,000.00	4
Environment		
Berkshire Hathaway	$1,000.00	2%
Enron	$1,000.00	2
Thermo Electron	$1,000.00	2
Total	**$50,000.00**	**100%**
Total Deflation	$12,000.00	24
Total Franchises	$17,000.00	34
Total Inflation	$18,000.00	36
Total Environmental	$3,000.00	6
Total Berk	$13,000.00	26

MEDIUM PORTFOLIO - CONSERVATIVE

Deflation Hedges		Percent
Straight Bonds	$60,000.00	12%
Zero Coupon Bonds	$45,000.00	9
Berkshire Hathaway	$50,000.00	10
Duke Energy	$5,000.00	1
Franchises		
Coke	$40,000.00	8%
Gillette	$40,000.00	8
Disney	$20,000.00	4
Pfizer	$15,000.00	3
Merck	$15,000.00	3
Berkshire Hathaway	$40,000.00	8
Inflation Hedges		
Small Stocks	$30,000.00	6%
REITs	$20,000.00	4
Gold &Gold Stocks	$20,000.00	4
Energy Service Cos.	$15,000.00	3
Large Energy Stocks	$35,000.00	7
Food Stocks	$20,000.00	4
Environment		
Berkshire Hathaway	$20,000.00	4%
Enron	$5,000.00	1
Thermo Electron	$5,000.00	1
Total	**$500,000.00**	**100%**
Total Deflation	$160,000.00	32
Total Franchises	$170,000.00	34
Total Inflation	$140,000.00	28
Total Environmental	$30,000.00	6
Total Berk	$150,000.00	30%

MEDIUM PORTFOLIO - AGGRESSIVE

Deflation Hedges		Percent
Straight Bonds	$20,000.00	4%
Zero Coupon Bonds	$40,000.00	8
Berkshire Hathaway	$40,000.00	8
Duke Energy	$20,000.00	4
Franchises		
Coke	$40,000.00	8%
Gillette	$40,000.00	8
Disney	$20,000.00	4
Pfizer	$15,000.00	3
Merck	$15,000.00	3
Berkshire Hathaway	$40,000.00	8
Inflation Hedges		
Small Stocks	$50,000.00	10%
REITs	$25,000.00	5
Gold &Gold Stocks	$25,000.00	5
Energy Service Cos.	$30,000.00	6
Large Energy Stocks	$30,000.00	6
Food Stocks	$20,000.00	4
Environment		
Berkshire Hathaway	$10,000.00	2%
Enron	$10,000.00	2
Thermo Electron	$10,000.00	2
Total	**$500,000.00**	**100%**
Total Deflation	$120,000.00	24
Total Franchises	$170,000.00	34
Total Inflation	$180,000.00	36
Total Environmental	$30,000.00	6
Total Berk	$130,000.00	26%

LARGE PORTFOLIO – CONSERVATIVE

Deflation Hedges		Percent
Straight Bonds	$240,000.00	12%
ZeroCouponBonds	$180,000.00	9
Berkshire Hathaway	$200,000.00	10
Duke Energy	$20,000.00	1

Franchises		
Coke	$160,000.00	8%
Gillette	$160,000.00	8
Disney	$80,000.00	4
Pfizer	$60,000.00	3
Merck	$60,000.00	3
Berkshire Hathaway	$160,000.00	8

Inflation Hedges		
Small Stocks	$120,000.00	6%
REITs	$80,000.00	4
Gold &Gold Stocks	$80,000.00	4
Energy Service Cos.	$60,000.00	3
Large Energy Stocks	$140,000.00	7
Food Stocks	$80,000.00	4.

Environment		
Berkshire Hathaway	$80,000.00	4%
Enron	$20,000.00	1
Thermo Electron	$20,000.00	1

Total	$2,000,000.00	100%
Total Deflation	$640,000.00	32
Total Franchises	$680,000.00	34
Total Inflation	$560,000.00	28
Total Environmental	$120,000.00	6

Total Berk	$600,000.00	30

LARGE PORTFOLIO – AGGRESSIVE

Deflation Hedges		Percent
Straight Bonds	$80,000.00	4%
Zero Coupon Bonds	$160,000.00	8
Berkshire Hathaway	$160,000.00	8
Duke Energy	$80,000.00	4
Franchises		
Coke	$160,000.00	8%
Gillette	$160,000.00	8
Disney	$80,000.00	4
Pfizer	$60,000.00	3
Merck	$60,000.00	3
Berkshire Hathaway	$160,000.00	8
Inflation Hedges		
Small Stocks	$200,000.00	10%
REITs	$100,000.00	5
Gold &Gold Stocks	$100,000.00	5
Energy Service Cos.	$120,000.00	6
Large Energy Stocks	$120,000.00	6
Food Stocks	$80,000.00	4
Environment		
Berkshire Hathaway	$40,000.00	2%
Enron	$40,000.00	2
Thermo Electron	$40,000.00	2
Total	**$2,000,000.00**	**100%**
Total Deflation	$480,000.00	24
Total Franchises	$680,000.00	34
Total Inflation	$720,000.00	36
Total Environmental	$120,000.00	6
Total Berk	$520,000.00	26

One caveat—the specific stocks referred to in our model portfolios are those that we would buy as of this minute. By the time you are reading this, things could have changed. Some of the stocks may already have appreciated too much, and we would then recommend substitutes. It's also possible that the favorable fundamentals of some of them may have altered, and again we would find alternatives. But for now, the portfolios presented in the six charts provided are what we would suggest.

HEDGES AND PLAYS

As you can see, for all categories of investors, we've divided our recommendations into four basic groups: deflation hedges, franchises, inflation plays, and environmental protection. Every investor should have some of each.

Deflation insurance ranges from 24 to 32 percent of each portfolio. The three more conservative portfolios not only have a larger total proportion of deflation insurance overall, they also have more of it concentrated in straight bonds and less in zero coupon bonds. The reverse is true for the more aggressive portfolios. The reason is that zero coupons will give you more bang for the buck if deflation strikes. With straight bonds, however, you gain the advantage of reliable income.

Zero coupon bonds should always be for the longest maturity possible, because the greater the maturity the more leveraged the investment is to economic events. And since the only reason you want zeros is to hedge against a deflationary event in which stocks will go down and possibly down sharply, you want as much leverage as possible. Many investors are not comfortable buying bonds directly. If that's you, there is nothing wrong with a mutual fund. Our favorite is American Central Benham Target 2025, whose phone number is 800-345-2012. The 2025 in the title refers to the year the zeros mature. Thus when it comes time to choose the fund, pick the one with the longest maturity (i.e., highest number). Just for the record, you don't need outright deflation for zeros to score big. In 1998 the deflation scare during the first nine months sent this fund soaring to a 24 percent return, far outperforming any stock market average. But again, don't expect good returns if inflation climbs. Indeed, even though this investment guarantees you a fixed long-term return, it will likely be under water and possibly considerably under water during times of high inflation. But insurance that you buy at a discount and that is guaranteed to mature at par is still pretty good insurance.

For straight bonds, too, you should also pick the longest maturity possible, for two reasons. As with zeros, the longer the maturity the better the gains if deflation comes to pass. The second reason revolves around the income you receive from a straight bond. Typically, the longer the maturity, the higher the yield. However, in periods of rising inflation, bonds with longer maturities may yield a bit less than shorter-term bonds. This is known as an inverted yield curve. Under these circumstances, you might be tempted to go for the shorter-term bonds to take advantage of their greater income. These bonds also, on the surface, might seem to have less risk, in that if inflation continued to rise, the impact might be greatest on the longer-term bonds, which, therefore, might decline more than the shorter-term ones.

Resist the temptation to go for the shorter-term bonds, however. For it is exactly at these times, when the economy and interest rates are most out of whack, that you should have as much deflation insurance as possible. In other words, when inflation is really soaring, the risks of all-out deflation ironically become the greatest. And while we don't want to start recommending trading systems, an inverted yield curve is typically a pretty dangerous situation. That's when it might make sense to add to deflation insurance at the expense of inflation plays. It also will be the time when you will have made a lot of money on inflation plays, and in this business being overly greedy usually doesn't pay.

Note that there is one omission from our deflationary plays, plain old cash. We wouldn't argue if you decided you wanted to hold a portion of your deflation insurance in cash. But we think bonds are better. Cash makes most sense in a neutral environment, where hedging and leverage are not that important. But in the environment we see unfolding, turbulence will be the overriding reality, and this means you want investments that are both solid and at the same time leveraged to the direction that the turbulence is running.

Franchises were the one category where, within each investment level, we treated both conservative and aggressive investors the same. That makes sense since by definition these are the investments that we consider the safest growth stocks. All of them are good investments, but as you can see by our allocations, while we like the drugs, we don't like them quite as much as the other franchises on our list. That's because to some extent drug companies are always competing against one another and, everything else equal, we would rather have a unique company than one that can be paired off against another. You also may have noticed that we haven't put in any of the franchiselike tech stocks such as Microsoft or Cisco. You can certainly feel free to purchase them, however, and to modify the allocations among the different franchises.

In the key section on inflation plays—key because we consider these the highest-potential investments—we were less specific than in the other three categories, suggesting groups rather than specific stocks. That's simply because there is such a diverse range of good stocks to choose from and it's hard to say which ones will be the best picks at the time you're ready to buy. Instead, we've indicated examples of each type of inflation play, and you can refer back to previous chapters for a discussion of each. You can pick and choose among them. For conservative investors, inflation plays represent 28 percent of the overall portfolio. For aggressive investors, the figure is 36 percent. For aggressive investors, there also is a somewhat greater emphasis on smaller-cap stocks and on energy service companies.

In buying small stocks, you can pick and choose among individual stocks, or you can invest in a small stock mutual fund. The advantage of this approach, of course, is that you get a lot of diversification for the same dollar investment. Moreover, if you pick the right fund you also get an expert money manager who spends his or her working hours ferreting out the best of the small stocks.

One small stock fund we have been recommending for many years is the Baron Asset Fund (800-992-2766). Managed by Ron Baron, the fund seeks the best of small stock franchises. And that's a tough thing to find, since the strongest franchises are always larger companies. Still, sometimes you can find market-dominant companies in relatively small packages. For example, in 1998 Baron took a big position in Sotheby's, which is the only publicly traded worldwide auction house. (Its only competitor is Christies, which was acquired in 1997.) Though the market for art is not massive, it is one that has been around for millennia and will likely be around for more millennia. If you ever want to participate in this timeless market as either a significant buyer or seller, Sotheby's will likely play a role in your life. Baron's approach is validated by superb performance in that despite his focus on a sector of the market that has underperformed the big-cap averages, he has outperformed.

THE VOLATILITY FACTOR

You might be wondering here about one thing: Why, if we're so convinced that inflation is one of the surest bets you can make over the next decade or longer, have we devoted just a third or so of our portfolios to all-out inflation plays? Why not invest 50 or 60 or 70 percent in these spitfire stocks and really cash in big? It's a good question, and it has several answers.

One is that investing is not gambling, and it's important to realize the difference. While millions of people may spend a few dollars every week or so to buy a couple of lottery tickets, only a few are desperate or loony enough to go for broke—to spend their last cent buying all the lottery tickets they can get in the hopes of striking it big. Constructing a portfolio is an exercise in balancing the probabilities, not in catering to all-out greed. And it's not that we're against greed on principle, it's just that we know that being too greedy isn't worth the potential cost.

Our pure inflation plays are by their nature inherently volatile. These stocks are directly leveraged to inflation, and they will be gangbuster performers when inflation is high and rising and growth is strong. But in periods of low inflation—and these can include times when inflation is rising but from a very low level—these stocks can be terrible underperformers. Adding to their volatility is the fact that many of the highest-potential inflation plays are relatively small companies, which in general have fewer cushions against any unexpected setbacks. Thus one reason we don't emphasize pure inflation hedges more is that we want to make sure that your portfolio has a certain level of built-in stability, over both the short and longer term.

Similarly, besides small-cap growth stocks, the other types of inflation hedges such as gold and oil service companies also tend to be populated by small companies, and even the companies in these categories that are not small, such as oil service giant Schlumberger, still tend to be very volatile.

Investing in volatile stocks requires that you adopt, if it doesn't come to you naturally, a certain mindset. The first thing to realize is that because these stocks can go down a lot, they require a lot of faith to hold onto. During the 1997–1998 period, for example, the oil drillers, which we expect will be among the best-performing groups in the next decade, dropped about 70 percent from their highs. Even if we are right and these stocks end up trading several times above their previous highs (i.e., rising more than tenfold from their lows) you doubtlessly would have lost a lot of sleep if they had been a major portion of your portfolio. And while oil drillers were admittedly a somewhat extreme case, in 1998 the typical small stock— even those that were not victimized by a fundamental event such as the temporary drop in oil prices—fell about 40 percent from its highs. While big drops like these are somewhat unusual, they not only are always possible, they are likely to become more common as the markets tend toward more turbulence.

Before you get scared off entirely, though, realize that the countervailing point about volatility is that it goes hand in hand with leverage. In the long run if we are right about overall economic trends, these stocks will go to many times their current prices. If you're on the right side of a trend, leverage translates into big—and we mean really big—gains. And this means that these stocks will end up being a much bigger share of your portfolio than they were to start with. By the time we reach the next chapter in economic history, a portfolio that began with 30 percent allocated to inflationary beneficiaries could find those stocks worth many times the portfolio's entire starting value. So in our view, to ask for more and to put a greater portion of your assets in the most volatile investments would be unnecessarily overreaching.

One other point. We've touched on the necessity for faith, and another virtue that goes hand in hand with faith is patience. If you've invested in a stock for sound reasons, you have to believe in your choice and be willing to wait for it to work out. Our predictions are for the long term. We expect them to pan out over the next decade or so, and while this may seem a long wait, if in ten years you suddenly realize that your initial investment has multiplied manyfold, you'll probably be very happy.

In her autobiography *Personal History* (Alfred Knopf, New York, 1997), former *Washington Post* publisher Katharine Graham refers fondly to Warren Buffett, who in the early 1970s became a major investor in the newspaper's parent company and was instrumental in its phenomenal success. During the time he made his initial investment in the company, the stock fell well over 50 percent. Graham was devastated but relates how Buffett remained serenely calm. The market, he told her, was severely underpricing the stock, and rather than panic, the idea was to buy more. In this as in his other investments, Buffett's shrewd patience was rewarded. Today the Graham family is worth more than a billion dollars and Buffett's original investment in the *Post* has multiplied many, many times.

Here is a sad and true story about patience from when we first entered the investment business. We had a friend who happened to be a really great guy with a terrific feel for the market—and especially for gold. In mid-1976 my friend made one of the greatest calls we've ever seen. He called, to the day, the exact bottom in gold—and we mean the exact bottom, $100. He was sure that gold, which at the end of 1974 had traded as high as $200 an ounce, was on its way up to much higher prices. He was absolutely right, as gold eventually topped out at about 800 in 1980.

Our friend's way of participating in what he viewed as a once-in-a-lifetime bull market was with a Philippine gold mine. So sure was he that this investment would pan out that he put most of his own money in the mine and talked many of his best friends into making big investments as well. The stock did almost nothing for about three years. It would climb a bit and then just when it seemed ready to launch into a major uptrend would fall back again. It seemed like a never-ending trading range.

Our friend was patient for about three years. But then—sometime in 1979, if we remember correctly—he finally threw in the towel and sold all his shares, and so did most of his friends who had invested in the mine. About a week later, the stock began to move up dramatically. Within several months it had climbed about tenfold above its previous high. Our friend was never the same after that—his spirit was broken. Eventually he got out of the investing business and began driving a limousine, for others, not himself. It wasn't just the loss of money—it was that he had given up on something he knew was right.

Enough of philosophizing. Moving right along to the rest of our recommendations, the environmental hedges round out our list and for each portfolio make up a relatively modest proportion of the overall allocations. But as with any company leveraged to particular events, these stocks could end up making up a substantial portion of your portfolio. If environmental concerns flare up, you'll be glad you own these companies.

You'll also notice that one stock is a three-in-one play—Berkshire Hathaway. As we've discussed in previous chapters, this stock qualifies as a deflation hedge, through its massive bond portfolio; as a franchise; and as an environmental play, through its merger with reinsurer General Re. For all portfolios it's the single largest position. It is the one stock that is at once a hedge against inflation, deflation, and environmental accidents. Moreover, as the U.S. company with the largest equity base, it is arguably the safest company in the world. If bond-rating companies were to assign ratings higher than three stars, Berkshire would probably merit a star class by itself. Note, too, that Berkshire has two classes of stock. In early 1999 one was trading at about $72,000 a share, which is obviously not suitable for many investors as just one share might exceed the total portfolio. The other class, the B shares, traded at about $2400. There is virtually no difference between the two classes, and thus opting for the B is fine.

Note that there is one big advantage to a high-priced stock—there are very low commission charges. When it comes to buying shares, commissions are almost always calculated on a per ticket and per share basis. And in this regard we just can't resist a bit of a jab at Wall Street. Berkshire, one of the most successful stocks of all time and the U.S. company with the largest equity base, had virtually no analysts covering the stock in 1997. For example, Bloomberg, a broad-based financial services company, listed just one covering analyst, who simply had an earnings estimate on the stock. To the best of our knowledge, until very recently no Wall Street firm has ever written a long report on Berkshire urging its clients to buy (or sell).

By contrast, a typical Internet company such as Excite, which in terms of market capitalization is about one-fiftieth the size of Berkshire and has no earnings and at best poorly defined long-term prospects, has about 15 analysts following it. The difference is that Excite can generate huge brokerage commissions. It is a gambler's dream, moving up and down ten or more percent on psychological whims. Daily trading volume tends to be enormous. And that's why Wall Street invests so much brain power in analyzing Excite—it attracts trading volume, and trading volume is what rings the cash register for Wall Street. With Berkshire you buy on the cheap and hold forever. There are no bucks there for Wall Street, but there are big bucks for investors. Buy Berkshire and don't ever sell it.

TIMING THE MARKET

You may have noticed that we haven't discussed market timing—getting in and out of and back in various investments as the economic background shifts. If you could time deflationary periods and scares, you could shift out of inflation plays at those moments and get back in when inflation heats up again. Obviously, you'd maximize your gains.

Market timing has a definite place, and in an earlier book, *Market Timing for the Nineties*, coauthored with Roger Conrad, we gave some rules for anticipating and acting upon market swings. The most useful and general rule is long-term oriented. It's to buy when there is a lot of slack in the economy and to sell when the economy has used up its excess capacity. And the book outlines several fairly simple ways to assess these conditions.

One problem, though, is that when economic conditions change dramatically, the timing rules that have worked well in the past may have to be modified. It would be tricky here to try to define exactly the guidelines you should follow. So rather than focus on timing, we've focused on insurance. The important point is that with a reasonable mix of investments, such as those in our portfolios, you should still come out well ahead over the long run without ever being too vulnerable.

In fact, market timing can become such an arcane and difficult business that even the best of the professionals tend to get beaten by it eventually. Our feeling is that for many analysts it becomes more a game than a genuine investment aid—and that far too much ego goes into trying to catch the exact lows and highs, when what really counts is being right for the long term.

A prime example of this is Joe Granville, the best known and probably the best market timer of his day. For several years Granville, a very bright and flamboyant analyst, had an extraordinary record—calling a number of market tops and bottoms almost to the day. His last great call was in January 1981, and it was an on-target sell signal.

Granville's system relied on market divergences. One of his rules, which he followed religiously, was that for a market trend to reverse, the Dow Jones Industrial Average had to make a new high or new low that was not confirmed by other averages. For instance, according to this theory, a bottom in the market could occur only if the Dow finished at a new low but almost all other averages did not. This notion plus a number of very creative indicators served him extremely well until market traders and ego got the best of him.

In a *Barron's* interview in early 1982, Granville said he would turn bullish if the market ever moved 100 points (which in those days was a pretty big move) against him. During the summer of 1982, stocks, which were down about 20 percent from their highs and 20 percent from the point at which Granville a year and a half earlier had given a sell signal, were approaching a major bottom, and the vast majority of Granville's indicators were bullish. For example, while the Dow was declining, the typical stock kept rising. But Granville kept waiting for the perfect moment, a day in which the Dow closed at a new low and no other major average matched its previous low. There were several days in which that condition was met prior to the closing runoff. On those days, somehow the final trades would always put the Dow just slightly above its previous low. Watching this with a friend, our suspicion was that market specialists might be causing this to happen, and doing so just because they did not want to be overwhelmed with buy orders the next morning, a near certainty if Granville gave a buy signal. It still seems plausible that is what was going on, though we have no proof.

The market exploded in mid-August. Granville insisted the rally was not to be trusted. In pretty short order, though stocks did move a hundred points above their lows to the then lofty level of about 880, Granville, ignoring his *Barron's* promise, remained resolutely bearish. And as the market rose, Granville's star set.

The next guru of the 1980s became Bob Prechter, which is a story for another book. But suffice it to say that Prechter did not turn bullish on stocks until they had reached 1000.

Our best advice for now is to focus not on timing but on buying one of the balanced and great portfolios we outline in this chapter.

They should serve you well. Start accumulating the recommended positions now, as long as you realize that while any one of our recommendations could take off quickly, some will undoubtedly take longer than others to bear fruit. But as we counseled, have patience. The turbulence and inflation we foresee ahead will be with us for at least the next decade and maybe even longer. The background conditions described in this book are powerful and promise to be protracted. All the portfolios we present are designed for the long haul. While letting you sleep at night, they should be profitable in all but the most dire conditions. And under those conditions, it might not make any difference what happens anyway.

EPILOGUE

In preceding pages we've discussed the slowdown in tech and what it means for your investments. Our time frame has been the next decade or so, which from an investment point of view is a reasonably long-term perspective. You might be wondering, though, about the even longer term. In particular, are we contending that the slowdown in technology is destined to persist for far longer—even forever? Or is there any reason to hope that at some point in the future true technological and scientific progress will resume? And if so, what might trigger the turnaround?

These are very good questions, even though they may not have immediate relevance for your investment decisions. They also happen to fit in quite nicely with a controversy that has burgeoned during the past year over a book written by *Scientific American* editor John Horgan and titled *The End of Science*. In his book, Horgan argues that science has nowhere left to go. It has discovered all that it can. All the big questions that are capable of being answered have been answered already, and whatever questions remain deal with matters that are inherently unknowable. Or so Horgan contends.

In many ways, as Horgan points out, many of the key scientific discoveries of this century would seem to support this pessimistic conclusion. After all, many of these seminal discoveries have to do with either the limits or the intrinsic opaqueness of basic scientific principles. In a sense, in fact, it seems as if the twentieth century has dealt science one blow after another.

One major scientific discovery, for instance, was quantum physics, elaborated by Neils Bohr and others in the early part of the twentieth century. Its basic premise is that the world cannot be defined in a causal way. One of its fundamental premises is that we can never observe nature without changing nature. Werner Heisenberg's uncertainty principle is an example of the quantum nature of microscopic phenomena. It states that we can never know both the position of a particle and its speed. One offshoot of this uncertainty is that we can never precisely measure either the position or the speed of a particle. A deeper corollary is that particles can act on each other at a distance. Thus if we measure the momentum, spin, or some other quality of a particle at one point it will determine the quality of another particle that can literally be billions of miles away.

Another major twentieth-century scientific thinker was Kurt Godel. His contribution was the incompleteness theorem, which basically says that our cherished systems of logic are either incomplete or inconsistent. This means that the axioms underlying something as basic as arithmetic will lead to statements that either are contradictory or cannot be proven. And finally, there was the development of chaos theory, which stemmed initially from the thinking of a late nineteenth-century French mathematician, Henri Poincaré, who realized that the celestial motion of more than two bodies could not be perfectly predicted. It is not surprising, in light of all these discoveries, that Horgan and some others have concluded that science has gone as far as it can go.

You might think that, given our view that technological progress is slowing down and that technological breakthroughs are not in the offing, we would agree with Horgan. Actually, though, we don't. We have not been arguing for the most part that science and technology have reached immutable limits—only that the way we are going about the process is short-circuiting the chances of success.

One reason we think that science still has a lot farther to go is the work of David Bohm, one of the most creative physicists of the twentieth century. Bohm was a leading contributor to quantum mechanics, which is the basis for much of our information technologies. He made a good case that many of the paradoxes of quantum mechanics could be explained by a deeper understanding of the phenomena, and indeed he put forward a theory that resolved many of the seemingly contradictory aspects of quantum mechanics. But his work was largely ignored by mainstream science.

Increasingly, it seems, scientists are starting from the assumption that it just isn't possible to gain a true understanding of nature's laws. Therefore, as Bohm himself put it, they are willing to settle for knowledge as opposed to understanding—accumulating data instead of trying to achieve deeper insights. In other words, the seminal discoveries of this century may have had a chilling effect on scientists' faith in their ability to penetrate the deepest mysteries of the universe. Scientists have narrowed their horizons and are looking merely to amass additional facts. And this goes hand in hand with the increasing reliance on computers as a research tool.

A good example of this narrow focus can be seen in efforts to develop artificial intelligence—thinking computers. Book after book has been written about the potential for thinking computers. But they all boil down to compediums of what computers can do and pie in the sky dreams of what they might someday do. They fail to point out that until we understand the nature of human intelligence—which we don't—artificial intelligence doesn't have a prayer. Roger Penrose, a brilliant British physicist and author of *The Emperor's New Mind*, makes the point compellingly. He argues in effect that the human mind is likely the most complex object in the universe with which we are familiar. As a result, the laws governing it are likely to be among the most complex that physics can offer. Yet we still have very little understanding of these laws, which is to say, of how physics operates on a microscopic level. A theory of quantum gravity, which Penrose feels is essential to understanding human intelligence, is not in view. Yet we continue to catalog computer achievements as if they represent giant strides forward.

As we said, our overreliance on the computer in carrying out research goes hand in glove with this narrowing focus. We discussed in Chapter 2 how computer-oriented research has contributed to the slowdown in technological progress, as we accumulate vast reams of data and hope to stumble upon useful answers through hit or miss computing tactics. This approach is almost certain to fail except at the margins. True progress will come only if we understand the limits of this approach and, as we suggested earlier, turn instead to nature for our inspiration. Henri Poincaré expressed this poetically. As quoted in the book *Insights of Genius: Imagery and Creativity in Science and Art*, written by Arthur Miller (not the playwright but the history and philosophy of science professor), he said, "The scientist does not study nature because it is useful, he studies it because he delights in it, and he delights in it because it is beautiful. . . . If nature were not beautiful, it would not be worth knowing, and if nature were not worth knowing, life would not be worth living."

Poincaré wrote well before the dawning of the age of computers, but his thoughts resonate even more strongly today. Scientists need to pull themselves away from their computers and study the mysteries of nature directly. There is no way that we can represent nature on a computer, for when we try to do so, we are laughably far from representing the real thing. It's like trying to understand human emotions by studying a robot. For there to be any hope of genuine scientific breakthroughs, science will need to reorient itself in some basic ways. It's an open question whether this will ever happen—but if it does, then a new age of scientific discovery may well be in the offing.

Computers, though, aren't the only culprits. A second factor also probably deserves some of the blame for the slowdown in technological and scientific progress—our obsession with immediacy, with short-term results. Wall Street, which has become the largest source of wealth in the economy, exemplifies the importance our society places on immediate gratification. Companies in the stock market are judged not by their long-term potential but by their quarter-to-quarter performance. One reason General Re gave for merging with Berkshire Hathaway was to escape the pressures of having to make its earnings grow year after year. In the insurance business (and others as well), sometimes maximizing long-term gains means taking risks that result in a year or two of declining profits. Wall Street, though, is quick to punish even a quarter or two of disappointing profits. This quarter-to-quarter mentality is undoubtedly exacerbated by the Internet and our whole information-dominated economy, where all results can be instantaneously disseminated.

How does this relate to the slowdown in science? Major technological breakthroughs may begin as intuitive creative insights, but to bring them to full fruition takes many years—years in which any profits from the insight will be nonexistent. Take the Internet itself, for example. It was conceived in 1964 as the ARPAnet. It wasn't until 1983 that networking became a tool for scientists, and not until the mid-1990s that consumers latched onto the net. The initial work, which lasted about a generation, was made possible by government funding. The hard part was this early development; the easy part has been making the net accessible to the public, as Len Bosack, one of the founders of Cisco, candidly admits. He says, "The only thing I actually did with regard to Internet technology was make it economic to build a large, fast Internet. People had surely built routers before me, and people had built fast networks. The question was how to do it economically." In other words, Cisco's genius lay in applying existing technologies, not in inventing new ones.

It is unlikely that the Internet could be developed in today's world, where immediate results are so worshipped. Similarly, it is unlikely that the transistor, the sine qua non of the information world, ever would have been developed. The transistor was nursed along for more than a generation. Very much tied into its history was the research powerhouse Bell Labs, the research arm of AT&T. In the good old days, Bell Labs provided the kind of no-immediate-payoff-required research environment that nurtured some of the major discoveries of our age. For example, in addition to the transistor, Bell Labs produced networking software, the first digital computer, talking motion pictures, evidence of the Big Bang, and information theory. There's not much mystery about how one lab could produce so much original work. It's because Bell Labs was willing to fund long-term projects without demanding assurances of bottom-line results. And right behind Bell Labs was the lab at IBM and the Palo Alto Research Corporation, which was the adjunct to Xerox. Together these research leaders gave us superconductivity, the scanning tunneling microscope, the laser printer and, yes, the personal computer. In fact, much of today's technology resulted from long-term research carried out under the auspices of one of these labs or funded by a well-heeled Defense Department.

Once AT&T was broken up, Bell labs became a shadow of its former self, no longer existing under the aegis of a benign monopoly. The other labs became hostage to the demand for immediate results. It goes against the grain of current antiregulation trends, but to get science going again it probably wouldn't hurt to have something like the old Bell Labs around again. The government right now is pursuing its antitrust suit against Microsoft and has been making noises about Intel. We'd prefer to see these companies permitted to be at least partial monopolies with one condition being that they must fund long-term research projects. Maybe it wouldn't produce much, but it would work better than anything we are trying now.

There's one more theme we want to return to and that's the Internet and technology. In Chapter 1 we made the point that the technology establishing the Internet is fairly well fixed, and that any changes will be evolutionary, not revolutionary. This, we argued, favored those companies that already have a firm grip on the technological reins, such as Cisco. Meanwhile, some of the hottest Internet companies on the retailing and content-providing side are likely to sputter. That's because while use of the Internet will proliferate, it is not likely to generate the kind of massive economic payoffs that would be necessary to justify the sensationally high valuations Internet companies have been awarded.

All that is true. But the relationships actually go a bit deeper than that. Not only will the Internet not bring on a new age of technological nirvana, as it spreads it is likely to reveal the limits of technology and to make us have to confront those limits sooner. In other words, not only will the Internet be useless in helping us overcome the limits of technology, it will expose those limits faster than may otherwise have been the case.

Let's look at this more closely. The frenzied rush in Internet stocks began in August 1998. And frenzied is obviously the operative word. To give just one example, E-Bay, an online auction house, was valued at over $10 billion despite the fact that the company had never earned a penny, had only 67 employees, and had tons of competition. By contrast, Sotheby's, one of only two major worldwide auction houses and the only publicly traded auction house, ended the year with a market capitalization of about $1.4 billion. And almost surely, Sotheby's, much better financed and much better known than E-Bay, will end up competing with E-Bay on line. The difference between E-Bay and Sotheby's is that the former has a technological aura surrounding it. Sotheby's, at least as of year-end 1998, was still viewed as a company with little technological appeal.

Similarly, the king of Internet stocks, America Online, finished 1998 with a market capitalization greater than that of Disney, one of our favorite growth stocks. Yet Disney's sites on the Internet were nearly as widely visited as AOL's, and over the long run Disney, thanks to its greater financial might and name recognition, will be better positioned to prosper from online commerce. But investors fell in love with AOL because it is a pure Internet play, uniquely linked to technology. Americans, in short, are still head over heels in love with technology. We can't help it—it's part of our national psyche.

Now for some interesting correlations. It's both significant and symbolic that in August 1998, when Internet mania was heating up, many major commodity indices such as the Commodity Research Bureau (CRB) futures index hit generation lows. Investors apparently were making a bet that technology was going to keep commodity prices low forever, thereby ensuring an infinitely bright future for us all.

August also was the month in which the U.S. dollar, which had been rising strongly since spring 1995, began to falter. By early January 1999, the dollar had dropped by more than 25 percent, one of the most intense declines on record. Historically a falling dollar tends to mean rising commodity prices, for two related reasons. First, most commodities are priced in dollars. Thus when the dollar falls, many commodities become cheaper to the outside world and demand rises. Eventually prices will rise as well.

Second, a cheaper dollar, particularly in relation to the yen, gives a boost to the currencies and economies of Asia. And the developing world is where growth in demand for commodities will be the greatest. As a result, economic strength in Asia goes hand in hand with recovering commodity prices.

The lag between a falling dollar and rising commodity prices can be anywhere from a few weeks to a year or more. But the relationship always holds. Once the dollar sinks, commodity prices rise. How does this tie in with the Internet? In the future, the most explosive growth in Internet usage will come from the developing world. More than 30 percent of the United States already is online, and while that percentage will grow, that growth will be minor compared to Internet proliferation in the Third World. For instance, according to nonprofit organization Worldwatch, the number of Internet users in China and India, the world's two most populous countries, will grow 15-fold in the next two years. And this growth in Internet use will work to further accelerate economic growth in those countries, by giving those countries easy access to existing technological knowhow. This, in turn, will put additional pressure on key commodities and intensify price increases.

In other words, because of the spread of the Internet—which involves technological proliferation, not innovation—the consequences of the limits of technology in terms of our ability to develop alternative energies or to increase food supplies will become evident sooner rather than later. Far from saving us or leading us to a new era of technological progress, the Internet will hasten our confrontation with the technological limits we've described in this book.

APPENDIX

Following is a list of the major scientific discoveries of the past four and a half centuries. The list is based on a variety of sources, and in particular on John Simmons' book *The Scientific 100* and the *Encyclopedia Britannica*.

The list makes plain that technological progress has slowed dramatically in recent years. Throughout the twentieth century up until the 1970s, there were at least five important discoveries per decade, and in many decades more than twice that number. In the 1970s, there were just three; in the 1980s, just one, and in the 1990s, none.

The Slowing Pace of Technological Progress

Year	Scientist	Achievement
1530	Copernicus	Sun-centered solar system
1610	Galilei	Modern astronomy
1627	Kepler	Planetary motion
1661	Malpighi	Capillaries
1673	Leeuwenhoek	Microscopic descriptions
1675	Huygens	Wave structure of light
1687	Newton	Laws of motion
1736	Euler	Systematized mechanics
1749	Buffon	Definition of species
1753	Haller	Catalog of body organs

1758	Linnaeus	Biological nomenclature
1772	Lavoisier	States of matter
1780	Herschel	Stellar astronomy
1784	Laplace	Celestial mechanics
1810	Gauss	Probability theory
1831	Faraday	Electromagnetism
1833	Lyell	Modern geology
1839	Virchow	Cellular pathology
1840	Liebig	Organic chemistry
1848	Bernard	Physiology of organs
1855	Kekule	Chemical reactions
1856	Mendel	Laws of heredity
1857	Pasteur	Bacteria and disease
1859	Darwin	Evolution
1862	Wundt	Experimental psychology
1865	Mendeleev	Categorization of elements
1866	Haeckel	Genealogical trees
1873	Cantor	Transfinite numbers
1873	Maxwell	Electromagnetic laws
1877	Boltzmann	Entropy
1882	Koch	Tuberculosis bacterium
1893	Poincare	Celestial mechanics, chaos theory
1895	Fischer	Nature of enzymes
1895	Rontgen	X-rays
1897	Thomsom	Electron
1898	Pavlov	Conditioned reflexes
1900	Freud	Psychoanalysis
1900	Planck	Notion of quanta
1900	Curie	Radiochemistry
1902	Bayliss	Hormone functions
1903	Dalton	Concept of the atom
1905	Einstein	Theory of relativity

1906	Sherrington	Functioning of nerve cells
1906	Hopkins	Vitamins
1907	Landsteiner	Blood typing
1910	Ehrlich	Chemotherapy
1911	Boas	Human mutability, modern anthropoloy
1911	Onnes	Superconductivity
1911	Rutherford	Nuclear physics
1912	Laue	X-ray diffraction
1913	Bohr	Quantum theory of atom
1915	Wegener	Continental drift
1920	Lamarck	Taxonomy
1921	Bjerknes	Warm and cold fronts
1921	Banting	Insulin
1924	Broglie	Quantum wave mechanics
1925	Schrodinger	Quantum waves
1926	Morgan	Genetic mechanisms
1926	Eddington	Nuclear astronomy
1926	Dirac	Quantum mechanics
1927	Heisenberg	Quantum uncertainty
1927	Piaget	Child development
1928	Fleming	Penicillin
1929	Hubble	Measurement of the universe
1931	Godel	Limits of logic
1931	Leakey	Early humans
1931	Pauling	Quantum chemistry
1932	Chadwick	Neutron
1933	Fermi	Beta decay
1936	Turing	Computational theory
1936	Bush	Analog computer
1937	Dobzhansky	Chromosonal theory
1937	Rabi	Magnetic resonance
1938	Bethe	Theory of stellar energy

1938	Lorenz	Animal behavior
1941	Mayr	Development of species
1943	Waksman	Streptomycin
1944	Von Neumann	Modern computer
1945	Feynman	Quantum electrodynamics
1947	Bardeen	Transistor
1950	Selye	Stress-related diseases
1952	Libby	Radiocarbon dating
1953	Basov	Laser
1953	Watson	DNA structure
1953	Gibbon	Open-heart surgery
1953	Bohm	Hidden variables in quantum mechanics
1954	Salk	Polio vaccine
1954	Sanger	Sequencing of complex molecules
1955	Chomsky	Cognitive linguistics
1957	Bardeen	Theory of superconductivity
1958	Crick	Molecular biology
1958	Glashow	Electroweak theory
1958	Levi-Strauss	Structural anthropology
1961	Gell-Mann	Elementary particle theory
1962	Kuhn	Nature of scientific theories
1964	Bell	Quantum anomalies
1965	Wilson	Evolutionary biology
1968	Margulis	Evolutionary role of bacteria
1970	Hawking	Quantum cosmology
1975	Mandelbrot	Chaos theory and fractals
1978	Elion	Antiviral medications
1983	Mullis	DNA replication

FURTHER READING

Aczel, Amir D., *Fermat's Last Theorem*, Four Walls Eight Windows, New York, 1996.

Bailey, Ronald, editor, *The True State of the Planet*, The Free Press, New York, 1995.

Barrow, John D., *Impossibility*, Oxford University Press, Oxford, 1998.

Baskin, Yvonne, *The Work of Nature*, Island Press, Washington, 1997.

Bohm, D. and Hiley, B.J., *The Undivided Universe*, Routledge, London, 1993.

Cohen, Joel E., *How Many People Can the Earth Support?*, W.W. Norton & Co., New York, 1995.

Conway, Gordon, *The Doubly Green Revolution*, Penguin Books, London, 1997.

Crick, Francis, *Life Itself*, Simon & Schuster, New York, 1981.

Daily, Gretchen C., Editor, *Nature's Services*, Island Press, Washington D.C., 1997.

Delsemme, Armand, *Our Cosmic Origins*, Cambridge University Press, Cambridge, 1998.

Denning, Peter J. and Metcalfe, Robert M., *Beyond Calculation*, Copernicus, New York, 1997.

Denton, Michael J., *Nature's Destiny*, The Free Press, New York, 1998.

Dyson, Freeman, *Imagined Worlds*, Harvard University Press, Cambridge, 1997.

Ehrlich, Paul R., *The Population Bomb*, Buccaneer, Cutchogue, 1976.

Ehrlich, Paul R. and Ehrlich, Anne H., *Betrayal of Science and Reason*, Island Press, Washington, 1996.

Ezrahi, Yaron, Mendelsohn, Everett, and Segal, Howard P., editors, *Technology, Pessimism, and Postmodernism*, University of Massachusetts Press, Amherst, 1994.

Flavin, Christopher, and Lenssen, Nicholas, *Power Surge*, W.W. Norton & Co., New York, 1994.

Fowler, T. Kenneth, *The Fusion Quest*, Johns Hopkins University Press, Baltimore, 1997.

Frank, Jerome D. and Frank, Julia B. 1961, *Persuasion and Healing*, Johns Hopkins University Press, Baltimore, 1961.

Fried, Stephen, *Bitter Pills*, Bantam Books, New York, 1998.

Friedman, Milton and Schwartz, Anna Jacobson, *A Monetary History of the United States*, Princeton University Press, Princeton,1963.

Galison, Peter, *Image and Logic*, The University of Chicago Press, Chicago, 1997.

Glantz, Michael H., *Currents of Change*, Cambridge University Press, Cambridge, 1996.

Hall, Stephen S., *A Commotion in the Blood*, Henry Holt & Co., New York, 1997.

Harrington, Anne, editor, *The Placebo Effect*, Harvard University Press, Cambridge, 1997.

Healy, David, *The Anti-Depressant Era*, Harvard University Press, Cambridge, 1997.

Horgan, John, *The End of Science*, Helix Books, Reading, 1996.

Hughes, Thomas P., *Rescuing Prometheus*, Pantheon Books, New York, 1998.

King, Daniel, *Kasparov V Deeper Blue*, Batsford Chess Books, London, 1997.

Landauer, Thomas K., *The Trouble with Computers*, MIT Press, Cambridge, 1995.

Leeb, Stephen and Conrad, Roger, *The Agile Investor*, HarperBusiness, New York, 1997.

Leeb, Stephen and Conrad, Roger, *Market Timing for the Nineties*, HarperBusiness, New York, 1993.

Lorenz, Edward, *The Essence of Chaos*, University of Washington Press, Seattle, 1993.

Lovelock, James, *The Ages of Gaia*, W.W. Norton & Co., New York, 1995.

Maddox, John. 1998, *What Remains To Be Discovered*, The Free Press, New York, 1998.

Margulis, Lynn and Sagan, Dorion, *Slanted Truths*, Copernicus, New York, 1997.

Marsa, Linda, *Prescription for Profits*, Scribner, New York, 1997.

Miller, Arthur, *Insights of Genius*, Copernicus, New York, 1996.

Moore, Thomas J., *Prescription for Disaster*, Simon & Schuster, New York, 1998.

Narby, Jeremy, *The Cosmic Serpent*, Jeremy P. Tarcher/Putnam, New York, 1998.

Nagel, Ernest and Newman, James R., *Godel's Proof*, New York University Press, New York, 1958.

Nowotny, Helga and Felt, Ulrike, *After the Breakthrough*, Cambridge University Press, Cambridge, 1997.

Oldstone, Michael B.A., *Viruses, Plagues, and History*, Oxford University Press, New York, 1998.

Pacey, Arnold, *Technology in World Civilization*, MIT Press, Cambridge, 1990.

Penrose, Roger, *The Emperor's New Mind*, Oxford University Press, New York, 1989.

Philander, S. George, *Is the Temperature Rising?*, Princeton University Press, Princeton, 1998.

Pollan, Stephen, *Die Broke*, HarperCollins, New York, 1998.

Porter, Roy, *The Greatest Benefit to Mankind*, HarperCollins, London, 1997.

Riordan, Michael and Hoddeson, Lillian, *Crystal Fire*, W. W. Norton & Co., New York, 1997.

Root-Bernstein, Robert and Root-Bernstein, Michele, *Honey, Mud, Maggots, and Other Medical Marvels*, Houghton Mifflin, Boston, 1997.

Rochlin, Gene I., *Trapped in the Net*, Princeton University Press, Princeton, 1997.

Rose, Stephen, *Lifelines*, Oxford University Press, New York, 1998.

Ryan, Frank, *Virus X*, Little, Brown and Co., Boston, 1997.

Schulz-Aellen, Marie-Francoise, *Aging and Human Longevity*, Birkhauser, Boston, 1997.

Segaller, Stephen, *Nerds 2.0.1*, TV Books, New York, 1998.

Seitz, Frederic and Einspruch, Norman G., *Electronic Genie*, University of Illinois Press, Urbana, 1998.

Shenk, David, *Data Smog*, HarperEdge, New York, 1997.

Sichel, Daniel E., *The Computer Revolution*, Brookings Institution Press, Washington, 1997.

Simmons, John, *The Scientific 100*, Citadel Press, Secaucus, 1996.

Simon, Julian L., *The Ultimate Resource 2*, Princeton University Press, Princeton, 1996.

Singh, Simon, Fermat's *Enigma*, Walker Publishing Co., New York, 1997.

Volk, Tyler, *Gaia's Body*, Copernicus, New York, 1998.

INDEX

ABOUT THE AUTHORS

Stephen Leeb, Ph.D., is editor of *Personal Finance*, one of the largest investment newsletters in the country, and *The Big Picture*, which recently celebrated its 35th year of publication. Consistently rated among the top 10 stock pickers by *Timer Digest* and *Hulbert Financial Digest*, Dr. Leeb also wrote or co-wrote *The Agile Investor, Market Timing for the 90s*, and *Getting In on the Ground Floor* (a main selection of the Fortune Book Club). He is a frequent guest on television and radio programs including Louis Rukeyser's *Wall Street Week*.

Donna Leeb worked with Stephen Leeb to found and develop his first investment letter, *Investment Strategist*. She has a master's degree in Journalism from Columbia's Graduate School of Journalism.